History's Babel

History's Babel

*Scholarship, Professionalization,
and the Historical Enterprise
in the United States, 1880–1940*

ROBERT B. TOWNSEND

THE UNIVERSITY OF CHICAGO PRESS   CHICAGO AND LONDON

ROBERT B. TOWNSEND is the deputy director of the American Historical Association, where he has worked for more than twenty years.

The University of Chicago Press, Chicago 60637
The University of Chicago Press, Ltd., London
© 2013 by The University of Chicago
All rights reserved. Published 2013.
Printed in the United States of America
22 21 20 19 18 17 16 15 14 13   1 2 3 4 5

ISBN-13: 978-0-226-92392-5 (cloth)
ISBN-13: 978-0-226-92393-2 (paper)
ISBN-13: 978-0-226-92394-9 (e-book)
ISBN-10: 0-226-92392-4 (cloth)
ISBN-10: 0-226-92393-2 (paper)
ISBN-10: 0-226-92394-0 (e-book)

Library of Congress Cataloging-in-Publication Data

Townsend, Robert B., 1966– author.
    History's Babel : scholarship, professionalization, and the historical enterprise in the United States, 1880–1940 / Robert B. Townsend.
        pages   cm
    Includes bibliographical references and index.
    ISBN-13: 978-0-226-92392-5 (cloth : alkaline paper)
    ISBN-13: 978-0-226-92393-2 (paperback : alkaline paper)
    ISBN-13: 978-0-226-92394-9 (e-book)
    ISBN-10: 0-226-92392-4 (cloth : alkaline paper)
    [etc.]
    1. Historiography—United States—History.   2. History—Study and teaching—United States.   3. Historians—United States.   I. Title.
    D13.5.U6T69 2013
    907.2'073—dc23
                                                        2012017474

TO THE MEMORY OF ROY ROSENZWEIG

Contents

Figures

Acknowledgments

Early in graduate school I was taught to look at acknowledgments as a useful tool for the reader—a valuable opportunity to puzzle out friends and intellectual antecedents for the work, as the author briefly drops the veil of scholarly objectivity. Over time, I've come to appreciate them as a valuable resource for assessing the rich set of interlocking communities of support for our profession, which puts the lie to one of the great myths of our discipline—the notion of the solitary scholar, struggling on in isolation. In my case, this study emerged out of two decades of conversations with historians and specialists working in a wide variety of settings, and I cannot do proper justice to them all. But a few names stand out, and merit particular notice.

This study took a rather long and tortured journey, germinating through almost twenty years on the staff of the American Historical Association before it was finally forced into written form. This book is dedicated to Roy Rosenzweig, who set me on the path to this project with a seemingly simple question about how new media might change history scholarship, and then coaxed me to pursue the answer to the end. He was exceptional both in his careful reading of early (and fairly awful) drafts and in his ability to nurture and inspire with his enthusiasm and careful questions. His death when this was barely half done was a personal loss that is still keenly and painfully felt.

I was exceptionally grateful and fortunate that Peter Stearns was willing to step in and guide the project to its conclusion. He applied gentle pressure to get me back on track and set speed records for returning comments that I know many writers can only envy. I also owe special thanks to Rosemarie Zagarri. She convinced me that American history was not the oxymoron that a young European history snob assumed. But

I benefited from her good advice and counsel through the years, and she provided invaluable comments and encouragement along the way. And Rosemary Jann deserves special appreciation. She offered very detailed and invaluable advice on critical chapters—sharpening the prose and forcing me to think about how this might work as a book for a more general audience.

Beyond those with a direct hand in the writing process, I also accumulated debts too numerous to mention to various members of the discipline who were under no obligation to assist. As executive director of the association, Arnita Jones provided more encouragement and support than I could ever have hoped or reasonably expected. And my other colleagues at the AHA helped carry the burden of my occasional absences and general distraction over far too many years. Outside the confines of the association, a remarkably eclectic array of scholars and historians—Robert Adcock, Joyce Appleby, Tom Bender, Richard Bond, Rebecca Conard, James Cortada, Julie Des Jardins, John Dichtl, Paul Forman, Linda Kerber, Lawrence Levine, Jerry Z. Muller, James Sparrow, Ian Tyrrell, and William Weber—all read pieces of this study at various steps along the way and offered thoughtful advice and suggestions, as well as general encouragement that kept this moving along to completion. And my dear friends in the Murky Coffee study group (Katharina Hering, Steven Saltzgiver, Sheila Brennan, Bill Carpenter, Roger Mellon, Jenny Lansbury, and Kevin Shupe) read a number of early proposals and drafts and posed a number of hard questions. To the extent I failed to heed any of the suggestions or critiques received over the years, the fault is entirely my own.

Professionally, I owe special thanks to the staff at the Manuscripts Division at the Library of Congress, whose model of a well-run archival collection first inspired my interest in that aspect of history work. But I also owe thanks to the archival staffs at Harvard University; Indiana University–Purdue University Indianapolis, the University of Minneapolis, the Briscoe Center at the University of Texas, the Wisconsin Historical Society, and the North Carolina Historical Commission for their assistance in finding materials for this study. And I owe a special word of thanks to Sarah Steinbock-Pratt, who assisted with some crucial last-minute research when the papers of the National Council for Social Studies opened up quite late in the writing process.

After the manuscript reached a relatively finished form, I greatly benefited from the good cheer and enthusiasm of my editor at the University of Chicago Press, Robert Devens. He made the entire process much easier than I expected. And I owe particular thanks to Jim Banner, both for putting me in touch with the press and for reading the manuscript at a number of stages along the way. Together with an anonymous reader for the press, he helped to expose a number of analytical weak points and provided essential guidance as I embarked on a second round of research.

Through it all, I incurred my greatest debt to Liz Townsend, who put up with the highs and lows of the entire journey, tolerated the occasional holes in the family finances to pay for my research sojourns and that "one last book I really needed," and ultimately polished up the final product with one of the sharpest editorial eyes in the business. She is, as ever, the true secret to my success.

Introduction

Casting an Olympian gaze over the work of the history discipline in 1910, one of the early eminences of the field, J. Franklin Jameson, envisioned history as a vast panorama of activity. As editor of the *American Historical Review* and director of the Department of Historical Research at the Carnegie Institution of Washington, he sat at the center of two national networks of historical activity—the first for scholarship, the second for the tools and materials of research. From that perspective, he fit the monograph writing of academics into a much larger array of historical practices, encompassing popular history making, school teaching, and the work of historical societies.[1]

A century later, Jameson's vision of a discipline that embraced a diverse array of practices seems a distant memory, scattered among a wide range of historical activities and professions—including academics, public historians, teachers, and digital humanists. And Jameson is only dimly remembered in the discipline as the rather fussy editor of the *Review* who helped history scholars center the discipline on themselves. Marking the distance between his time and ours, in a seminal article for the public history movement in 1979, Joan Hoff singled out Jameson for focusing the notion of a history profession (a term barely used in his time) on academics.[2] Jameson's image of a larger tapestry of historical work was erased, and in its place she described a discipline ill prepared for sharp shifts in the academic job market and challenges to its scholarly authority in the public sphere.

For Hoff, and many others in the public history movement, the ascent of academic history was complicit in a general decline in the discipline—an escape into obscurantism and the ivory tower. These sentiments are echoed by many teaching specialists, who criticize academics for their distance from and naiveté about the challenges of teaching at the K-12 level.

How, then, did we get from there to here? Hoff's invocation of a history profession points to the root of the change. Our understanding of the discipline seems trapped in a paradigm of professionalization that centers the narrative on academia. In the standard conception of the field, historians emerged from a dark age of amateur and "gentlemen" historians in the first decade of the twentieth century and acquired the characteristics of a profession. On this reading, the "professional historian" of the present is understood as someone with a history PhD, who is employed at a research university and an author of significant books or articles—characteristics that tend to be marked off from a much larger and often undifferentiated group, typically designated as amateurs or "the public."

Hoff's article is merely one among many jeremiads on the discipline extending down to the present, which are built on the separation of "professional historians" from the public and other history workers. This notion is so pervasive that many of those who object to aspects of this division find it difficult to think outside these categories. In each case, the authors trace a problem in the field arising from the divide between historians and the public, but their efforts to describe how the separation arose and prescribe a solution tend to be undercut by the assumption that academics are the normative definition of history professionals. While the problems they note are quite real, by framing their thinking and reading of their subject in a relatively fixed professional/public framework, they tend to reinforce the very barriers they want to break down. This in turn feeds a sense of frustration and anger that their particular concern seems so intractable and inevitably leads to a diagnosis of moral failure on the part of academics for allowing such divisions to grow.[3]

To get a better handle on these problems, I decided to recenter the story about history on an expanded vision of the historical enterprise that tries to encompass the entire terrain over which academic historians have claimed some jurisdiction or authority over the past 130 years— claims that have arisen in debates about school curricula, disputes over interpretations offered at historic sites, or arguments with archivists and librarians about the way they organize and release materials. In place of the many narrowly focused great-men/great-books histories of the discipline, I will highlight a number of separate microprofessionalization projects in history that facilitated the current divided state of work in history. Examining how competing spheres of professional identity and practice developed in the historical enterprise from the late nineteenth through the early twentieth centuries—and treating the larger sphere of academia as just one among the others—helps to explain why it now seems so difficult to speak across these lines to others engaged in closely related efforts.

In recent years, a growing number of monographs and essays have tried to articulate a more holistic view of the entire field of historical activity—positioning written scholarship in a wider set of relationships with others working in the field of history as well as the general public.[4] Often inspired by the public history movement, these studies challenge the longstanding focus in the historiography that treats academic research as the sum and total of work worthy of note in the discipline. I have tried to build on and synthesize those efforts. Rather than treating historical societies or efforts to reform history in the schools either on their own or in relation (and sometimes in opposition) to the academic community, I hope to show how all of these communities were wrestling with very similar problems of professionalization in ways that established wedges between the different communities and continue to affect them to this day.

Too often, the terms *history discipline* and *history profession* are used interchangeably, as if they designated the same thing. But as the many different types of work in the historical enterprise demonstrate, the way history is practiced as a profession and the body of historical knowledge that constitutes a discipline may overlap, but they are different in critical ways. This book is constructed around the notion that what constitutes a discipline as an organized body of knowledge and what constitutes a profession as an organized form of work are actually quite different. The two can clearly overlap, as some form of knowledge inevitably underpins every form of work. In history, for instance, what is broadly understood as a discipline at a college or university is simply a "subject" in the schools. And what is often loosely imagined as a profession at a university is often a very tightly structured area of work in a variety of cultural institutions. Rather than engage in hairsplitting about where the line between a discipline ends and a profession begins, I use the term *historical enterprise* here to denote the broad range of activities where such knowledge about the past is produced and used in an organized or systematic way. When, how, and why particular areas of work under the larger sign of history became professional will be the subject of this book.[5]

In the late nineteenth and early twentieth centuries, the historical enterprise functioned with a more capacious understanding of how the various pieces of history work fit together. The personnel linked with it were employed in more diverse and overlapping pursuits, and the cultural and social resources linking them together were more visible. When leaders of the discipline such as Jameson described the "modern work of history" in the early twentieth century, books represented the apex of their imagined hierarchy of activities, but teaching and the collecting and publishing of historical materials were also seen as integral parts of the whole. Given that, it is reasonable to ask when and why so many of the people who now practice history (often under highly professional standards) were written out of the narrative. Answering those questions exposes many of the social and cultural forces that now separate academics from their closest collaborators in the work of history.

Unlike many of the works that focus on the division between professional historians and the public as a problem, this analysis does not trace a story of clear and inevitable decline. The professionalization of activities such as teaching and archival management was quite positive in many ways—elevating the quality of classroom instruction and assuring the availability of records that researchers now rely on—just as the expansion of academic research into new subjects, new methods, and new sources was a net gain for our understanding of the past. These changes can only be recast as problems, such as "fragmentation" and an alien intrusion of "educationists," when they are treated in isolation and measured as a net loss from a narrow and static view of what constitutes professional history.

In contrast to a broader understanding of those who feel they are engaged in and have a stake in history, most assessments of the discipline generally accept that the work of research scholars represents the center of the discipline (either for good or ill).[6] In an attempt to bridge this divide, I recentered the narrative about history in America on a broader set of professional practices that extend well beyond academia. This encompasses history work taking place in a wide variety of forms and settings by a diverse group of people, including the writers of academic monographs, the staff at historical societies and public archives who collect and organize historical materials, the public historians who shape history for various audiences, and the teachers who impart history in a variety of classrooms. These activities constitute professional work under almost any definition—as they are conducted in an organized and systematic way, based on training in specific knowledge and skills, and done to earn a living.[7]

Taking a larger perspective also allows for a more accurate view of the development of history in academia, since the current normative definition of a professional in the discipline only applies to a very small proportion of those engaged in the work of history. Today, only about half of the students completing history PhDs are employed in academia, and barely a third of academic historians are employed at institutions that support substantial writing and research.[8] This suggests the limits of a definition of history work based narrowly on academic employment and significant scholarly production. From this perspective, the concerns that haunt many works on the discipline, such as questions of objectivity and relativism, seem largely irrelevant.

One of the best examples of what we can learn from this wider perspective on historical activity can be found in the professionalization process that took place in history teaching at the precollegiate level. As history emerged as a modern discipline around the turn of the century, discussions about teaching played a significant role in determining the boundaries with other disciplines. Some of the earliest efforts to define and describe specialized history in the United States sprang out of dissatisfaction with history teaching at the secondary level.[9] Efforts to improve history teaching in the schools also helped advance the academic professionalization project by feeding students and resources into college history programs. Conversely, the academics' unwillingness to engage with an emerging professional literature about precollegiate teaching in the early twentieth century significantly diminished their standing in discussions about the history curriculum from World War I to the present.[10]

There is a similar story to be told from the perspective of the public history movement, which formally emerged in a time of crisis for the history discipline in the 1970s. When a sudden and unexpected collapse of the academic job market left hundreds of newly minted history PhDs without academic positions, historians rediscovered large areas of employment outside of academia. But public history has a much deeper and richer presence in a range of historical organizations that fashioned themselves into separate systems of professional work, and have been and remain vital partners in the work of the discipline.[11]

In addition to providing a perspective on current problems afflicting the historical enterprise, expanding the optic to include this wider range of activities reveals that the field has been much more dynamic than the academic perspective often allows. The boundaries of the historical enterprise were shaped and defined in a wide variety of work contexts—through engagements with issues related to history teaching, efforts to shape history for public audiences, and cooperative projects to catalog and collect the materials of the past. These efforts are generally excluded from the larger narrative about history, so it should come as little surprise when academic historians find they have very little standing in, or even access to, many of the arenas where these issues are being negotiated.[12]

The narrowing and hardening of a particular notion that equates professionalization in the discipline with the historiographic arguments of historians in research universities makes the underlying causes for these divisions increasingly difficult to see, and the resources available to address these problems increasingly remote. Anyone engaged in history work should be concerned about its health in all areas, even if academic blinders sometimes make it difficult to see the larger picture.

The postwar enclosure of disciplinary professionalization within the frame of academia is certainly not unique to history, as it fits into a larger transdisciplinary literature about academic professionalization.[13] Histories of other disciplines generally mirror the work on the history field—defining the field by those holding the PhD and employed at research universities and assessing the profession by looking at those who had written significant monographs or programmatic statements for the discipline. Most of these studies demonstrate a tendency to acknowledge a role for nonacademics in the discipline but then use similar rhetorical and structural strategies to bracket them out of the larger narrative. They tend to fall back to a recurring argument that, "unlike the other disciplines, we have a significant nonacademic branch (involved in or interfering with) the discipline's development, but its role is peripheral to the real work being done in academia."[14] This is stated quite explicitly by Peter Novick, for instance, who observed that "unlike the situation in other disciplines, nothing approaching a thoroughgoing monopoly by certified professionals was ever achieved" in history.[15] Viewed collectively, histories of the disciplines display a common and mutually reinforcing tendency to define away all work that takes place outside of research universities.

In all of these histories, the national disciplinary associations play an essential role in defining and delimiting the narratives, as their establishment and the status markers of their elective offices provide essential milestones. They are generally treated as a neutral forum (save for biases of class, gender, and race) in which the academic professionalization project was worked out. The disciplinary histories also tend to develop their framing chronologies around events in the main disciplinary association for the field.[16]

This book will be no different, but only because the activities and membership of the American Historical Association (AHA) provide ample evidence about other emerging professions in the discipline. Looking more widely at the people in the AHA and the activities taken up by the leadership of the organization demonstrates the changing ideals and practices of history—understood not merely as the products of original research but more broadly as a wide range of activities concerned with creating and disseminating a better understanding of the past. Through changes in context—the development of new technologies, literatures of best practices, and professional organizations, for instance—new professions emerged first within, and then through formal separations from, the AHA.[17] Taking a more systemic view of professionalization encourages a careful rethinking of the institutional context for these shifting relationships, particularly on the borders between academia and other institutions that either support their work (as in the libraries and archives) or amplify their work to a larger public (such as the high school classroom or a museum).[18]

Unlike most other histories, this book takes the AHA founders' original (and oft-repeated) statement of purpose—to work "for the promotion of historical studies, the collection and preservation of historical manuscripts and for kindred purposes in the interest of American history and of history in America"—as a true description of their aspirations. On this reading, the association is more accurately seen as originating in an ideal—often only partially enacted and limited by a variety of institutional and demographic factors—that cast its doors wide to "professors, teachers, specialists, and others."[19]

Admittedly, this book relies heavily on a very particular type of person—those who are attracted to the work of systematization that is an essential part of professionalization. To compensate, this book also relies on a social view of the types of people attracted to organizations that serve the same interests. To bring in these other voices and perspectives, traditional source material from the AHA (drawn from committee reports and pronouncements from leaders of the organization) is situated in a social analysis of the association's membership, supplemented by comparisons to other regional historical associations (such as the Mississippi Valley Historical Association and the Association of History Teachers of the Middle States and Maryland) and a closer look at when and why a number of professional organizations emerged out of the AHA in the 1920s and 1930s (including the National Council for the Social Studies, the Society of American Archivists, and the American Association for State and Local History). This more expansive optic, read through a narrative of professionalization, shows how the AHA gradually pared its ambit of responsibility down to the interests of college professors and monograph writers, arriving at a point by World War II when teachers at the secondary and collegiate levels and specialists in the archives and historical societies were essentially defined out of the larger project and voted with their feet by leaving the organization.

This story is organized into a relatively linear form, covering three stages in the development and fragmentation of the historical enterprise. The first period (roughly 1880 to 1910) was marked by rapid expansion across a wide range of activities and an effort to establish a broad notion of who was party to the historical enterprise under the umbrella of the association. The leaders of the AHA reached out to anyone with a "scientific" interest in history and sought the resources to engage in a wide array of historical activities. In the second period (roughly 1911 to 1925), the association provided the site and resources for a set of micro-professionalization activities within the larger historical enterprise—still maintaining a wide and diverse membership but also fostering activities that facilitated the professionalization of diverse forms of history work. In the third period (roughly 1926 to 1940), these microprofessionalization activities formally scattered into separate professional spheres, facilitated by an increasingly hostile attitude among the research university faculty in the AHA's leadership.

To provide some shape to the story, this story can be read either straight through or across the three parallel threads of analysis. The first chapter in each time period focuses on the development of an academic worldview centered on the research universities. Each of these chapters starts with a fairly conventional examination of the interests of faculty and doctoral students but then turns to a wider look at the membership of the American Historical Association to situate historians in academia within the larger historical enterprise. The second chapter in each section focuses on a variety of types of history work that generally fit under the label of public history today. These chapters consider work in a range of historical organizations but focus primarily on the development of professional identities related to the gathering and dissemination of historical materials. The third and final chapter in each section focuses on the development of the teaching profession—initially viewed as a continuum extending from schools to universities but ultimately as a discrete profession that primarily connected school teachers to specialists in education.

By 1940, the lines of difference between these professional spheres were sharply drawn both conceptually and institutionally. For all practical purposes, the "professional historians" had retreated into an enclave of universities and had an uneasy relationship even with academics employed in colleges with teaching missions. Meanwhile, archivists and historians employed at historical societies were looking at the academics (and the AHA in particular) as a foil in their efforts to develop separate professional identities. Likewise, history teachers and even some faculty in smaller colleges were integrated into separate professional networks connected to the educational community and proponents of the social studies.

Following World War II, the historical enterprise was irrevocably broken. After a lull in training and institutional development caused by the war, a host of young men and women entered the various fragments of the historical enterprise through a variety of different doors and through a plethora of different professional training grounds. Shaped in the training apparatus and institutions formalized before the war, they were acculturated into distinct professions and began to forget their common history. While members of the historical enterprise could still work together on issues of common concern, their relations tended to be rather ad hoc and across clearly marked professional lines. It was only with the rise of the public history movement and establishment of an AHA Teaching Division in the mid-1970s that leaders of the association acknowledged some sense of loss—and even some complicity—in the divided state of the historical enterprise.

Without a more expansive understanding of historical practices and

development, discussions about how certain aspects of the historical enterprise became alienated over time can easily get lost in simplistic distinctions between historians and "educationists" or academics and public historians. If today the historical enterprise seems too divided by the
work its members perform at the expense of the discipline they serve,
we should look to the past to find when and why those divisions first
appeared.

PART I

Building the Historical Enterprise, 1880 to 1910

CHAPTER ONE

Establishing a Framework for "Scientific" History Scholarship

Shortly after the American Historical Association was established, the organization's first secretary, Herbert Baxter Adams, exulted that it marked "a new historical movement."[1] As he described it, the movement's novelty consisted of the new forms of training and employment taking hold in American research universities, the development of "modern" and "scientific" research practices, and the establishment of new disciplinary networks for publishing and association. The first glimmerings of a history profession began in his efforts to use the AHA as a platform to develop and promote these efforts—abstracting from the work of a few young scholars to try to promote a new set of standards for historical research and writing.

When he was first appointed to a position in history at the new Johns Hopkins University in 1876, Adams joined less than a dozen other historians employed in academia. But with a convert's enthusiasm for German training methods, and Hopkins's basic research orientation supporting his efforts, he advanced this new form of history with a missionary zeal. At a superficial level, the historical work Adams promoted seems quite familiar. He advocated the authorship of "original work" based on research in the sources, training based on the seminar method, and the PhD as the highest form of certification. But this description obscures a number of fundamental differences from the standards of the present. For instance, the original sources used in the scholarship of the day generally came out of printed collections, the seminar method and PhD were only just being adapted from a German model, and the work of gentlemen historians remained the high point of history writing in the minds of many.

Establishing an Academic Identity for History

Over the next twenty-five years, the discipline developed four basic elements of a professional identity for history scholarship—an idealized site for employment in academia, an ideology centered on the "scientific" study of history, a system of training and certification, and an institutional apparatus for disseminating the fruits of the new scholarship. The establishment of the AHA is often viewed as the fifth element of professionalization in the discipline, but its role remained rather ambiguous in this period. Even though the association was established to serve the particular interests of research scholarship in the discipline, the leaders of the organization quickly sought a loose accommodation with more traditional practices of historical research and writing while also extending its corporate interests to include other areas of the historical enterprise.

The number of historians employed in academia increased by about 10 percent per year between 1880 and 1910, though the often blurry lines between disciplines make a precise count difficult. From the beginning, the key departments conferring history PhDs were explicitly aligned with political science. At Johns Hopkins and Columbia Universities, the departments were both constituted as history and political science and remained so for decades. Similarly, the history program at Harvard University was integrated into a Department of History and Government, and by 1910, included overlapping courses and faculty members in economics, politics, and sociology. In all three programs, historical studies and staff were subdivided into two principal categories of American and European studies.

The disciplinary ambiguity at the departmental level was often reflected at the individual level as well. Early studies on history teaching at the college level (and the membership rolls of the AHA) included a number of faculty members who subsequently identified themselves with other disciplines, such as Francis Walker and Richard Ely (usually counted among the founders of economics) and John Burgess (usually considered one of the founders of political science).[2] For his part, Adams saw history as encompassing all these other disciplines, and his doctoral students went on to serve as important figures in their development (including Woodrow Wilson in political science and Albion Small in sociology). As late as 1911, almost a quarter of the membership of the AHA still listed at least partial affiliation with another discipline, reflecting considerable ambiguity at the disciplinary boundaries that we now see as fairly solid.

Even with that as a caveat, however, the available evidence indicates significant growth in the number of academics who identified with history as a discipline in this period. From barely two dozen history faculty in 1886, the number of historians in academia grew to almost six hundred scattered across the country by 1910.[3] This growth was not isolated to the history discipline, as higher education in general expanded both geographically and intellectually. By one estimate, between 1900 and 1910 alone, the number of teaching faculty in American colleges and universities increased by more than a third (from 26,500 to 39,500).[4]

At the time, higher education was expanding to encompass a wide range of institutional types (land-grant colleges, teachers colleges, women's colleges), but the history discipline found its first real home in the research universities, which allowed for greater specialization with their discipline-based department structures and larger faculty sizes.[5] Faculty at these universities provided the intellectual force for history in this period, writing most of the prescriptive studies on the discipline and conducting much of the research and writing that was highly prized in academia. But the experiences of university faculty were hardly the norm. Faculty at a wide range of other institutions were teaching history at colleges and universities, even if they were not truly specialists in the subject or conducting research. By 1910, a significant portion of the AHA's academic members were employed at colleges and universities with teaching missions and little or no support for research. Many others in the lists were employed at community and teachers colleges. This suggests a significant gap between the historical evidence that remains about the development of history in higher education—which focuses on the expectations and ideals of historians in research universities—and the realities of what it meant to teach in the more obscure colleges of the country.

Even at the research universities of the time, the PhD was not necessarily the essential pass into academic employment that it is today. Many of the academics at the founding of the association in 1884 lacked any substantive training, and instead entered college teaching through positions in the schools or even careers in politics and business (though often a substantial published work aided their promotion into the academic ranks). As late as 1905, graduate students from Harvard reported back that they felt no particular pressure to finish their doctoral studies, as they were already well set up in a college teaching position.[6] It is only in 1919 that one student observed that this tendency was fading, and he reported an obligation to hurry back to finish the degree.[7]

Regardless of where they were employed, historians who self-consciously viewed themselves as practicing history in the "new" way were acutely conscious of the fact that they represented a very small minority of those actually writing and teaching history. And the discussions among this new breed of historian reflect considerable ambiguity about where to draw the lines separating them from their predecessors. In their references to a "profession" of history, their definition of the term seemed more akin to the act of public speaking than to a particular occupation. When they used the term, it often encompassed gentlemen or amateur historians, such as Francis Parkman and the businessman-turned-historian James Ford Rhodes.[8]

Likewise, the syllabi of texts used in the classroom by Herbert Baxter Adams and other academic historians at the time indicate the struggles of the younger generation as they tried to separate themselves from their "literary" predecessors. At their direction, students in the late nineteenth and early twentieth centuries read collections of original sources and short essays by other academics, as well as works by the gentlemen historians for background or context.[9] The older works were more synthetic and wider in scope, and they continued to shape thinking about the past at the time—even in graduate history seminars.

And the older historians still loomed large in the public consciousness of the discipline as well, so maintaining a connection provided substantial credibility for all forms of history work among the general public. Adams worked to assure that George Bancroft was selected as the third president of the AHA for precisely this purpose, and he was not alone in this perspective. In an article summarizing the best historical writing at the turn of the century, H. Morse Stephens (a professor at Cornell University) did not include a single academic on his list. He lamented, "The absorption of the work of teaching, the absence of leisure, and the lack of advantages for traveling to study material and of means to provide for paying for copies of material preserved in distant archives combine to prevent the undertaking of large tasks."[10]

Fashioning an Ideology of Modern History

In making a case for why their brand of history should be recognized as a separate discipline in academia, the younger historians tried to harness the public respectability of the older historians to the scientific ideals of the new class of research universities. As part of his effort to encourage other scholars to promote the discipline, Adams emphasized, "It must be made clear that the claim of history to rank among the sciences is founded in fact—the fact that it has a scientific method."[11] This notion of history as science tended to be vaguely defined and loosely used, but it generally included elements of the scientific method of fact gathering and inductive reasoning, treating primary documents as the foundational elements of such work, and avoiding the introduction of opinions or other literary flourishes when presenting the results of research. In an early book review in the *American Historical Review*, Maurice Bloomfield observed that the new methods set them apart from their predecessors, because "the professional scholar alone is capable of measuring and presenting the measurements of the difficulties and uncertainties that attach to any line of facts."[12]

Early on, historians connected their claim to scientific status to Charles Darwin's effort to trace change over time, and many cited Darwin directly as providing the basic framework for their efforts. Charles Francis Adams (president of the Massachusetts Historical Society), for instance, cited "what we of the new school regard as the dividing line between us and the historians of the old school, the first day of October, 1859, the date of the publication of Darwin's 'Origin of the Species.'"[13] In practice, Darwin's methods tended to be mediated through the work of the social scientist Herbert Spencer, who more clearly demonstrated how the scientific method could be applied to large-scale temporal studies of human populations.[14]

The adoption of ideas from Darwin and Spencer included more than just notions about the scientific method; it also extended to the application of evolution as a concept. A number of the projects taken up by the advanced scholars training new history PhDs (most notably in the leading graduate programs at Harvard, Hopkins, and Columbia) involved gathering their students to work on a common project, demonstrating how a particular institution "evolved" into its present form. Typical of this, Adams promoted the Teutonic "germ theory"—the notion that the antecedents of many local government institutions in the United States could trace their origins to Germany.[15] The editor of an early series of academic monographs, Albert Bushnell Hart (of Harvard University) likewise concluded that each of the authors "consciously or unconsciously learned from Charles Darwin, who is the great historical master of our age in that he has taught us how, in the world of the mind as in the material universe, there is a steady progression from one condition to another; for human institutions also follow a law of natural selection."[16] This modeling after Darwinian methods extended even to a number of religious historians of the period.[17]

As part of their identification with scientific methods, the emerging cohort of historians also singled out a new form of evidence—the primary document—that set them apart from their predecessors. The earlier "literary" historians were viewed with suspicion, because they relied heavily on secondary sources and used primary sources uncritically when they did. As James Harvey Robinson later recalled:

> We enjoyed a certain sense of superiority in our emulations, and looked down with some condescension upon our predecessors. We had made a very essential discovery, the distinction between the primary and secondary sources of historical knowledge. We inhaled the delicious odor of firsthand accounts, of the "original document," of the "official report." We had at last got to the bottom of things. Earlier writers had of course used primary sources, but in a reckless and irreverent manner as it seemed to our heightened sense of criticism.[18]

Part of the shift in the use of primary sources was a matter of circumstance. Given the near absence of public archival institutions at the national, state, or local level, much of the early historians' research in the sources could only be haphazard at best. Quite often they needed to spend their own resources to acquire manuscripts and their own libraries for research—making personal wealth a prerequisite for acquiring their sources as well as the leisure time needed for writing.[19] But as private and state institutions in the United States and abroad began collecting (and in many cases publishing) primary source materials in significant numbers, the expectations about using and citing such sources rose accordingly.[20]

The development of the scientific view of history research also promoted a social notion of the historian's work—adopting the idea that re-searchers should be able to replicate and build upon the work of others just like scientists. This ideal set the work of the newer generation apart from the "private" activities of its predecessors, whose work was writ-ten in isolation and often for partisan purposes. The newer historians envisioned themselves as participating in a larger community, mediated by their students at the local level and by other scholars at a more gen-eral level. This larger social framework provided part of the rationale (at least overtly) for eschewing partisanship and remaining objective in their classrooms and in their scholarship. It also set certain expectations about how to present one's work, ensuring that other scholars could fol-low the same trails. Hart expressed a common critique of an older his-torian, who "does not see fit to append those foot-notes which are a re-straint upon a writer, an opportunity to examine his ground, and a useful equipment for later investigators."[21]

But the social notion of the construction of knowledge also opened the door for some exceptionally dull prose. Constrained by potential criti-cism from their peers, and generally urged to bring new evidence to light, the scientific scholars accepted that there was a price to be paid for their methods in a loss of synthetic ideas and engaging prose. As Jameson con-ceded, in contrast to "picturesque historians" such as Francis Parkman,

> If there is not produced among us any work of a supereminent genius, there will surely be a large amount of good second-class work done . . . in respect to purely literary qualities. Now it is the spread of thoroughly good second-class work . . . that our science most needs at present; for it sorely needs that im-provement in technical process, that superior finish of workmanship, which a large number of works of talent can do more to foster than a few works of lit-erary genius.[22]

Others criticized this perspective as failing by another traditional measure—making the past widely accessible to the public. Benjamin Andrews of Brown University lamented the narrow factualism of many scholars: "In most directions one finds a stronger zeal for the knowledge of history than for the understanding of history. We are so busy at gath-ering facts that no time is left us to reflect upon their deeper meanings."[23] And the editors of the *Nation* (some of whom were members of the AHA at the time) regularly lamented this problem, complaining in one edi-torial about the "hundreds of ill-digested books in which the historian has rashly claimed the scientist's immunity from the requirements of form."[24] The difficulties inherent in writing history in a technical mode for academic peers quickly set up a recurring point of tension between the scientific pretensions of the younger historians and their aspirations to supersede their literary predecessors.

Preparing a New Generation of Scientific Historians

The development of history PhD programs served as the core of the emerging academic history profession, given the personnel they employed, the students they trained, and the materials they produced. But before 1910, there was considerable diversity between programs at the most fundamental level, as the basic standards and characteristics of doctoral training were slowly articulated and refined.

Although departments began conferring history PhDs sometime earlier in the nineteenth century, they only began to confer such degrees on the basis of substantial study or research (typically with a two-year time requirement) in the 1870s. The training of scholars in the field was increasingly built on a more proactive method of instruction, generally credited to the seminar method used in German universities.[25] Fundamentally, the seminar method placed an emphasis on the active production of "clear and original statements of fact and opinion." To assist this, at Johns Hopkins Adams developed a carefully organized room with a variety of aids to support discussion and reading. Adams contrasted his teaching methods with those of older scholars—most of whom taught history as just one among a number of other subjects—for their "passive methods" and reliance on standard textbooks.[26] The establishment of new programs of historical study by younger scholars with PhDs from German universities at Johns Hopkins, Columbia, and Harvard Universities in the mid-1870s and early 1880s set a new standard for the PhD, and created a much more vibrant and energetic base of history doctoral study.

Harvard conferred the first PhD as a research degree in 1873, but the Johns Hopkins department awarded almost 40 percent of the doctorates in the discipline up to the end of the century. After Adams's death in 1901, however, Hopkins quickly faded behind a number of other programs—most notably at Harvard and Columbia—in both numbers and prestige. Overall, history PhD programs conferred approximately 448 doctoral degrees between 1880 and 1910, and the ranks of programs conferring such degrees grew by an average of almost one new program per year.[27]

The history department at Hopkins had a distinct advantage over most other programs before 1900, because it was only a few years old and not encumbered by a long-standing tradition of undergraduate education. But it also benefited from a conscious effort at the university to develop a program based on graduate research from the beginning. In contrast, departments at institutions such as Harvard and Yale had to graft research activities onto their undergraduate programs. In his comprehensive survey of history teaching in American colleges in 1887, Adams credited Harvard as the first university with a true history program in the United States but lamented the persistence of older methods of instruction. He observed that "in importing the German *Seminar*, young Harvard instructors have secured only a secular evolution of that old theological and tutorial system, once the common property of England and Germany."[28] As a result, these more traditional institutions proved to be more resistant to methods that encouraged the active engagement of student's original work.

But the seminar method elicited considerable enthusiasm from faculty at colleges and universities with less entrenched traditions. After reading Adams's monograph on *Methods of Historical Study*, one southern historian enthused about promoting the seminar method at the University of North Carolina "to excite a spirit of historical research and investigation among the advanced student," and reported that the faculty there "determined to form an historical seminary modeled as nearly as possible upon your own."[29] And the perception of rupture between the prior methods of history training and the development of this new model helped to facilitate the sense of a significant new turn in the work of history scholarship, and a nascent sense of professionalizing activity. J. Franklin Jameson celebrated the fact that historians no longer had to learn their craft in "isolation," but could now enjoy "apprenticeship in the communicable portions of the art."[30]

The development of new PhD programs through this period reflects the uneven geographic distribution of departments and students. Before 1884, Johns Hopkins was the only history doctoral program established outside of the Northeast, and over the next quarter century doctoral programs grew up in other regions of the country very slowly. By 1910, history PhD programs had only just been established as far west as California and as far south as Tennessee. The number of students earning PhDs from these newer programs remained fairly modest, but they did promote a set of attitudes quite at odds with the more traditional views of the schools in the Northeast—both by promoting different worldviews (such as the "western" history articulated by Frederick Jackson Turner at Wisconsin) and a different perception of the possible relationship between history departments and historical societies. The societies in the Midwest were more "scientific" in outlook than their New England counterparts, and as such, they provided better partners for historical research and a legitimate area of employment for history doctoral students.

While the new methods of training elicited enthusiasm, the actual standards for the degree remained quite diverse from university to university. In 1893, Ephraim Emerton (a professor at Harvard University) surveyed the quality of history doctoral training and found it haphazard at best. A number of universities were still conferring doctorates based only on an extra year or two of study and successful completion of an examination. In its place, he recommended at least two years of focused and continuous study after the baccalaureate degree, under the direction of a specialist in the field, and resulting in the production of some form of new scholarly research.[31]

At the time Emerton wrote, the departments at Johns Hopkins and Harvard were still conferring the largest number of new history PhDs, but the History and Political Science Department at Columbia University surpassed them both by the turn of the century and conferred the largest number of history doctorates almost every year from 1900 to 1930.[32] These remained the three dominant departments throughout this period, but they each loomed over different aspects of the field—Harvard for its scholarly production (facilitated by its exceptional library), Columbia for its historiographical leadership (from William Dunning to James Harvey Robinson and Charles Beard), and Johns Hopkins for the organizational leadership of its faculty and students (first Adams, then his students J. Franklin Jameson, Charles Homer Haskins, and John Spencer Bassett).

Developing New Models of Scholarly Publishing

The training and institutional infrastructure for research relied heavily on the development of new publication networks to disseminate the growing volume of scholarly work in the scientific mode. The early descriptions of the history seminar programs treated the production of new knowledge as a happy byproduct of this form of teaching.[33] But by the turn of the century, the production of a substantial piece of original scholarship increasingly became an end in itself for doctoral training and the emerging profession of history. And a number of doctoral programs, including those at Harvard, Columbia, Bryn Mawr, and the University of Pennsylvania, instituted policies requiring publication of the dissertation as a criterion for receiving the degree.[34] This significantly raised the bar for younger scholars, who felt significant pressure to make their presentations worthy of publication and to find venues for the publication of their work.

The expanded emphasis on original historical research was facilitated by a rapid growth in the number of outlets for publishing such work, which at this time consisted primarily of articles. Before the turn of the century, the departments at Johns Hopkins and Columbia each initiated programs to publish series of monographic studies, which provided an outlet for their students' work and promoted their programs.[35] When announcing the Johns Hopkins University Studies in Historical and Political Science, Adams described its value in the social terms of the emerging profession, as serving to publish "kindred contributions in historical and political science so that individual efforts may gain strength by combination and become more useful as well as more accessible to students."[36] This series, and similar efforts that grew up over the following decade, encouraged a sense of identity among the often far-flung members of the discipline, while also providing models of the new type of scholarship. As one correspondent observed, "They possess the merit of being at once a model for higher academic study, in keeping with the most advanced thought and method, and are also most valuable products of original investigation."[37] Even the department at Harvard felt pressure to establish a similar publication series. Shortly after the department was constituted in 1892, faculty members there quickly converted an endowment fund to support the publication of theses and monographs.[38]

Under Adams's direction, the AHA established a similar publishing program shortly after it was established in 1884, using papers delivered at the association's annual meeting. *The Papers of the American Historical Association* (1884–89) and the *Annual Report of the American Historical Association* (1890–) served as an early journal of sorts for the discipline, including reports on the development of the historical enterprise and the work of the association, followed by essays of widely varied quality.

Collectively, these collections played a vital role in the dissemination of knowledge at the time, because the definition of a monograph was much more modest. Like the dissertations that often served as their point of origin, works labeled as "monographs" back then were rarely more than long journal articles by today's standards.[39] Nevertheless, writing in 1895, Harvard historians Edward Channing and Albert Bushnell Hart set these short-form monographs at the pinnacle of scholarly study in history, describing them as the "highest and most difficult kind of written work for students in history."[40]

But the formal structure of these publishing programs bore little relation to scholarly journals of the present. There was no substantive peer review for the papers published, and the authors were quite diverse—encompassing academics in an array of disciplines, unaffiliated writers, and politicians. The work published consisted primarily of research studies, ranging from reviews of notable historical events (which were often the work of more traditional authors) to complex studies on more obscure topics that often originated as dissertations. Regardless of whether the papers were the work of politicians or new PhDs, in topic and method they were quite similar. The presentations typically focused on political subjects, drew their material primarily from government documents or private letters, and presented their findings largely through extensive serial quotation rather than analysis. Even the basic apparatus of scholarship—such as the form and content of scholarly footnotes—was still a matter of debate and discussion for those seeking to set the discipline on a properly "scientific" footing.[41]

In an effort to boost the amount of content from junior scholars, Adams even sought additional funds to provide "bounties" to attract more original research.[42] Like the Johns Hopkins Studies, he set a lofty goal for the AHA *Papers*, which he envisioned as communicating the work of the association's members to other historians, libraries, and "American and foreign historical societies," with the goal of ultimately developing into "an *American Historical Review* under the auspices of the Association."[43]

But the AHA constantly ran up against financial barriers, as the cost of putting ink on paper often exceeded the organization's revenues in its first three years. To solve this problem, Herbert Baxter Adams and a few of the elite members in Washington, DC, (most notably Massachusetts Senator George Frisbie Hoar) engineered a congressional charter that included a publication subsidy for an "annual report," to be published through the US Government Printing Office. This arrangement greatly increased the AHA's public profile and provided an outlet for other forms of historical activity, including original documents and studies on best practices in archives and historical societies. While this created a durable foundation for the association's work and a national presence, it proved to be a mixed blessing. The Government Printing Office's publication schedule was "irregular at best," and the often haphazard pace of publication became a recurring problem over the next six decades.[44] The irregularities in the publication programs exacerbated subsequent tensions between the AHA's constituencies, some of whom relied on the reports as an essential outlet for their work.

The establishment of the *American Historical Review* in 1895 is generally seen as a vital step in the process of professionalization in the discipline, and to some extent, a rejection of the quality of the material being published in the other serial publications of the AHA. This perception is reinforced by the financial backing from history departments at five major research universities.[45] As Adams had feared when the *Review* was first founded, the best pieces from academic historians quickly began to shift over to the *AHR*, particularly after the AHA adopted the *Review* in 1898.[46] As a result, by 1905 the association's annual reports were largely devoid of original research scholarship. While the occupations of the authors of articles and book reviews in the *Review* quickly diverged from those publishing in the association's reports, the actual content did not substantially differ from its predecessor. The form, content, and methodological underpinnings of much of the work remained quite similar. The articles still focused primarily on political activities, presented material largely from government documents and private letters, and generally demonstrated their findings through extensive quotation rather than analysis. In contrast to the criteria that shaped the assessment of scholarship a few decades later, the *Review* started with only two criteria for inclusion: "accuracy and literary merit."[47]

Many of the procedures subsequently taken as guarantees of scholarly gatekeeping—such as peer review—were largely absent. Articles in the *Review* were comprised heavily of submissions from members of the board of editors and their students, with other articles often accepted based on little more than a recommendation from an author's doctoral advisor.[48] The networks of scholarship reflected in the institutional affiliations of the authors helped to reinforce the association between academia and original research. At least one member of the board of editors insisted that there was no intentional bias against historians working in other venues or even amateur historians, insisting that "we have tried repeatedly for Roosevelt, for Mahan, and other men of that type, and we simply cannot get them without paying as much for one article as we pay for all the reviews in a number."[49]

By 1910, the journal's relatively passive system of gathering articles was increasingly viewed as a problem. As he left the editorial board of the *Review* in 1909, Albert Bushnell Hart admonished the other members to engage the broader discipline by becoming more proactive in soliciting articles that reflected the best work of the moment, to "tell more upon the progress of historical investigation and thought in this country . . . instead of leaving the choice of subjects mainly to the casual initiative of writers, we should systematically try to engage articles which solve definite and important questions or treat specific subjects."[50] J. Franklin Jameson, then serving as managing editor of the journal, took this admonition to heart and circulated the recommendation to the other members of the editorial board.

In addition to its role as a forum for original scholarship, the *Review* also provided space to the larger historical enterprise. The original plan for the *AHR* encompassed the publication of original documents and discussions of pedagogy, alongside the publication of original and synthetic essays. This expanded notion of scholarship carried over into the first issue of the *Review*, which consisted of a broadly synthetic work by William M. Sloane on "History and Democracy," four articles, three document collections, and a complement of twenty-six book reviews. The articles highlighted the diversity of research forms, with an "article" by Henry Adams that was little more than an annotated correspondence and an essay by Frederick Jackson Turner that included a foldout map hand-drawn by the author.[51] The nature and form of early articles in the *Review* were markedly different as well. The articles themselves were written with a more leisurely pace and in a more florid tone—reflecting the enduring influence of the literary historians in their work. And reflecting the smaller base of interpretive scholarship to contend with, the articles had comparatively few footnotes, and references to earlier authorities (both in the text and the footnotes) often cited only the last name of the author. This diversity of historical modes earned praise in a review of historical periodicals in 1918, which cited the *Review* as "the premier historical journal of the country" that contains "articles which are the result of research, documents which are worthy of preservation, book reviews, and news notes."[52]

The periodical literature seemed to provide the primary outlet for published scholarship in the period before 1910, but a growing book publishing industry provided alternative outlets for historians as they developed longer analyses. In 1903, the first bibliography of *Writings on American History* indexed work from 155 publishing outlets. By 1910, that list had grown to 233 publishers, and there was a separate list of journals and periodicals, indicating the large and rapid expansion of literature in the discipline. Reflecting this growth, between 1900 and 1920 Harvard College's special library for history doubled in size.[53]

The book review section of the *AHR* indicates the diverse body of work in the discipline. Of the 1,671 titles reviewed in the *AHR* between 1895 and 1901, 137 were textbooks for students of different ages (such as *A Student's History of the United States* and *A Child's Guide to American History*), and almost 400 titles were source materials of some sort, either document collections for materials from around the world (e.g., *Correspondence of William Pitt* and *Collection de documents inédits sur l'histoire économique de la Révolution française*) or tools for research (e.g., *Dictionary of American Biography* and *Atlas of European History*). Of the remainder, a remarkably large proportion—over 300—were either simple biographies (e.g., *The Life of Adam Smith*) or used an exemplary life to study a period or place (such as *Theodore of Studium: His Life and Times*). What is striking in surveying the reviewed book literature of this period is how different it seems from the research scholarship of the present, as the academic historians of the period tried to develop new forms of book-length scholarship.[54]

Charles Kendall Adams's *Manual of Historical Literature*, first published in 1882, reflected the intellectual environment into which the new "scientific" historians had to accommodate themselves. Adams, then the history chair at the University of Michigan, assembled his bibliography for "students, general readers, and collectors of books." The manual highlights two aspects of this transitional phase—first that history scholarship was still perceived as having a public audience, and second that the body of historical literature (from American to "universal history") was small enough that one scholar could attempt to summarize it all without embarrassment.[55] By the turn of the century, it became increasingly common to observe that the literature on US history alone had grown beyond any one person's ability to survey, much less write properly.[56] Part of the change from 1882 to 1900 was a substantial increase in the output from scholars in academia. Notably, the *Manual* consisted largely of longer works by gentlemen and amateur historians (with only the mildest criticisms of small flaws in the writing or organization of their work) and excluded the emerging scholarly literature appearing in serial publications.

Remarkably, a discussion of "The Present State of Historical Writing" by three leading historians almost twenty-seven years later indicated that the discipline was still struggling with many of the same issues of the relationship between publishing and practice. J. Franklin Jameson (then at the Carnegie Institution of Washington, DC), Edward Channing (Harvard University), and John Bach McMaster (University of Pennsylvania) collectively worried that more than a generation of scientific history had little to show for its efforts. Jameson made it clear that the number of American history scholars had not yet reached a critical mass, noting that it was still difficult to produce book reviews in the *AHR*, because "we have not developed so large a class of persons who, whether they themselves write or not, are accomplished judges of what historical books should be."[57] More generally, the three authors seemed to agree that the new breed of historian was still struggling to supersede its literary predecessors in anything more than technique. Channing and McMaster even held out the work of the literary historians as examples of the kind of synthetic writing that the new generation of historians should aspire to.[58] So despite ready access to a publishing infrastructure for history scholarship in the scientific mode, the new generation of historians still found itself in the shadow of its predecessors.

While scholars did not generally identify "professionalism" in academia with the discipline of history at the time, they did occasionally apply the label to emerging notions of scholarship (or, in Jameson's rather punning phrase, to "professional or professorial history-writing"). But there is an undertone in some of the writing that identifies the university as only a temporary or transitional home for history. Jameson, for instance, conceded that the college or university was the only secure place for someone to earn an income writing history at the time, but warned that the other pressures and commitments of academic employment detracted from the full flowering of history writing.[59]

Representing "History in America":
The AHA and the Historical Enterprise

From its inception, the American Historical Association contained similar tensions between the past and future of history. Although the establishment of the AHA is often taken as a point of origin for professional history in America, in practice, the association was only an imperfect indicator of a rising spirit of professionalism in history scholarship.

The initial impetus to establish the AHA came from historians scattered at colleges and universities from Boston to Michigan to Baltimore, but it built on an emerging sense of history as a distinct field of activity taking root in a variety of institutional settings (schools, universities, and historical societies) and new efforts to systematize the collection of historical materials (particularly evident in Justin Winsor's *Narrative and Critical History of America*).[60] The first public call to an organizational meeting for the AHA reflects this diversity, pitching the request to "professors, teachers, specialists, and others interested in the advancement of history in this country" to join together in conference to "widen their horizon of interest and cause their individual fields of labor to become more fruitful."[61]

As a first step, the AHA had to separate from the American Social Science Association (ASSA). The ASSA represented an early impulse to gather "learned men" to discuss national reform efforts, and its annual meetings covered a range of the standard progressive subjects, ranging from tariffs to schools to temperance.[62] A number of the early leaders of the AHA had been gathering at ASSA meetings for years, and Adams had even delivered an address on "New Methods of Study in History" the year before. But the ASSA held to a rather diffuse notion of "social science," one that provided little room for more specific disciplinary interests. So in light of the growing recognition of historical study as a discrete branch of study, and following the establishment of a learned society for the modern languages in 1883, a number of historians issued a call to establish a new organization to promote a more disciplined study of history.[63]

While academic historians were instrumental in the effort, the twenty-five men gathered for the first meeting in September 1884 tangibly demonstrated the breadth of the historical enterprise at the time, drawing together university presidents and history faculty from seven colleges, the Harvard librarian and author Justin Winsor, the US Commissioner of Education, representatives from three historical societies, publisher Clarence Winthrop Bowen, as well as "several other college graduates and men of affairs."[64]

As this range of personnel indicates, history making in this period encompassed a rather large tool box of different skills, which included writing and original research alongside the gathering, assessment, and publication of historical source materials; history teaching in different settings; and the application of historical knowledge to other spheres of life. But the need to define history as a discipline was particularly important to the small number of academic historians, because they were trying to gain recognition and space for their work in institutions where traditional subjects (such as classics, math, and science) still reigned.[65] As part of their mission, they placed a premium on the promotion of original research in history, which nominally aligned the interests of the academics with the research activities of many gentlemen historians.

While the early members of the association represented a diverse range of occupations, they reflected a fairly narrow portion of the country, as most of the new members were either employed or raised in New England. This was partially a matter of regional chauvinism, but also reflected where the core of advanced study in the discipline was to be found at the time.[66] As an organization intended to reduce the isolation of historians through face-to-face meetings, naturally the center of gravity reflected those origins. From the beginning, the leaders of the new organization recognized the problem of becoming too firmly identified with New England. Part of Adams's appeal as the association's first secretary was that he was conveniently positioned along the most obvious regional fault line at the time, between North and South.[67] But by 1910, doctoral programs and more sophisticated historical societies were springing up in the West and South, and the association's regional bias became more visible, creating a recurring point of discord in the organization.

And notably, in contrast to their enthusiastic appropriations of European models of scholarship, in establishing the AHA the leaders of the new association were looking to indigenous models of associational activity, not abroad. Even up to the present, history scholars in other countries rarely organize and gather in voluntary membership organizations that aspire to set professional standards and speak for the discipline at large.[68] In contrast to the types of societies that grew up abroad, the association represented a uniquely American form of social striving even before it framed its goals in explicitly professional terms. The association was organized to serve a range of interests that encompassed social recognition of the discipline, material aid and support, and the networking of ideas and employment opportunities.

Over the course of the AHA's first twenty-five years (from 1885 to 1910), membership in the AHA grew almost thirteen-fold—from 220 charter members at the end of its first year to 2,763 by 1910. A significant part of the growth before 1910 came from an enlargement of the organization's activities, from a narrow focus on discussions about original research to a larger effort to encompass the full breadth of the historical enterprise. Most notably, the association obtained a congressional charter in 1889 that expanded the organization's focus to include "the promotion of historical studies, the collection and preservation of historical manuscripts, and for kindred purposes in the interest of American history and of history in America."[69]

The enlarged scope of activities and additional resources and exposure that resulted from the congressional charter led to a near doubling of the membership between 1888 and 1891. That growth accelerated after 1896, when the organization began to tangibly put those ideals into practice by taking substantial leadership roles in the areas of secondary school teaching, archival work, and the publication of original source materials. This was reinforced by the adoption of the *American Historical Review* two years later, which provided a more regular and tangible benefit of membership.

The promotional literature published by the organization from 1890 to 1910 reflects this widening embrace of the entire historical enterprise. While the original call to members stressed sociality and the promotion of original research, a promotional flyer from 1904 described the association's purposes and scope as focused on other aspects of the historical enterprise, such as its Historical Manuscripts and Public Archives Commissions. The brochure also promised that the association intended to go further and "enter upon new and important historical activities." And the membership of the organization had grown much more expansive as well, as the authors observed, "In organization, the distribution of its members, in initiating the historical enterprises, the American Historical Association is truly national, and deserves the support of the wider public than has yet been admitted to membership. The [governing] Council believes that not fewer than three thousand persons in the United States are eligible to membership, and would take a warm interest in the work of the Association."[70] Notably, the *American Historical Review* was not even mentioned in the 1904 flyer. Likewise, in a promotional flyer distributed five years later, the association highlighted four primary activities: "Publication" (in which the *AHR* was listed after the *Annual Report*), "The Teaching of History," "Historical Societies," and "Archives and Manuscripts."[71] In its activities and self-presentation then, the AHA was attempting to represent something larger than just original scholarship.

The changing demographics of the governing council and membership of the association reflected the enlarged scope of the organization. The first council included two university presidents, three university faculty members, a university librarian, two historical society staff, and one publisher. But the charter members of the association were significantly more diverse, with barely a quarter of the membership employed in academia. Only three of the men on the initial governing council and barely 5 percent of the charter membership held a history PhD (most from foreign universities).

As the membership grew over the next twenty-seven years, the representation of academic historians in both the leadership and the membership was further diluted as the AHA sought to represent all historical interests and occupations. Much of the growth, at least measured by members' institutional affiliations, came from precollegiate teaching or staff at historical organizations (fig. 1.1).

Regardless of the AHA's limitations as a vessel for the aspirations of academic historians, however, the organization's membership rolls and correspondence provide ample evidence of a growing sense of identification among academic historians between 1884 and 1911. Throughout this period their numbers were expanding and spreading to remote sections of the country. In 1884, just five members of the AHA identified themselves as employed at a college or university (though estimates are that the actual number of employed history faculty was closer to a dozen). By 1900, the number of academic historians in the membership increased to 79 and more than doubled to 189 a decade later. Among the early history PhDs who had joined the AHA, more than three quarters found employment in colleges and universities, but the employment of history PhDs who joined the AHA became more diverse in the period up to 1911. Among PhD recipients before 1900, almost all had a position in a college or university by the turn of the century. In the decade after 1900, however, growing numbers of history PhDs can be found taking up jobs

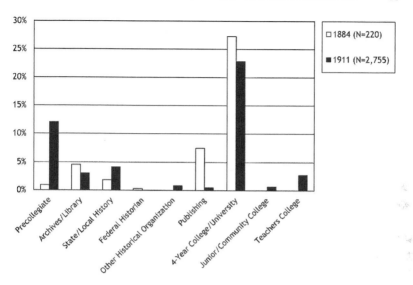

FIGURE I.I. History-related workplaces of AHA Members, 1884 and 1911 (nonhistory employed not shown)
Source: Tabulation of AHA members listed with employment information. Membership information published in *Papers of the American Historical Association*, vol. 1, and *AHA Annual Report 1911*.

in a variety of other workplaces, including schools, government offices, and historical societies.[72]

Despite his enthusiasm about a "new movement" in history, Herbert Baxter Adams spent most of his sixteen years as executive secretary trying to establish an organization that could bridge the divisions in the historical enterprise—between old and new in history writing, teachers at various levels, and those gathering, organizing, and disseminating primary source materials. His interests could seem half-hearted at times, and his appeals to those with a more traditional interest in history were often self-serving—particularly the energy with which he ingratiated himself to political leaders in Washington. But in doing so, he was recognizing the simple reality that the ranks of academic historians remained tiny, providing very few resources to advance their cause. And by that measure he had a fair amount of success, most notably by developing a diverse membership base and obtaining a large (though not always regular) federal subsidy for the association.

But this balancing act was often difficult. Early on, older members with more traditional interests resented the narrow attention to presen-

tations of academic research. Just four years after the association was established, Edward Eggleston (a Methodist minister and author who was
later to become an AHA president) resigned his membership, complaining that the association "seems to be in the interest of college professors
only and to give those who are not of that clan the cold shoulder."[73] Conversely, academics were quitting that year for precisely the opposite reason, citing the apparent lack of commitment to academic interests and
because they felt underutilized and underappreciated.[74] A few years later
their disappointment at the association's expansive focus prompted the
independent establishment of the *AHR*. In the period before the turn of
the century, the tension between traditional and scientific views of history writing tended to manifest in complaints about the mix of speakers
at the annual meeting—with the academics privately deriding the "old
bulls" invited to deliver talks and nonacademics protesting the pedantry
of the academics.[75]

The conflicting interests became much more public after Herbert
Baxter Adams retired from his post in 1900. (He cited nervous exhaus-
tion and died barely a year later.) This set off a battle between the association's assistant secretary, A. Howard Clarke (a curator at the Smithsonian Institution), who expected to replace Adams, and some of the
academics on the AHA Council (most visibly Albert Bushnell Hart of
Harvard) who felt the organization needed the leadership of "a scholar."
In an effort to balance some of the competing interests in the historical enterprise, the council divided the secretariat into two positions—
leaving Clarke with the day-to-day management of the association's affairs while creating a new "Secretary to the Council" position to be filled
by the medieval historian Charles Homer Haskins (who was then moving from the University of Wisconsin to Harvard). Haskins served as the
public face of the association.[76]

It would be easy to read this as reversing the organization's growing
embrace of the diverse aspects of the historical enterprise, but the correspondence from the period indicates that this was primarily a matter
of personality. Projects focused on other areas of the historical enterprise continued apace, and after Clarke left eight years later, the council
selected another nonacademic historian who enjoyed much greater ad-
miration and support. When Waldo Leland Gifford of the Carnegie Institution succeeded Clarke in 1909, he made the position a much more
powerful and significant position in the association.

Despite the tensions evident in these transfers of power in the organization, by 1910 the AHA had built up the infrastructure and personnel to represent the wider historical enterprise. Indeed, the organization had already taken up a number of projects to develop and promote efforts to support other aspects of the historical enterprise, particularly work on the tools and materials of historical research and the interests of improved history teaching. While the interests of the academic historians remained the most clearly defined area of professionalizing activity taking place under the disciplinary umbrella of the association, the organization had emerged as a leader for a much wider range of practices in the discipline.

Developing the Tools and Materials of History Research

Reflecting the shifting alignments of personnel in the historical enterprise, after almost a quarter century in academia, J. Franklin Jameson left his position at the University of Chicago in 1904 to take up a position that "presents more largely the kind of work I like to do" at the Carnegie Institution of Washington's Department of Historical Research.[1] Jameson continued to serve as a leader in the discipline's scholarly production (particularly as editor of the *American Historical Review*), but the shift to the Carnegie Institution represented the culmination of his efforts to elevate the discipline's work on the tools and materials of research. His efforts to encourage the collection and publication of primary source materials and to promote better archiving practices, and his shift from academic to nonacademic employment—activities often lumped together under the umbrella of public history today—all marked the emergence of other forms of work in the historical enterprise.

From the AHA's earliest days, thinking about these activities was framed by the examples of early collectors and societies in the United States and more extensive state-sponsored projects in Europe. The early leaders of the association were often critical of the preceding generation of historians for failing to press for reforms of archival conditions and practices at the state and national levels.[2] Some of the prescientific historians, such as Hubert Howe Bancroft and Peter Force, took an active interest in gathering and collecting materials but did so as private citizens relying on their personal wealth. In other areas of the country, modest collecting was done by state libraries and historical societies, but not in a particularly systematic or consistent way. It was only with the rise of the scientific historians and their enthusiastic attitude toward source materials that the historians began an active program to promote and support the collection, preservation, and dissemination of documents.[3]

Establishing a New Responsibility for Historical Documents

In 1880, this area of historical activity had barely developed even the precursors to a professional identity. Very few of the institutions that would come to represent these interests existed, and the few that did were highly idiosyncratic in their approach to their work. This is perhaps best evident in the work of the historical societies of this period, which took widely different views of their missions and work. The Massachusetts Historical Society, for instance, was viewed primarily as a preserve for the antiquarian interests of the elite of the state, with a rather haphazard collecting policy of books, newspapers, and pamphlets.[4] By the end of the century, many of the newly emerging science-minded historians were grumbling about these older societies, and the president of the society worried that "I have often—more frequently too of late than formerly—heard it intimated that the day of usefulness of historical societies . . . was over."[5]

But this skepticism was particularly focused on societies in the East. As a model in the West, the Wisconsin Historical Society served as an extension of the state government, funded to serve the interests of the people of the state and intimately connected to the main state university.[6] By the turn of the century, Wisconsin served as a model for similar relationships between faculty and staff at historical organizations and societies that were springing up in Illinois, Missouri, and Minnesota, though as one historian noted, "The relations of the college departments to the societies is one of little more than friendly interest."[7]

While all of the societies gathered historical materials and made them available in a variety of media, what they collected and how they shared their collections with researchers and the general public were fundamentally different. Archival work in the period—to the extent it could be said to exist—was performed largely as an extension of other activities—typically either antiquarian collecting or administrative recordkeeping. As it emerged into a separate sphere of activity, archival work was generally subordinated to the production of interpretive scholarship—drawing on the same scientific ideology and notions of the social construction of new knowledge in the discipline. Nevertheless, by 1900, 3 percent of the AHA members with PhDs can be identified as employed in this area of work. And even among historians employed in academia, many, if not most of them, accepted a relatively crude form of collecting and dissemination as an essential part of their own work. In one of the earliest essays about monographic history research, for instance, Edward Channing and Albert Bushnell Hart of Harvard admonished authors to "append the text of rare and important documents, exactly transcribed."[8] H. Morse Stephens of Cornell explicitly cited this convergence of activities as a vital part of the work of academia, observing that "in the production of monographs, in the selection and editing of documents, and in the training of men to do the necessary pioneer work among historical materials, the professors in American universities have taken their part in clearing the way for more accurate knowledge."[9]

While Herbert Baxter Adams regularly upheld the same ideals in his own work, he was fairly reticent about using the resources of the American Historical Association to promote it as an organized area of activity. The *Papers* and annual reports of the AHA offered very few case studies of archiving work (or the research process, for that matter). But Jameson stepped forward in the 1890s to articulate a more expansive notion of the historical enterprise that encompassed this larger field of work—promoting the imperative to gather and disseminate original materials.

When the AHA was established in 1884, the societies also provided institutional points of reference for the early leaders of the organization. Although the subject of tools and materials for research was not part of the formative description of the AHA, the early leaders did include this sort of work among the potential activities of the organization. As they saw it, an essential purpose of the association's meetings was to provide opportunities for sharing information about the location of sources.[10] The scope of their ambitions was shaped in part by the examples of foreign activities to promote research. The *Monumenta Germaniae Historica*, a massive state-funded project for the publication of original historical documents in Germany, served as a particularly important model for many in the first generation of scientific historians. It was cited as a model of collective historical activity and the advantage of bringing government resources to bear on the study of the past, but also as an institutional hub around which to form a particular "school" of study.[11] With that example in mind, as the officers of the association lobbied for a congressional charter they specifically listed among their goals "the collection and preservation of historical manuscripts."[12] This effort to expand the legitimacy and potential resources for gathering and publication of historical materials led to the enlarged perceptions of who should serve as a leader in the association, and who should join as a member.

The defining emphasis on documentary sources, and a shift in topical attention among newer historians, supported this growing interest in American historical materials. Among those who had received history PhDs in the United States up to 1884, barely half had written dissertations on US history, and the work of only one of them extended chronologically past 1816. By the turn of the century, however, two-thirds of the PhD recipients were doing their dissertations on some aspect of US history, and they were increasingly tilted toward the history of the United States between the Revolution and Reconstruction.[13] The materials used in original articles published between 1885 and 1900 also show a growing turn toward archival sources in this period. The number of citations to published documents dropped steadily in the *Papers* and *Annual Reports* and accelerated in the pages of the *American Historical Review* after 1895, while the number of citations to archival records rose steadily.[14]

Despite the relative decline in citations to printed source materials, they were still used extensively in both scholarship and pedagogy, so there continued to be a strong sense that significant documents (particularly those dealing with political and military subjects of "broad and general interest") should be organized, edited to a high standard of quality, and published for wider use.[15] As a result, documentary editing became a significant area of interest and concern for a number of AHA members, as well as the staff in a variety of historical organizations.

Developing an Institutional Infrastructure for History Materials

The extension of an ethos at the individual level to support the gathering and dissemination of source materials was diffused somewhat by an often chaotic network of institutions to carry out this type of work in the late nineteenth century. At the national level, the association focused a considerable amount of attention on pressing the government to establish a central repository for its records and commit to a regular practice of publishing significant documents. Below the national level, historians had to work with and through a wide variety of institutions and authorities.

Despite similarities in name, the historical societies varied widely in their programs, structure, and personnel depending on their location and sources of support. In the East, the societies were often privately supported and tended toward the antiquarian—generally gathering materials from elite families and exceptional figures in a fairly unsystematic way. Further West (and sometimes in the South) younger societies were often supported by public funds and tended toward a more democratic view of the materials worth preserving. Beyond the organizations specifically labeled as historical societies, the role of gathering state materials (broadly conceived to include a wide variety of objects, personal histories, and paper records), classifying them for use, and sharing them with a wider audience took place under a variety of institutional guises. In some states, this sort of work was done through the state libraries, in others, under the label of a "historical commission." As the historical societies began to organize themselves and take on a discrete identity in the early twentieth century, they tended to embrace all of these different institutions, regardless of the specific label.[16]

In the late nineteenth century, much of the collecting work was done under the auspices of the library and was largely restricted to printed objects—books, newspapers, pamphlets, and maps. In Wisconsin and Missouri, for instance, the societies annually reported on highly quantified collection efforts in the numbers of printed works added to the collections. But they also started to add other ephemeral material, such as government documents and correspondence, and also began to invite letters and recollections from significant historical figures in the state.[17]

Collectively, these institutions provided a vital service to history researchers, as well as an emerging area of employment for students from history graduate programs. But these institutions did not yet constitute a well organized or systematic area of work. The gathering and preservation of materials and documents were often haphazard (as many acknowledged at the time). Members of staff also tended to blur many of the bright lines of subsequent professional work in historical institutions. Most visibly in this period, they often straddled lines between personal and official work for the institution. The correspondence shows a number of cases where staff at these institutions were collecting for the institution, for instance, but publishing the best of the materials they gathered under their own names. In a description of his activities, for instance,

William Egle of the State Library of Pennsylvania reported dividing his time between "official" tasks of arranging and classifying material for eventual use, and "personal" efforts to publish genealogical and military records.[18] Nevertheless, the establishment of this scattered set of state-supported institutions provided an institutional context and point of reference for a new type of history work outside of academia.

The growth in history-related institutions was promoted by the interests of historians, but it was also connected to changes in the training and availability of personnel in the discipline. Quite a few students from history graduate programs (including history PhDs) were taking up employment outside of academia, in the growing number of historical societies, archives, and other history-related institutions such as the Department of Historical Research at the Carnegie Institution of Washington. And a number of the history PhDs who took leadership positions in the AHA would become determined advocates of new forms of history work developing outside of academia, including J. Franklin Jameson at Carnegie, Herbert Friedenwald at the Library of Congress, Joseph Schafer and Louise Kellogg at the State Historical Society of Wisconsin, Benjamin Shambaugh at the State Historical Society of Iowa, Solon Buck at the Minnesota Historical Society and National Archives (who served as treasurer of the AHA and helped found the Society of American Archivists), and Charles Crittenden of the North Carolina Historical Commission (who led the Conference of Historical Societies out of the AHA). Aside from those with PhDs, the list of AHA leaders who did not earn the PhD but gained distinction in the AHA for work in the wider historical enterprise was also quite long.

Much of this change derived from the proliferation of history-related institutions at the state, local, and federal levels that provided employment to those working in the field of history but also helped to facilitate new types of research in the United States. But the linkage of employment and new types of historiography made many in the discipline acutely conscious (and increasingly concerned) about the perilous condition of many of these materials. An early survey of the historical societies found that each of them tended to rely on "the efforts and enthusiasm of a few individuals" and tended to reflect "the growth of historic interest in the community which it represents."[19] As a result, the societies were highly dependent on factors at the local level. This created a patchwork of coverage and activities, and very different (and not always healthy) relationships between the societies.[20]

As an institutional hub for these different interests, the *AHA Annual Report* served a vital early role in drawing these disparate parts of the historical enterprise together. Beginning in 1895, the annual reports provided a wealth of resources for the particular interests of archivists, documentary editors, and bibliographers, including documents, calendars of manuscripts, and reports on archival materials. The reports also gave them a sense of place within the AHA and the larger historical enterprise.

The resulting publications now fill a large bookshelf, but the diversity of interests vying for space in the reports and a cap on the federal subsidy for publication imposed significant limits on how much could be published. This created an economics of scarcity in the organization that provides a useful barometer for some of the professional boundary disputes in the historical enterprise. Within a decade of its first publication, for instance, the limits on available space in the *Report* opened up rifts that set those concerned about disseminating manuscript materials against those promoting better archival practices, and also pitted the historical societies against those interested in disseminating bibliographies of scholarly work.

Shortly after the arrangement with the federal government had been finalized, Jameson called on the association to use its annual meetings to vet original documents and publish them in the *Report*.[21] The governing council rejected the idea, because it was still hoping to convince the federal government to take up such publication activities on its own, but also because it recognized that such a project required a protoprofessional system of editorial oversight and review before publication.[22] As a result, the early reports of the association largely excluded such materials despite pleas from the first editor of the *Report* that the AHA should "properly be the medium for publication of much material that is of national importance."[23] Adams remained ambivalent about focusing so much effort on the materials of research rather than promoting interpretive advances in the field, wondering whether the costs of Jameson's manuscript proposal should be better spent on "bibliographic work showing the progress of historical science in America."[24]

However, as optimism about the federal government taking up publishing work began to fade, in 1895 the AHA formed the first independent committee in the organization—a Historical Manuscripts Commission to "collect information regarding the manuscript materials relating to American history, especially those which are in the hands of private persons or institutions."[25] Jameson's dual role as chair of the commission and managing editor of the *AHR* provided a platform for proselytizing about the commission's work, and he predicted in a subsequent issue of the *Review* that, "if the work of the commission is successfully conducted, its establishment must surely be regarded as a step of great importance in the promotion of scholarly research in American history."[26]

The members of the first Manuscripts Commission reflected the diversity of interests on this issue, drawing together academics from the three major sections of the country as they conceived them at the time (Jameson at Brown, Frederick Jackson Turner at Wisconsin, and William P. Trent at the University of the South) with Douglas Brymner, the national archivist of Canada, and publisher Talcott Williams of the Philadelphia Press. This encapsulated the identity politics of the association, in its effort to reach across the regional divisions of the day (North, South, and West) while also bringing together academics, archivists, and publishers.

The initial efforts from the commission offered a good measure of the scale of Jameson's ambitions, as it quickly sent out dozens of letters to institutions and individuals that might be holding materials or have information about them.[27] The results of the survey filled almost 560 pages of the next *Report*, encompassing a bibliography of printed guides to archival materials and a range of documents from Britain and North America.[28] And work on these materials was not limited to the five members of the commission. Reflecting the wider ethic in the discipline to support the dissemination of such source materials, the AIIA's executive council spent a great deal of time reviewing the quality of the materials going into the commission's reports, discussing other potential collections for publication, and assuring enough funding to ensure a wide distribution of materials.[29] In many ways, having a practical focus seemed to vitalize the association's governing body, which up to that point had largely consisted of just "very brief and informal affairs."[30]

The success of the Manuscripts Commission generated considerable enthusiasm about the other kinds of leadership and materials the AHA could offer, so the council established a Public Archives Commission in 1899, "to investigate and report, from the point of view of historical study, upon the character, contents, and functions of our public repositories of manuscript records."[31] Although the distinction between manuscripts and archives seems somewhat anachronistic now, historically the division followed the sequence in which the two commissions were established and the different interests they represented. Manuscripts were designated as private documents (such as personal papers), while archives were collections of materials produced by government officials and entities. The territories marked out by the two commissions provided conceptual distinctions that endured for generations (to the subsequent chagrin of some in the library and archival communities).[32] In addition to fostering divisions among those assigned to care for the source materials, this separation also neglected important classes of materials that are of considerable interest to historians today, particularly the records of nongovernmental entities such as businesses, labor unions, and churches.[33] But at this point there seemed to be a broad consensus that political leaders and institutions were the most significant subjects for historical research, and that therefore their materials were the most worth preserving and making available.

The Public Archives Commission adopted a very different structure from the Manuscripts Commission—instead of a representative five-person committee, the new commission had only four regular members with the power to appoint "adjunct" members to draw in expertise from around the nation to investigate conditions at the local level. The four initial members of the Public Archives Commission were academics and once again represented an effort at regional balance, with William MacDonald (at Bowdoin College in Maine), James Harvey Robinson (at Columbia), Lester Bugbee (at the University of Texas), and Howard Caldwell (at the University of Nebraska). The commission had quick success in commissioning reports on conditions in twenty-two states, and within a year gathered and published ten reports covering states ranging from Massachusetts down to North Carolina and as far West as Nebraska.[34] Despite the discipline's heavy emphasis on political and military issues at the time, the commission's reports ranged widely through materials being created by various governmental entities, encompassing records and materials that later provided the basis for social and economic histories. The surveys of municipal records in New York and Philadelphia, for instance, included records from the board of health, the bureau of highways, and the orphans' court.[35]

The commission's reports served three functions in facilitating the subsequent professionalization of different aspects of the historical enterprise. For academic researchers, the reports provided valuable guides to otherwise inaccessible source materials to promote new areas of research.[36] Perhaps more importantly, the archives commission's reports also demonstrated the appalling treatment of most state and local records. By bringing such neglect to light, and giving it national exposure in a federal report to Congress, the commission focused attention on these issues and helped to generate additional funding for their proper care and management at the local, state, and national levels.[37] Finally, the reports also began to articulate basic models and standards of archival practice in the United States, which helped to generate the essential resources and institutional basis for the archival profession.[38]

After its first decade, the commission could plausibly claim credit for archival legislation in more than a dozen states and provided the foundation for lobbying efforts to support a "hall of records" in the nation's capital.[39] It would take more than three decades to establish a proper national archives, but the general agitation on these issues (supported by a number of hereditary and patriotic interests at the local level) fostered a proliferation of new institutions focused on history. Within two decades after the commission began its work, almost a quarter of the states had developed centralized archival programs for their records, and most of the others had begun to develop less systematic programs to preserve at least some of their records. While still small in number, these new institutions provided employment for dozens of people gathering and classifying records generated at the local, state, and national levels. Many of the newly employed record keepers had graduate training in history, if not a history PhD, and served as the nucleus for the archival profession.[40]

Creating New Homes for History at the State and Local Levels

The association's efforts to provide substantive leadership for this type of history work at the state and local levels was often frustrated by a plethora of competing institutional arrangements, where "the archival function had to find a place among a whole range of state agencies that could include a state library, law library, historical society, state museum, library commission, and a legislative reference bureau."[41] While the state historical societies had been around for many years (more than a century in some parts of the Northeast), state-owned and state-operated archives only really started with the establishment of the Alabama Department of Archives and History in 1901.[42] The histories of similar organizations generally seemed to start in a similarly haphazard manner, often with modest collection and publication programs by one or two state agencies, ultimately leading to a more active engagement between state officials and faculty in a variety of history departments. But at least until 1910, many states (and many scholars) considered the publication of records an adequate substitute for the proper preservation of original documents.[43] After an initial flurry of activity inspired by the Public Archives Commission, the growth in the proportion of states with a specific body assigned to care for the public records of the state (and paid accordingly) grew painfully slowly.

Alongside the establishment of state-owned and state-supported institutions, a number of other historical societies benefited from the interest and attention generated by the two commissions. Around the turn of the century, some of the association's activities were focused on addressing the diversity in structure and forms of historical activity at the local level. The relationship between the national organization and these more local interests tended to be uneven at best. Jameson's disparaging comment about historical societies in 1897 (scoring them for focusing on history that is "purely local and nothing else") is often cited as indicative of a growing academic hubris in this period.[44] In the perception of many, the nature of the relationship was one-sided, with societies and individuals at the local and state levels assigned the role of gathering raw materials while academics processed and disseminated them for a national audience.[45] But the actual relationship between the state and local historical societies and between the societies and the academics was more dynamic and complex. Jameson's comments were generally targeted at the historical societies of his home region of New England, where privately owned societies reflected the narrow and antiquarian interests of their patrons and rarely measured up to his high standards of historical craftsmanship.[46] The leaders of some of the historical societies in the West shared his perspective on this point. Reuben Gold Thwaites, the head of the Wisconsin Historical Society, referred to them with near-equal derision as the "so-called learned societies in the East."[47] Jameson was considerably more enthusiastic about the state-supported historical societies west of the Alleghenies. As these organizations established themselves around the turn of the century, their leaders found greater welcome in the AHA, as Thwaites and Benjamin Shambaugh (head of the State Historical Society of Iowa), ascended to high positions in the association.

As early as 1897, Lucy Salmon put forward an idea for "the affiliation of local historical societies with the American Historical Association," but her taxonomy of the societies suggests considerable ambiguity about their definition. She classified them by geographical scope as "National" (lumping together the AHA with the American Baptist Historical Society), "Local" (drawing together state, sectional, county, city, and town historical societies under one heading), and "Kindred Associations" (including the American Geographical Society). Despite the lack of precision in her definitions, she accurately diagnosed that "each society is absolutely independent in its work and maintains communication with other similar societies only through irregular correspondence and exchange of publications. The result is often ignorance of what has been done by others, lack of system, duplication of work and in the same locality, duplication of library facilities."[48]

Her observations are amply borne out in the correspondence among the societies and related organizations of the period, as much of the correspondence before 1905 focused primarily on basic policy and fiscal matters—such as exchanging advice on funding levels and the legislative language that empowered their various activities.[49] To break down the differences, Salmon proposed an "organic connection between National and Local Societies," which would "avoid duplication of work"; "make possible the circulation of information in regard to methods of administration that have been found helpful by individual societies"; and provide a "central organization" that "would serve as a clearing house for individual students who are looking for special subjects to be investigated." Despite some initial enthusiasm for the idea, the leaders of the association deferred the proposal, concerned over the additional costs for a new organization. And as the leaders of the association explored the matter further, they found "comparatively few local societies which have sufficient vigor to lead their members to desire conferences with the representatives of other local societies."[50]

Despite continued misgivings, the council of the association finally convened a Conference of Historical Societies in 1904. Initially, the conference only consisted of a separate session within the annual meeting, intended to promote "greater cooperation" with the societies, and minimize "unwise and unnecessary duplication of work" among them.[51] Thwaites organized and chaired the first conference, even though he shared Jameson's sense that only a handful of his peers could be considered "up to the modern standard."[52] Throughout his correspondence in the preparations for the conference, he emphasized his desire to bring the leaders and staff of the historical societies up to a standard as "professional history workers," but conceded that "most of them have nothing but hopes, enthusiasm, and a very limited supply of experience."[53]

Nevertheless, the establishment of this conference alongside the archives and manuscripts commissions visibly opened up a space in the AHA for a wider range of history work in the interests of the association. It also served a professionalizing function for the history specialists employed in those organizations.[54] This proved to be quite timely as the number of historical societies recognized by the association nearly doubled over the following decade, from 215 in a 1905 survey to 375 in 1916 (fig. 2.1). In addition to the growth in quantity, there was a marked change in the qualitative characteristics of these organizations, with a notable increase in the number of organizations with more than one paid employee, elaborated structures that included systematic collecting and publishing programs, and increased financial support from local or state legislators.

The issue of financing dominated the discussions at the first meeting of the conference, indicating a range of differences about the societies' institutional autonomy and responsibilities to the larger historical

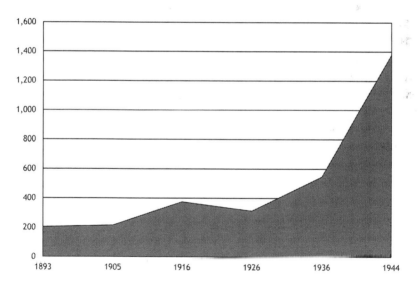

FIGURE 2.1. Estimated number of state and local historical societies, 1893–1944
Source: Tabulation of institutions listed in "Historical Societies of the United States," *AHA Annual Report, 1893*; and AHA Conference of Historical Societies reports in the *AHA Annual Reports* (1906 and 1916), *Handbook of American Historical Societies* (1926), and *Guide to State and Local History Societies* (1936 and 1946).

enterprise. Thomas M. Owen, head of the first state Department of Archives and History, in Alabama, asserted that a direct connection to state government was the only way to assure suitable funds and responsibility to care for state records. But Warren Upham, secretary of the Minnesota Historical Society, maintained that a direct connection to state institutions created a "danger of being subjected to political influence." Other speakers lamented the diverse and overlapping types of institutions in many states, which led to duplication of efforts and opportunities for materials to fall through the cracks and be lost.[55]

The following year, Thwaites surveyed the societies to clarify the apparent differences. The resulting report offered a more precise taxonomy of the societies than the one earlier offered by Salmon. He broke up his list into four types, separating national societies from "sectional societies," "state societies and departments," and "local societies." In the course of developing the survey, however, Thwaites and others struggled to find a definition that would exclude "patriotic" and genealogical societies, such as the Daughters of the American Revolution. In the end, they established two basic functions of a historical society: the collection of materials related to its subject and the dissemination of those materials.[56] These goals aligned the historical societies with the interests of academic researchers but also offered new opportunities for history employment in research, archiving, and documentary editing. The authors of the final report observed that the societies represented a diversity of structures—with some owning an entire building, including a library and museum, while others comprised little more than a room—and relied on diverse and often contingent funding sources, including member dues, endowments, and varying levels of government appropriations.

In an effort to build closer ties to this area of the historical enterprise, Thwaites was appointed to the governing council of the AHA to represent the "best methods and work on the part of state and local historical societies."[57] Under Thwaites leadership, the society in Wisconsin held a premier position in this area. Its staffing and funding were the envy of other societies with scientific aspirations, and Thomas McAdory Owen observed, "Wisconsin has an enviable place at the head of the historical enterprise."[58]

Despite Thwaites's representation, there was still a perception that the association's connection to the societies remained "shadowy" in dealing with the "Historical Society problem," and efforts to create more systematic affiliations with the societies in 1905 and 1906 quickly failed.[59]

One society leader complained that "states are too independent . . . and their societies too conscious of ego to unite in such an undertaking."[60] Nevertheless, Thwaites received regular requests for offprints of his report about the societies over the next three years, which one of his counterparts noted could "prove of much value toward unifying future historical work and enterprise, and in properly pointing the way to new fields of activity."[61]

New Institutions, New Networks

After 1905, it becomes difficult to separate the AHA's direct role in these kinds of activities, particularly at the national and international levels, from the activities of the Department of Historical Research at the Carnegie Institution of Washington. Even before he assumed the management of the department, Jameson had convinced the institution to subsidize the clerical and editorial activities of the AHA, an arrangement that lasted twenty-five years.[62] This also led to a tacit division of labor between the AHA and the department. Even though the original mandate for the Public Archives Commission included federal archives, the association did very little at the national level—at first in the hope that the government could be convinced to address these issues, but later in deference to the Carnegie Institution. The department's first substantial report (described as "the first historical enterprise" of the institution) was a *Guide to the Archives of the Government of the United States in Washington* by Claude Van Tyne and Waldo Leland. Their study brought to light many of the flaws in the federal government's archiving practices and provided real impetus to the movement for a national archives.[63] In contrast to a number of the reports from the Public Archives Commission, this report focused heavily on traditional political and military subjects. The authors sniffed, "From the papers of the Continental Congress or the journals of the Confederate Congress to correspondence relating to the pay or dismissal of a janitor there is considerable depreciation in value."[64]

The connection between the AHA and institution became even closer in 1909, when Leland took over as secretary of the association. Leland rarely makes much of an appearance in histories of the discipline, because he was not an academic, never completed his doctoral studies, and never published a major scholarly work. His distinctions were in archival cataloguing and theory, organizing the international history community, and working across disciplinary boundaries.[65] His work on the *Guide to Archives*, his surveys of manuscript materials in the southern states and France, and his close connection to Jameson helped secure his initial appointment at the AIIA.[66] Over the next decade, however, he played a critical role in the professionalization efforts of a number of areas of the historical enterprise. And Leland's elevation demonstrates that a nonacademic professional could gain significant status and respect in the discipline in this period. Although he lacked a PhD, his graduate training at Harvard, his commitment to scientific principles in the preparation of manuscripts and the management of collections, and his status on the international stage all served as a bond to the academics.

Like the association, the societies quickly recognized that the institution could play a vital role in their efforts. Initially, some of the societies were concerned that the department would duplicate, and perhaps even supersede, their efforts. But by 1909, they were enthusiastically subsidizing the department's services to make transcribed copies of federal records by various federal agencies about their respective states.[67] Following this model, the societies also started to develop the necessary systems and infrastructure to start sharing their collections and materials, both among themselves and with distant scholars.[68]

Further west, the establishment of the Mississippi Valley Historical Association (MVHA) as an organized body in 1907 further elevated the interests of the societies. The initial plan for the MVHA was developed by leaders of historical societies in the region to coordinate and promote their efforts to publish source materials related to the history of the valley.[69] A few of the society leaders in the West, particularly Thwaites, were deeply ambivalent about the endeavor at the outset, noting that an initial meeting for the group was "so thoroughly genealogical in its character, and in a general way amateurish, that I did not take kindly to the movement." Even though he would later serve as president of the MVHA, he observed that—initially at least—he thought it "hardly worth the serious consideration of professional students of history."[70]

Nevertheless, the members of the MVHA quickly formed an interest group that had a direct influence on the AHA. At the 1907 meeting, a number of leaders from the AHA promoted a national version of the MVHA's plan for cooperation between state historical societies and history departments in "the collection and publication of historical materials in the form of transcripts of original documents." The resulting project—a calendar of manuscripts in French archives about the Mississippi Valley—was tailored to the interests of the MVHA, in part because it represented a large voting block at the Conference of Historical Societies, and in part as an effort by Jameson and others to co-opt the group. The project ultimately took more than ten years to complete. And though it was started with support from the AHA, it was ultimately only brought to completion by the Carnegie Institution.[71] As this suggests, at least until 1910, the AHA was still viewed as the primary vehicle for collective action by the historical societies at the national level. Even as he was presiding over the first meeting of the MVHA in 1907, Thomas McAdory Owen (of the Alabama State Department of Archives and History) was actively engaged in trying to expand the work of the Historical Manuscripts Commission to press the historical societies to do more for the materials under their care.[72]

The AHA also proved instrumental in providing a platform for the early professionalization of archivists. In his first year as secretary of the association, Leland helped to organize a conference of archivists within the AHA.[73] At Leland's urging, the Public Archives Commission acknowledged recent developments in archival economy, and declared that "the time has come when some occasion should be provided for archivists and other officers in charge of public records to come together for the discussion of problems of common interest."[74] Leland described the work of the conference in protoprofessional terms, to lay "the foundation of an archive economy, sound in principle, and in practice adapted to American conditions, in conformity to which all our public archives, federal, state, county, municipal, and town, and perhaps even our private archives, shall in time come to be administered."[75]

The shape of the first meeting indicates how far the scattered archivists in the country were from recognition as a discrete professional identity in the historical enterprise. Leland's introduction to the conference was followed by five academics discussing "the lessons of" the British, Italian, Dutch, Spanish, and Swedish archives.[76] Only one practicing archivist spoke at the conference, as Victor Hugo Paltsits discussed "tragedies in New York's public records"—primarily their loss and destruction to thieves, fire, and mismanagement. Reflecting the larger framework of discussion in the discipline, discussions about archives took place in the idiom of "scientific" practices and focused on political and institutional subjects.[77]

The conference marked the establishment of yet another space for both societies and archives in the meetings and activities of the AHA. While written scholarship held a privileged place in the association, by 1910 the leaders of the AHA recognized the historical societies and archives as a growing area of employment in the historical enterprise. Academics were direct participants in activities such as the conference of archivists, openly acknowledging their dependence on historical organizations outside of academia. With the establishment of permanent bodies within the AHA to facilitate their work, and coordinate their efforts with other areas of the historical enterprise, the leaders of the association recognized that archivists, documentary editors, and historical societies had a vital role to play in the development of scientific history in America. Nevertheless, the correspondence of the period is filled with small asides about the limited financial rewards to those who chose this area of employment. Thwaites and Owen regularly worried over the way limited state support was starving the historical societies in their efforts to develop a more substantial infrastructure and networks of communication. And Jameson warned one historian interested in this type of employment that the jobs require "learning and competence" but were "not customarily rewarded with good pay."[78]

Despite these challenges, by 1910 a growing number of societies and archival agencies began to assume responsibility for systematically gathering, curating, and sharing historical materials for their areas of responsibility. And with the development of an emerging infrastructure of commissions and conferences within the AHA to support their interests, they began to develop the necessary networks for professionalization.

CHAPTER THREE

Defining a Profession of History Teaching

While work in historical organizations struggled for recognition in the emerging historical enterprise, history teaching played a highly visible role from the beginning. Teaching in the schools played a fundamental part in establishing history as a profession, since much of the impetus for the American Historical Association arose from a changing educational context that established history as a discrete subject for teaching at the secondary and postsecondary levels. The origin story of the discipline taught in history graduate seminars today generally starts with the introduction of upper-level studies in the history seminars of the late 1870s, but the establishment of history in the teaching curricula of American schools and colleges after the Civil War provided the necessary precondition for more advanced study—a career path for those with advanced training in the discipline. Elevating history teaching to a vital part of the story presents a useful challenge to whiggish narratives about the progress of advanced learning in the field, however, because history gained a toehold in the curricula for very present-minded and unscientific reasons.

Establishing History in the Schools

History emerged as a separate school subject in the period between 1830 and 1860 but accounted for only a tiny fraction of the courses and student enrollments before the Civil War.[1] It appears history first took root in the early grades of the schools to serve a civic purpose—"to show that it cost much in life and treasure to establish, preserve, and maintain republican institutions."[2] In the period before the war, this utilitarian rationale for history instruction undercut efforts to advance history as a subject worthy of more advanced study at the upper levels. Schooling beyond the elementary level was largely the province of the urban elite (barely 5 percent of the eligible student population in 1890 was enrolled at the high school level) so history had to compete with the solidly established subjects more closely associated with college-level education, such as Latin and the classics.[3] To justify the adoption of history in the upper levels, proponents of history adopted more traditional justifications for school subjects, emphasizing history as a form of mental discipline that could teach good judgment.

These two rationales for history as a school subject—as civic good or as mental discipline—coexisted uneasily in the various pronouncements from history organizations in the late nineteenth and early twentieth centuries. The mental discipline argument could more easily be accommodated to a research-oriented and scientific perspective and encompassed in histories of all times and subjects. In contrast, civic good arguments proved more effective for political purposes—such as convincing state and local politicians and school boards of the value of the subject for their children. But this approach created a bias toward subjects closer to home, as well as a tendency to maintain relevance to current concerns.

The tension between these two perspectives undercut subsequent efforts to establish standards for history teacher training or a coherent rationale for history's role in the curriculum in the face of other disciplinary and educational interests. Nevertheless, by pushing both arguments for history, as the situation required, the discipline was well established in the high school curricula before the AHA became actively engaged in curricular issues. By 1890, almost 28 percent of secondary school students were enrolled in history courses, making history the third most popular subject behind the fields of Latin and algebra (fig. 3.1).[4]

Even as history was becoming established in the schools, however, the subject was already being criticized for the poor quality of instruction and a history of failed reforms. Speaking to the Massachusetts Teachers' Association in 1875, Thomas Wentworth Higginson lamented, "Great energy and new methods are constantly being brought to bear on [the subject], and yet it results in general weariness on the part of the pupil and disappointment on the part of the teacher," because "the maximum of facts and dates have to be crammed into the child's mind without reference

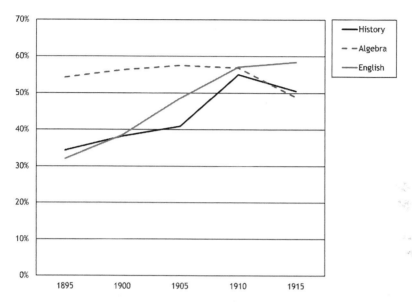

FIGURE 3.1. Proportion of public high school students enrolled in courses in select fields, 1895–1915
Source: Jessen and Herlihy, *Offerings and Registrations*, 28 (table 1).

to the ideas, emotions, and principles of history."[5] Writing a few years later, Charles Kendall Adams continued the refrain, emphasizing the poor training of history teachers, as well as the burdens of "other work" that inhibited teachers' efforts to develop more creative courses.[6]

As part of early efforts to professionalize teaching, in the late 1880s child psychologist G. Stanley Hall initiated a new "pedagogical library" to provide guidance to teachers in discrete fields. Hall decided his series should start with history, because "after much observation in the schoolrooms of many of the larger cities in the eastern part of our country, the editor . . . is convinced that no subject so widely taught is, on the whole, taught so poorly." He offered a long catalog of now familiar sins—that the textbooks were "dry" and overused, the teachers spread thin over a number of different fields, and the subject compressed into a single term or year.[7]

The resulting volume is intriguing not just for the familiarity of the complaints, but for the diversity of topics and authors assembled. Almost half of the authors went on to serve as elected leaders of the AHA, but the volume also included essays by Richard T. Ely (often mentioned

among the founders of economics) and John Burgess (a founder of political science). Both of them were members of the AHA at the time, reflecting the still-blurred lines between history and other disciplines that
would soon be arrayed against it among the social studies.

When the AHA was established in 1884, the founding members recognized teachers as an essential constituency for the new organization.
Nevertheless, pedagogy received very little attention in the initial meetings and activities of the association. The ancillary correspondence about
how the early meetings were assembled reflects a general assumption
that those interested in history would only be interested in, and drawn
together by, discussions about new research findings.[8] So narrower questions of practice—both research techniques and teaching—were not of-
ficially taken up for discussion at the first dozen meetings of the AHA.
Similarly, even though the *AHR* initially listed teaching activities as part
of its scope, the *Review* allocated very little space to issues of pedagogy.
The editors did include short news items about meetings of teachers' associations and significant publications in the field, but aside from a few
reviews of books on the subject, extended treatments of teaching were
generally left to the association's *Annual Report*.

Fusing the Interests of Academia and the Schools

While the AHA as a body did little to engage with teaching issues directly over the next twelve years, many of its most prominent members
were quite active on teaching-related issues at the secondary and postsecondary levels in private capacities.[9] In this emergent period of the discipline, the lines between teachers at the collegiate and precollegiate levels were less distinct and fostered a greater awareness of and engagement
with history teaching at all levels.

Albert Bushnell Hart, a Harvard professor who helped found the
American Historical Review and also served on all of the major history
curricula committees between 1892 and 1908, provides a good measure
of this. In an essay on "The Teacher as Professional Expert," to kick
off the new journal *School Review*, Hart described an emerging "profession of teaching" that extended from the schools to the universities. This
was a hierarchical relationship, to be sure, one that envisioned more advanced students employed in universities while less advanced students
(many lacking even a baccalaureate degree) teaching in the schools. But

in terms of their professional preparation, Hart prescribed the same type of pedagogical training founded on research skills, and urged an effort by teachers at all levels to assure a common level of professionalism through better training and greater self-confidence in practice.[10] This blurry notion about what it meant to be a professional teacher of history recurred in statements from AHA leaders up to the First World War. Unfortunately, this perception of similarity tended to serve as a substitute for a substantive knowledge or interest about what it meant to actually become a professional teacher at the precollege level.[11]

Even though leaders of the historical enterprise recognized the importance of teacher preparation as an area of professional interest, and rarely discussed school issues without offering a superficial and critical opinion on the subject, the AHA generally focused its collective efforts on more abstract curricular issues. Early on, curricula committees proved relatively simple and effective means of exercising the kind of national influence the leaders of the AHA craved. The first substantial effort at a national curriculum, sponsored by the National Education Association (NEA) in 1892, drew together a number of the AHA's most distinguished academic members and provided a framework for articulating the value of history to a national audience.[12]

In this effort, generally known as the Committee of Ten report, the discipline was situated under the broad umbrella of "History, Civil Government, and Political Economy."[13] The interconnection of the disciplines under that umbrella was reflected on the subcommittee that drafted this part of the report. Five of the committee's ten members subsequently served as president of the AHA, but two of them, Hart and Woodrow Wilson, also rose to the presidency of the American Political Science Association, while a third, James Harvey Robinson, was instrumental in the social studies movement two decades later. And throughout the committee's report, even though history was treated as the dominant subject (as indicated by the recurring phrase "history and kindred subjects") American history was tied with civil government as a single course.[14] While history provided the method of analysis, American politics provided the core content.

History had already gained substantial acceptance in the curricula, as the committee reported that a survey of college students found most received some history instruction in school (though the precise subjects of that instruction varied widely). Although the committee devoted the bulk of its report to a justification of history's place in the curriculum and proposals for the allocation of time to specific subjects, more than a third of the report focused on practical and professional matters, laying down a template for most of the curriculum committee reports to come over the next thirty years.[15] Based on its surveys, the committee characterized history teaching at the elementary and high school levels as too dependent on old and out-of-date textbooks and too dependent on rote memorization and recitation, which undercut efforts to accomplish their primary goal for history instruction—training in good "judgment." And typically, the committee lamented the quality of most teachers in the subject, complaining that they lacked "the spirit or apparatus to carry their classes outside these narrow limits" and offering a few modest recommendations on teacher training and improvements in teaching methods and materials.[16]

The committee's report fused two arguments for history in the schools—support of the civic good and promotion of "mental discipline" under the notion of "training of the mind"—which made the ability to the think historically a larger societal good. The prevailing disciplinary ideal about "history as past politics" played a critical part in this fusion. As the committee members described it, "the chief object is the training of the judgment, in selecting the grounds of an opinion, in accumulating materials for an opinion, in putting things together, in generalizing upon facts, in estimating character, in applying the lessons of history to current events, and in accustoming children to state their conclusions in their own words."[17] The prevailing politically oriented history was ready-made for the argument that history was the essential laboratory and best teacher of politics. Francis Thorpe (University of Pennsylvania) observed in a circular distributed by the US Bureau of Education, "Every American who becomes a true citizen enters upon responsibilities which he should have the privilege of studying before assuming. This is the just claim for American history as a study in the public school."[18]

The connection between history and politics helped to establish history in the curricula, but proved to be a very unstable foundation, particularly as political scientists began to define themselves as a unique and separate discipline. Specialists in education and other emerging social science disciplines seized on the "civic good" rationale to argue that the other disciplines, either individually or collectively, could and should contribute to those same ends. Speaking to the NEA shortly after the Committee of Ten issued its report, B. A. Hinsdale, professor of teaching at the University of Michigan and author of another early volume on

"How to Study and Teach History," promoted the correlation of history with civics and the larger integration of subjects, so that each reinforced the other and could "save time and secure better results" toward "forming the national mind and character."[19]

The Committee of Ten report was a small part of a much larger discussion about modernizing the curricula in the midst of a rapid expansion of the educational system and an increasingly diverse student population. In the last decade of the nineteenth century, the number of students in high school more than doubled (from 297,894 to 630,048), while the proportion of fourteen- to seventeen-year-olds attending high school grew from just 5.2 percent of the eligible population to 10.2 percent (fig. 3.2).[20]

This rapid growth had a disruptive effect on the entire educational system, fostering a dramatic increase in the number of institutions serving those students. Local and state governments developed new educational bureaucracies to administer these changes, and new networks of national organizations emerged to provide direction and disseminate information about innovations in methods and practice. The NEA was

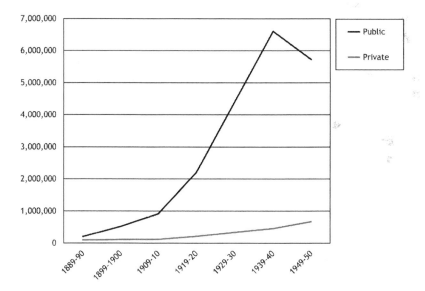

FIGURE 3.2. Number of high school students (grades 9–12) enrolled, 1889–1949
Source: US Department of Education, National Center for Education Statistics, *Annual Report of the Commissioner of Education, 1890 through 1910*; and *Biennial Survey of Education in the United States, 1919–20 through 1949–50.*

the most visible organization, but similar organizations emerged for other levels of the educational hierarchy, such as the American Association of School Administrators. The development of a professional infrastructure for teaching also extended to the nation's colleges and universities, which began to develop departments of education to train the rapidly growing population of teachers and administrators and provide sites for experimentation in curricula and pedagogy. The development of these larger institutional arrangements for education in the early twentieth century made it increasingly difficult for a small disciplinary organization like the AHA to be heard.

To be effective, the AHA had to attach itself to much larger organizations, such as the College Board or the NEA. While this created some notable successes, it also left history vulnerable to changes in leadership and policy at those organizations. History initially benefited from early efforts to establish a testing regime for college admissions. As early as 1896, the faculty in the Harvard history department tried to articulate basic standards and guidelines for history knowledge (extending even down to the elementary school level).[21] Almost as soon as these ideas gained some traction with the College Board, however, they began pushing the now familiar counterargument that cramming of facts would do a poor job of ensuring "proper methods of teaching history in preparing students for college," thus setting up the now familiar tension between pedagogy and testing in the discipline.[22]

A Charter for History in the Schools

The AHA did not directly intervene in school issues until 1896, when the NEA asked for advice on the role of history in college entrance requirements. Herbert Baxter Adams recognized this as an ideal opportunity to place the association on a national stage for the promotion of history in the schools. He gathered some of the organization's most distinguished members into a Committee of Seven to use the NEA's request as a springboard for a more general study of history in the schools. The committee was chaired by Andrew C. McLaughlin (a future editor of the *AHR* and president of the AHA), together with Adams; future AHA presidents Albert Bushnell Hart, Charles H. Haskins, and H. Morse Stephens; school headmaster George L. Fox; and Lucy M. Salmon of Vassar College. To assure the success of the report, Adams cajoled the treasurer of the association into allocating a significant portion of the organization's budget to pay for a series of meetings by the committee, conduct surveys of "representative schools," and travel to a number of European countries to investigate history teaching there.[23] This was quickly perceived as a major initiative of the association, and a session to elicit comment and discussion on the committee's work at the 1897 meeting drew a large audience (contrary to past assumptions by the AHA's leadership).[24]

The report that ultimately emerged from the committee tends to be idealized as the defining statement of history's role in the curriculum. As Robert Orrill and Linn Shapiro recently described it, "the AHA and the Seven effectively gave birth to modern history education in the United States."[25] Subsequent critics of the committee report in the social studies movement also characterized it as "the most influential report ever prepared in the field of the social studies curriculum."[26] But these perceptions focus rather narrowly on the report's curricular significance, not on an assessment of its full impact on history education. Read in the larger context of the fast-evolving educational system of the late nineteenth and early twentieth centuries, the report appears more contingent—the result of a fortunate convergence of events.

From the outset, the members of the committee differed on a number of issues that would become recurring problems for history teaching over the coming decades—the relation between history and other disciplines, the balance between particular subfields in the discipline, the best methods for teaching history, and finally, the professional alignment between history teachers at the different levels (from elementary school to university). At their first meeting, for instance, they "sharply debated" whether economics should be treated as part of history and whether "civil government studied in connection with American history is a suitable subject for the schools."[27] In the end, they decided to exclude economics but keep government as a core part of study in American history. They also differed among themselves about the proper balancing of different subject fields and treatment within the discipline. The minutes of the committee's meetings record "lively dissent" against the idea of combining Greek and Roman history, teaching the subject under the rubric of "general history," and assigning particular areas of European history (with English history dominant). They also differed sharply about whether "intensive" study of history could even be recommended at the secondary level.[28]

Oddly enough, the feature of the report that had the most enduring significance—the articulation of four-year "blocks" of ancient history, medieval Europe, English history, and American history and civics—represented the easiest part of the committee's work. As a practical matter, however, these recommendations were not particularly original at the time. These blocks had been described by other education reformers and administrators for a number of years.[29] These blocks were so self-evident that, despite its internal disagreements, the committee approved this program at its very first meeting, only leaving open the question of where to draw specific chronological divisions.[30] So rather than truly leading on this issue, the report merely articulated an emerging consensus on the broad contours of a curriculum for history. Nevertheless, the AHA Council held the four-year program as articulated by the committee relatively sacred for the next forty years—setting up a number of conflicts with educators trying to fit other subjects into the school systems and meet other needs.

The four blocks proved to be the easy part of the committee's deliberations, as it spent another two years surveying, studying, and debating a range of other issues about the teaching of history. These discussions highlight a number of areas where the committee papered over highly contentious issues that subsequently undermined the long-term standing of its report. For instance, members failed to resolve a number of basic issues about how to convert their relatively abstract plans into guidelines for actual practices in the classroom. The minutes report "a strong divergence of views" and "warm discussion" about methods of teaching at the secondary level—with disagreements about whether teachers should continue with the recitation method (making students present memorized portions of history texts aloud) or adopt something more akin to the seminar method involving student research and writing. Ultimately, the committee only agreed to lay out a fairly open-ended catalog of teaching methods in use at the time, from textbook recitation to study in original sources.[31]

In retrospect, the points of compromise and contradiction on the committee represented weaknesses in the seemingly solid edifice of history teaching and its place in the curriculum. The members failed to articulate a clear professional relationship between history research and teaching, or to offer the kind of practical advice that teachers needed to implement the program in the classroom. And while the committee made a strong case for history, they failed to offer clear guidance on the future relationship between history and other emerging social science disciplines by opening the door to civics but not economics.[32] The decision to tie American history to civics and allocate three-fourths of the subject blocks to European history reflected the college requirements of the day and the disproportionate number of European historians on the committee (and in the association). This balance became much harder to sustain in the face of emerging concerns about a truly public education system that extended into the twelfth grade and the rising discontent of a growing number of Americanists in the discipline. Questions that are now remembered as only emerging with the social studies movement were very much present at the birth of "modern history education" and an essential part of the dynamics of the discipline at this early date.

Regardless of the differences papered over by the Committee of Seven, the AHA's timely engagement in curricular discussions solidified history's role through the much larger shift from a classical to a modern curricula. According to the US Bureau of Education, in the 1890s only about 6 percent of the students were enrolled in history courses. By 1910 (and through the following decade) almost half of all students were enrolled in a history course in any given year.[33] In real terms, this translated into a net increase in the number of students enrolled in high school history courses from approximately 71,000 students in 1889 to almost half a million by 1909 (fig. 3.3).

Beneath these broad changes, however, there was a profound change in perceptions about the normative "student" for these curricula. In the 1890s, barely 7 percent of high school age students were spending more than eight years in the school systems, but a significant proportion of those who made it through twelve years in the schools were going on to college. But as the population in the nation's public high schools expanded rapidly in the early twentieth century, the proportion of students ending their education somewhere before college increased as well. This made conceiving of high school solely as preparation for college less tenable. The high schools increasingly became a site where students could move beyond fundamental skills and knowledge, and more advanced learning could serve larger utilitarian functions—educating students to be better citizens of the community, nation, or world.

As the history organizations tried to negotiate the rapid changes in the educational system in this period, they also had to contend with a rapid transformation in the constituency of history teachers. As the number of students in the classroom exploded, the resulting high demand for

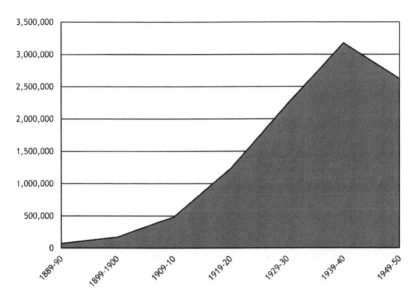

FIGURE 3.3. Estimated number of high school students (grades 9–12) enrolled in history courses, 1889–1949
Source: Based on calculations from data in Jessen and Herlihy, *Offerings and Registrations*, 28 (table 1); US Department of Education, National Center for Education Statistics, *Annual Report of the Commissioner of Education, 1890 through 1910*; and *Biennial Survey of Education in the United States, 1919–20 through 1949–50*.

new teachers meant widely disparate types of teachers were drawn into (or "thrown into") the history classroom. From the descriptions in surveys of teachers and the professional literature, the vast majority of history instruction in the schools was being done by teachers with very little background in the subject. This included long-term employees who had only limited training or interest in the discipline (marked even then as comprised of large numbers of coaches on sports teams) and teachers with limited training who only taught the subject for a few years. The true history specialists in the schools—teachers who had either majored in the subject in college or held an advanced degree, and who had the opportunity to spend all or even most of their time teaching history— were a tiny minority among secondary school instructors teaching the subject.[34]

The wide variations among history educators marked out very different sets of professional skills and networks that academic historians rarely recognized. The growth in the number of new teachers opened up opportunities for increased specialization and (for some) a path to professionalization more narrowly as a teacher of history. Around the turn of the century, members designated as "teacher of history" or chair of history departments at academies and private schools began appearing as more regular participants in meetings of the AHA. At the same time, regional associations of history teachers began to form, most notably the New England History Teachers' Association (1897) and the Association of History Teachers of the Middle States and Maryland (1904), which offered specialized professional networks for high school and college teachers.

But the history teachers participating at this level were the exception, not the norm. One schoolmaster observed that "the vast majority of those who are engaged in history teaching are also teaching other subjects and hardly claim or aspire to be called specialists in history."[35] This problem was exacerbated by rapid growth in the schools and the commensurately large proportion of new teachers in the classroom. As of 1904, more than a quarter of them had been teaching for less than five years—a proportion that remained fairly consistent in subsequent studies.[36] The large proportion of new teachers, as well as the large number of teachers splitting their time among history and a variety of other subjects, diluted the efforts of expert teachers in the history classroom.[37] This diversity and regular turnover in personnel teaching at the secondary level helps to explain the widely disparate comments about the quality of history teaching at the time, as well as the limited success in the recurring efforts at reform.

Putting the Committee of Seven into Practice

The Committee of Seven served as a vital point of reference over the next thirty years—for friend and foe alike—but its impact was mixed. A year after the committee issued its report, one school administrator observed, "The present condition of the subject is chaotic. It is taught unscientifically, at wrong times, and not continuously enough to permit of bringing its incentives to bear effectively."[38] Fifteen years later, the US Commissioner of Education reported that "the evident, though not overwhelming, distribution of the so-called 'four blocks of history' manifests the influence of the report of the Committee of Seven." He found that less than a third of the 7,197 schools surveyed (2,172 in all) had implemented the full four-year plan articulated by the committee. On average, schools only required 2.5 years of history, while offering a wide range of elective history courses.[39]

This reflected a perpetual problem for the AHA (and other education reformers). Efforts to design national reforms repeatedly ran up against the highly localized structure of American education. The AHA's first foray into school reform successfully articulated a program intended for all secondary schools, but it could not assure that these proposals were adopted nationwide—even though the support of the National Education Association (which disseminated the committee's report nationally) gave the report significant visibility and influence.[40] The Committee of Seven's report offered little advice on classroom practice, so its implementation relied heavily on intermediaries, particularly the regional associations of history teachers, which began to develop programs of training, syllabi, and guides based on the committee's report. Syllabi keyed to the four-block program from the New England History Teachers' Association had particularly enduring importance over the next two decades. Meanwhile, the Middle States Association of History Teachers focused much of its early attention on filling the gaps on professional issues—taking as one of its first tasks an analysis of "the amount and kind of preparation furnished to teachers of history by colleges or normal schools, and required of them by school boards, principals and superintendents."[41] As the AHA developed further revisions to the curriculum and attempted to embrace the professional role of history teachers over the next two decades, they relied heavily on the regional associations.[42]

The problems entailed by the changing educational structure extended even into the colleges, as the AHA Council felt compelled to organize a conference on "the first year of college work in history" in 1905. The committee's chair, Charles Homer Haskins, lamented the "comparatively new" problem for the college teacher of "introducing his students to college work in history but must also take his share of the task of introducing them to college work in general."[43] Many of the proposals offered by the conference simply extended recommendations from the Committee of Seven, with the added element that the teacher should be able to rely on "assistants" to provide more in-depth discussion of the collateral readings and to a lesser extent tutorial services. As a number of participants at the conference pointed out, however, this was an ideal that was really only practical at larger universities with graduate programs.[44] While there was no substantive follow-up to this conference within the association, the effort demonstrates a similar groping for improved pedagogical methods at the college level in the face of a diversifying student population.

At the same time, the colleges were increasingly viewed as serving a variety of professionalizing roles for the historical enterprise. For the schools, history faculty at a number of the colleges began to participate in a variety of professional development programs for school teachers—including summer school programs and other forms of continuing education. These courses were viewed as a way of improving knowledge for students otherwise separated or underserved by training. These courses varied widely, from "enrichment" lectures intended to inspire teachers' enthusiasm for the content to classes that could work actively with teachers in the development of courses and improvement of their pedagogy.[45] At the same time, senior historians also came to view history teaching at smaller colleges as an opportunity for younger historians to "broaden" their knowledge and get past thinking in terms of their dissertations.[46]

Between 1900 and 1910, the association made two more attempts to maintain the authority established with the Committee of Seven, first by offering a report on elementary school education (1909) and then by trying to adjust the committee's recommendations on secondary school curricula (1911). However, neither report had an impact comparable to the Committee of Seven. The 1909 report, *The Study of History in the Elementary Schools*, was undertaken along the same lines as the Committee of Seven, with surveys of a representative sample of schools and practices in European nations.[47] The composition of this committee was quite different, however, with a majority of its members "in actual touch with the work of the elementary schools" (three school superintendents and two teachers in normal schools). And the academic historians tended to be better known for their work on teaching-related issues and administration than their scholarship. While they tackled their subject with considerable seriousness, the report had limited impact on the association or on the school systems at large. One education specialist observed that the report was undercut because "teachers with less specialized training were in charge of the elementary grades" and attributed the general lack of interest in the report "to the lack of control from above such as the colleges exerted on the secondary schools."[48]

But the report does provide another indicator of growing resistance to the Committee of Seven report in the larger educational community. As the authors of the report describe it, "Fundamentally, our plan is based on the proposition that history teaching in the elementary school should be focused around American history . . . to explain the America of today, its civilization, its institutions, and traditions."[49] While they emphasized that this did not mean excluding the history of other regions of the world, it marked a fundamentally different point of orientation from the Committee of Seven report, which devoted three-quarters of its time on other parts of the world. In addressing the elementary schools, the committee tried to balance the different levels of knowledge and receptivity of students in lower grades with the utilitarian goals of forming a diverse student population into citizens.

Similar tensions surfaced in the AHA's reassessment of the Committee of Seven report a couple years later. Prompted by a request from the College Board and a petition from New England Head Masters to clarify the dividing line between the first two blocks of European history in the Committee of Seven's recommendations, the surviving members of the committee along with Columbia professor James Harvey Robinson and the educator Horace Mann came together in 1908 and 1909 to reassess the earlier report.[50] The response to this reopening of the subject demonstrates the changing context for the practice of teaching at the secondary level, as this time the committee received unsolicited opinions from organized groups of teachers from New England and the Middle Atlantic states.[51] In direct testimony to the committee, Edmund Noyes, a teacher at Central High School in Washington, DC, complained about the "vise of the text-book on the one side and the college examination on the other."[52] The net effect of the committee's discussions led to some modest tweaks, trimming back on the coverage in the ancient period and modestly expanding emphasis on the modern period. Criticisms like those voiced by Noyes clearly had some modest affect, as members of the committee debated how much supplementary material—particularly specific course syllabi—they should add to help clarify the new program. In the end, they decided against offering anything beyond their general report and recommendations.

When it was finally published, the report was largely seen as just reaffirming the plan of the Committee of Seven, but its fairly banal recommendations papered over a number of sharp divisions that were growing up within the discipline. In the course of the committee's discussions

Robinson took a fairly hard line in favor of history instruction focused on the modern period and closely informed by present-day concerns— actively promoting ideas that he would soon fashion together under proposals for a "New History."[53] This term designated an emerging school of thought in the discipline that advocated for greater attention to social and economic issues and argued that the value of history should be measured by its "utility in the present."[54] This was to be a very loose movement, but it comprised a number of themes that disrupted the discipline and ultimately led a number of historians to side with the social studies critique of history teaching.

The Committee of Five report ultimately elided many of these contested issues by focusing narrowly on the question that prompted the report—the chronological dividing line between the two blocks of European history in the first and second year of high school study. In sending the report to the AHA Council for final approval, the committee's chair, Andrew C. McLaughlin, reassured them that the final recommendations were "conservative and undestructive" of the Committee of Seven orthodoxy.[55] However modest the changes might have been, the new report was quickly touted as a new standard for textbook authors and publishers.[56]

Even before the committee completed its report, the AHA was becoming less engaged with teaching issues. The leadership of the association had begun to treat the Committee of Seven report as settled doctrine and sought to minimize opportunities for either reform or dissent. And the association's new secretary, Waldo Leland, had many interests in the history field but teaching was not one of them. His correspondence on teaching-related issues in this period tends to be quite desultory, generally lacking the inspiration that made his subsequent work on archival issues of such enduring importance.

In the absence of any clear leadership from the AHA for a time, the most important national voice for history teaching shifted to the *History Teacher's Magazine*, established in 1909 by Albert E. McKinley, a history professor at the University of Pennsylvania. Despite the magazine's title, and McKinley's position in a history department, the disciplinary boundaries of the new magazine were fairly expansive from the beginning. The initial description of the magazine, for instance, declared its purpose as "devoted to the interest of teachers of History, Civics, and related subjects in the fields of Geography and Economics," which re-

flected practices in the schools and the regional history teachers' associations.[57] By most accounts history remained the foundation for study of
these other subjects—civics was taught using historical examples, for instance—but this also acknowledged that many teachers covered multiple
subjects as well.

The magazine also promised a more expansive professional function
as well, offering to "describe recent methods of history teaching, and
such experiments as may be tried by teachers in different parts of the
country." McKinley also took a broad view of those included in the "profession" of teaching, encompassing those trained at a "normal school,
college, or graduate school," and going on to employment at "a high
school or small college."[58] But the early issues of the magazine reflected
the broad commonality of interests between teachers at different levels
on issues of teaching methods and syllabi preparation. A majority of the
authors of articles held a PhD and worked at a college or university, and
almost all of them were members of the AHA.[59]

The magazine quickly established itself as an important vehicle for
discussions of pedagogy. Evarts B. Greene, the secretary of the AHA
Council in 1911, praised the magazine for "developing the sense of common interest between the college and secondary school teachers of
history."[60] And within its first year, the subscription base of the magazine reached a little over 1,500, at a time when barely 400 members of the
AHA reported employment in schools or teachers colleges. Analyzing
the overlap in membership in 1911, McKinley reported that two-thirds
of the subscribers to the magazine were not members of the AHA. He
predicted rather ominously that a "large proportion of the eleven hundred teachers—and hundreds of others who are not subscribers to the
Magazine—are ready to join a national association which would advance
their professional interests both in its meetings and its publications."[61]
There was a certain amount of special pleading in this, however, as the
subscriber base failed to translate into a healthy financial situation for
the magazine. At the end of 1910, publication of the *Magazine* was suspended, leaving the AHA once again as the only national voice for history teaching.[62]

By 1910, the AHA had established itself as a leader in the area of history teaching, as its Committee of Seven report continued to set the standard for the discipline's place in the school curriculum. But aside from
fairly abstract curricular issues, the organization seemed unsure about
how to exercise true leadership for the professional aspects of this area

of the historical enterprise. Barely twelve years after the Committee of Seven report, there were growing rifts over the content of the courses and their relationship to the other social sciences, rifts that would soon be exacerbated by new pressures from outside groups and growing intellectual divisions within the discipline

PART II

Cracks Appear in the Edifice of History, 1911 to 1925

CHAPTER FOUR

Seeking Refuge in Professionalized Scholarship

By 1910 leaders of the historical enterprise had ample evidence that their visions of a unified discipline were falling apart. Broad arguments for a "New History" and growing numbers of graduate-trained, employed historians pursuing increasingly esoteric subjects made it difficult to view the larger field as a unified whole. All this was exacerbated by increasing differentiation and complexity in the structure of academic employment, as ever larger numbers of historians took their new PhDs into positions that placed a premium on teaching and gave little or no support for research.

As a counter to these intellectual and social disruptions, historians began to articulate a more abstract collective notion of historical scholarship that adopted many of the characteristics of a profession—even drawing direct analogies to the medical and legal professions. The term *profession* was only rarely applied to the craft of historical research in this period, but functionally, history faculty in academia began to behave as a profession and developed new efforts to elevate standards and promote their economic self-interest. In the process, academic historians increasingly looked to the American Historical Association to serve in the role of professional association for the discipline, both to police transgressions and encourage greater research activity. Many in the leadership continued to view the organization as representing the entire historical enterprise, but by 1926, intellectual and demographic pressures in the discipline promoted an inward turn by many in the academy. As they tried to get a handle on fragmentation in their own area of the historical enterprise, they left specialists on the tools and materials of research and history teaching feeling increasingly marginalized.

Fragmenting History Scholarship

The AHA's 1910 meeting was marked by a number of signs of the emerging intellectual divisions in the discipline. Intellectually, the meeting was bookended by presentations intended to promote the "new" in a discipline that many felt had become too settled in its approach to the past. In an opening presidential address to the association, Frederick Jackson Turner called on members to set aside their traditional attachment to political and military subjects, insisting that "we must deal with the connections of geography, industrial growth, politics, and government. With these we must take into consideration the changing social composition, the inherited beliefs and habitual attitude of the masses of the people, the psychology of the nation and of the separate sections, as well as of the leaders."[1]

Where the relatively conservative Turner made his case in rather abstract terms, James Harvey Robinson leveled charges directly against the social structure of the discipline. In a plenary session set aside at the end of the meeting to discuss his views, Robinson set out a list of proposed goals that seemed similar to Turner's—drawing new questions and new methods into historical research from other social science fields. But where Turner appealed to the interests of historians as individual scholars—by suggesting interesting new topics they might explore—Robinson addressed the collective interests of historians as an emerging profession. Robinson charged that "the usual training" and uniformity in the "general spirit and content of historical works . . . stands in the way of the proper development of historical study."[2] In its place he called for a "New History," which retained many of the assumptions of scientific history—such as the value of primary sources and the social construction of knowledge—but encouraged individual historians to stretch out in new methodological directions drawn from other disciplines.

Taken together, the two papers constituted a forceful challenge to a discipline still largely oriented to producing political histories extracted from official documents. As a number of the commentators recognized at the time, following Robinson's recommendations to their logical conclusion would unsettle the established ways of writing and teaching history. George Lincoln Burr, professor and librarian at Cornell University, warned that his proposals would upend the discipline's proper leadership role in the social sciences, noting that "there will still remain for history a field broad enough and noble enough for any study, and woe betide the social sciences themselves if we forget it."[3]

A wide variety of historians spent the next two decades debating whether Robinson's proposals were as novel as he suggested, or if any member of the discipline was actually producing the kind of work he recommended. Skeptics of his program insisted it offered nothing new, while friends of the program complained that it had little effect on actual scholarship well into the 1930s. In many ways Robinson's New History was more of a rhetorical stance than a substantial break with the past, even though some historians were offering courses on "social history" as early as 1911.[4] In general, the New History was relatively devoid of any actual content or meaning, except insofar as it represented an umbrella concept to encourage the adoption of new perspectives, new methods, and new sources into the traditional mix—usually drawing on the more scientific behavioral models of disciplines that had separated from history around the turn of the century, while also drawing in a more populist view of the subject of history. This represented only one large, and particularly visible, thread in the more general ferment in methods and sources of the discipline, but it seemed to serve as a touchpoint (both pro and con) for substantial amounts of discussion in the council and committees of the association.

As a marker designating a new method of scholarship, the New History movement had relatively little to show throughout this period. It took decades to articulate how the concept might actually work in practice, to develop the source materials for this new work, and ultimately to produce histories in this new form. Regardless of its effect on the production of actual scholarship, the publication of Robinson's essays in *The New History* in 1912 served as the banner for a large and divisive change in the discipline, as a wide variety of historians slowly began to consider social and economic issues in their work (both as teachers and researchers) and to apply the ideas in assessing the work of others. Reflecting this change, for instance, one of the few new primers on the writing of history to be published in this period, a revision of an earlier textbook, made frequent references to "social facts" where the previous volume only advised students on their use of "facts."[5]

Robinson and Turner were joined in this effort by Robinson's colleague at Columbia, Charles Beard, and a number of former students and other historians who quickly took up the idea, including Arthur Schlesinger, Guy Stanton Ford, James Schafer, Carl Becker, and Solon Buck—all of whom served as critical figures in the development of the historical enterprise over the next thirty years. By 1925, the diverse methods and questions loosely gathered under the New History banner had disrupted many of the methodological assumptions at the heart of the first generation's notions of scientific history.[6]

The effects of these ideas had a more immediate effect on relations with other areas of the historical enterprise. The earlier generation's focus on political issues simplified the relationship between archivists and researchers, for instance, by limiting their work primarily to documents and correspondence by politicians and government officials. By introducing methods developed in disciplines that had broken away from history (including economics, political science, and sociology), as well as other disciplines (such as geography and psychology), historians gathered under the New History banner challenged this relationship by encouraging historians to start using other historical materials to get at their "social facts." This placed new pressure on archivists and documentary editors to gather a wider range of materials, and led to often heated discussions about allocating resources to gathering and disseminating source materials about "everyday life" alongside traditional political and military subjects.

The themes gathered under New History also disrupted the relationship between academic historians and the area of precollegiate history teaching. For Robinson the historian's goal was to serve as "the critic and guide of the social sciences whose results he must synthesize and test by the actual life of mankind as it appears in the past."[7] While this drove Robinson and many of his colleagues to engage with teaching issues, it also undermined their perceptions of history's singular role in the school curriculum, since they were philosophically more inclined to see history as just one branch of the social sciences.

The public articulation of the New History idea was the most attention-getting aspect of the 1910 meeting, but the gathering also provides evidence of more fundamental changes in the discipline. This was only the second gathering to formally split the meeting into concurrent sessions for historians working in different fields of specialization. Since 1907, meetings had included a few concurrent sessions, but they consisted of less formal discussions among specialists or members focused on different practices (such as conferences for teachers and historical societies). But after much soul-searching on the council, in 1910 the association institutionalized the delivery of specialized research papers into separate concurrent sessions. This formally recognized the growing size and differentiation of the discipline—trying to provide more opportunities for members to speak and conceding that historians working in different geographical and chronological fields could no longer be interested in each other's work. The session divisions were still fairly expansive and done under the label of "conferences" for "Ancient History," "Modern European History," and "American Diplomatic History."[8] But this plainly recognized that history scholarship was expanding beyond the limits of any one historian's particular interests.

By the following year, Jameson complained that these "sectional sessions were distinctly less successful than the general" because they had "for the most part come to be mere sessions for the reading of short papers, unrelated and undiscussed."[9] And other historians, such as Hart, became increasingly concerned about the fracturing of the discipline evident in the "subdivision of the Association into smaller bodies."[10] Regardless of their ill opinion, other members strongly preferred the narrower focus. By 1925, the meeting featured four concurrent sessions (now called "group meetings") on subjects as specific as the "Personalities of Tudor-Stuart England."[11]

Finding a Home in Academia

This change simply reflected the growing size of history faculties in the research universities, which allowed ever-greater specialization as teachers and scholars. By 1911, the number of history faculty in American colleges and universities had grown well past the widely scattered numbers of the late nineteenth century. Within the membership of the AHA alone, there were 552 four-year college and university faculty members on the rolls, employed at 232 institutions in the United States. And the AHA did not represent the full universe of academic historians by any means (using other data, it appears less than 60 percent of the historians in academia were members at this time).

At the same time, the nature of the work performed in institutions of higher education was becoming increasingly diverse. While the total number of academically employed historians was growing, some were finding employment in research universities, but many more were finding employment in institutions that hired their faculty primarily or solely to teach. And academic employment for historians did not necessarily mean employment in a history department. In 1911, more than a third of the faculty members in the AHA's rolls indicated that their position was either principally in another subject (such as professor of economics) or combined history with a cognate field (such as professor of history and geography). Perhaps because of this heavy overlap in departmental affiliation there was relatively little public discussion about the definition of disciplinary boundaries outside of the protests of the New History movement early in this period.

The number of faculty and institutions of higher education grew fairly steadily between 1910 and 1920, which provided sufficient employment for the small but growing number of history PhDs. But as higher education expanded, the structure of history departments became progressively more hierarchical, as the social capital in the elite departments increased. Programs such as Harvard, Yale, and Princeton could "call" a rising young historian from smaller and less prestigious programs elsewhere in the country. In 1910, for instance, Harvard was able to draw Frederick Jackson Turner from Wisconsin, and Yale pulled Charles McLean Andrews from Bryn Mawr.[12] Turner and others cited the size of Harvard's library, access to other primary sources, and the diminished teaching load as particular incentives.[13] The enticements were apparently so strong that the history department at Harvard generally took it for granted that they could pluck another young professor from a state university in the Midwest just for a one-year trial appointment.[14] And one professor indicated he was even willing to take a 20 percent pay cut for the chance at a one-year appointment.[15]

But with growing numbers of campuses and history faculty employed across the country, the proportion of academic historians who could reasonably hope to achieve this sort of upward mobility rapidly diminished. As a result, there was a growing gap between the work increasingly held out as normative for academics—that of a scholar producing and publishing research—and the reality of academic employment for many in the discipline. Jameson estimated in 1909 that "more than half of our historical professors do not produce anything at all, and most of the others produce only very slowly," but he conceded that "doubtless the prime duty of a college teacher is to teach, and the multitudes clamoring more or less actively for historical instruction should receive it."[16]

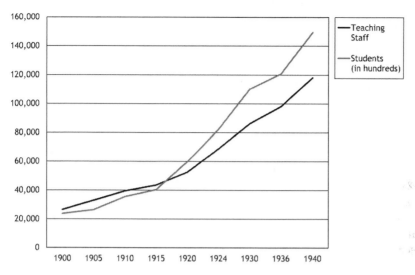

FIGURE 4.1. Approximate number of faculty and students in higher education, 1900–1940
Source: Data from Stigler, *Employment and Compensation in Education*, 29 (table 17).

By 1926, the leaders of the discipline were much less willing to make such a concession to teaching, due in part to rapid growth in the number of historians employed in teaching-focused positions after World War I. The number of students enrolled in colleges and universities more than doubled between 1919 and 1926 (fig. 4.1), which placed growing pressure on institutions to hire new faculty—including historians—to meet the rising demand for undergraduate instruction. The Bureau of Education estimated that the overall number of faculty increased from about 48,400 to 76,500 between 1915 and 1926, and the number of four-year colleges increased by about one-third over the same span.[17]

The sudden sharp growth in the number of students reinforced the emphasis on pedagogy in most institutions. By one estimate, the average number of students per faculty member in higher education increased substantially after 1915—rising from 83 in 1915 to almost 120 by 1926. This forced history departments away from their nominal ideal—teaching based on substantive research—toward teaching methods that treated students en masse—through increased numbers of lecture courses and (where possible) the use of graduate teaching assistants.[18] The rapid growth in the number of institutions of higher education trying to serve this growing student demand also produced a large increase in the proportion of history departments focused primarily on a teaching mission.

Almost two-thirds of the history faculty on the AHA membership rolls in 1911 appeared as the only members from their institutions, which reflected the realities of academic employment for most historians in this period. A 1928 census of colleges and universities found that even at that late date, 65 percent of all academic historians were employed in departments with only one or two other faculty in the discipline.[19] This inhibited efforts to establish a professional identity based on the ideal of a teacher-scholar in academia, since it provided little opportunity for historians at those institutions to specialize in a particular subject or field, as they were called upon to teach large swaths of American, European, or "general" history. And in many cases, they were not given any time or support to conduct research.[20]

The growing demand for new faculty, particularly after 1920, slowly reverberated down into the system of training for new PhDs. In the decade leading up to World War I, there was little change in either the number of PhD programs or the number of doctorates awarded each year. Nationally, only three departments started conferring history PhDs between 1910 and 1920 (raising the total to twenty-nine programs). And collectively, they conferred an average of about thirty doctorates per year over that decade. But after the war, both numbers increased rapidly. Twelve additional programs began conferring doctoral degrees in the five years after 1920, and the number of students receiving doctorates in the discipline more than tripled, to an average of 102 new degrees per year by the end of the decade (fig. 4.2).[21]

There are no substantive reports on training practices at history doctoral programs in this period, but there is ample evidence of rising standards and expectation for new PhDs. The published dissertations in this period show a clear shift from short essays to book-length works. In the period before 1910, well over half of the dissertations were short enough to be published in serial publications, but by 1925, all of the published history dissertations were either books or articles that comprised only a "part of his thesis."[22] The expansion of the requirements also increased the amount of time students spent in doctoral studies. Between 1905 and 1925, the average number of years between the students' last undergraduate degree and the doctorate expanded from below 6.5 years to nearly 10 (close to where it remains today).[23]

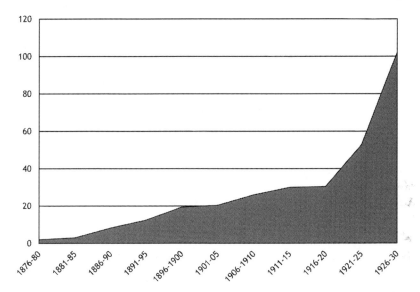

FIGURE 4.2. Average number of history PhDs conferred annually, 1876–1940
Source: Data tabulated from Kuehl, *Dissertations in History*, supplemented by the AHA's
online database of completed dissertations (available at http://www.historians.org/pubs
/dissertations/index.cfm).

Refining and Expanding the Outlets for History Scholarship

The rapid growth in the production of published dissertations and other
scholarly monographs relied heavily on a commensurate increase in publishing outlets. The development of the university press system played an
essential part, as these presses published a majority of the history dissertations by 1925. But the entire publishing industry had evolved to the
benefit of history scholarship, and by 1927, 38 commercial publishers,
39 university presses, and 69 "other" entities published scholarly history
books.[24]

Alongside the expanding and diversifying range of book publishers,
the number of outlets for shorter works of history scholarship also increased rapidly. The number of serial publications indexed in the annual
Writings on American History jumped from 322 to 451 between 1910
and 1920, although most of the growth occurred in publications that either did not systematically publish history or were published outside the

country (such as the *Princeton Theological Review* and *Revue Anthro-pologique*). The only criterion for inclusion at the time was the publication of an interesting or important article on history over the past year.

But the period also saw the introduction of a number of specialized history journals, starting with the *Mississippi Valley Historical Review*, which was established in 1914 to serve the interests of "the fraternity of western historians."[25] This was followed by the establishment of journals for specialists in Catholic history (1915), "Negro" history (1916), and Latin American history (1917).[26] All four journals were modeled on the *AHR*, with a section on articles followed by primary documents and book reviews, concluding with news on their respective areas of the discipline.

In addition to these structural similarities, these publications generally lacked many of the professional norms of peer review that now define a scholarly journal. Even the *AHR* had very little in the way of substantive peer review—as they often only sent articles to the editorial board member with the closest proximate geographical specialization for review.[27] There was, as yet, little sense of concern that articles should be assessed by someone truly expert in the materials and methods used by the author.

The leaders of the association were slow to appreciate the effects of growing specialization in the discipline, and rather blithely agreed to a new bibliographic "manual of historical literature" to replace the long out-of-date manual prepared by Charles Kendall Adams (the final edition had been published in 1888). But the editors quickly found themselves overwhelmed by the amount of material to be reviewed and catalogued. In the end it took five principal editors, thirty section editors, and almost five hundred historians (most employed at academic institutions) more than a decade to complete. When the final volume was published in 1931, it included citations to more than ten times the number of books listed in Adams's volumes. And in an effort to assuage the concerns of specialists about superficial treatment of the literature in their particular subfields, the editors felt obliged to describe their lists as only intended for nonspecialists. The editors characterized their goal as providing information on the best scholarly literature to public libraries, schools and their teachers, and "the scholar who wishes guidance in fields other than his own."[28]

The *AHR* was forced to make its own adjustments to address the rapid expansion in the annual production of new books by devoting a growing

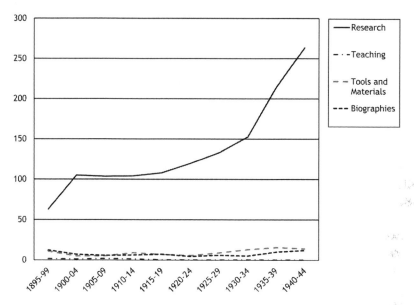

FIGURE 4.3. Number of books reviewed in the *AHR* by category, 1895–1944
Source: Based on a simple tabulation of book reviews in the *AHR*. "Books on Teaching"
include textbooks and primers on pedagogy. Books counted in "Tools and Materials" include all edited document collections and primers on that area of work. "Biographies" are
works limited to a specific historical person.

portion of its reviews to original monographs. Between 1910 and 1925,
the number of reviews of new works of historical scholarship grew from
an average of 105 per year to 130 (fig. 4.3). But the books taken up for review only represented an increasingly selective sample of the actual production of works in the discipline, which averaged about 550 new titles
and editions annually between 1910 and 1927.[29] To make space, the *AHR*
largely discontinued reviews of textbooks after 1911, deferring them to
specialized publications on pedagogy. And even though the journal continued to review publications of documents and guides to sources, the
editors increasingly relegated them to brief items in a "Minor Notices"
section at the end of the reviews.[3]

The growing fragmentation of the discipline into increasingly narrow subfields posed an even greater challenge to the editors, as it undermined efforts to establish a common understanding of the standards and
methods the journal was supposed to uphold. First, it made it harder to
rely on a common language and tools for assessing the quality of schol-

arship. Where scholars could previously focus their assessments on the quality of the official sources used, and the historian's fidelity in reproducing those documents, reviewers placed an increased emphasis on original interpretation (instead of extensive quotation from documents, for instance) and suggested different measures and new tools for assessing the work of other historians. Given the diversity of the reviewers and the authors and the increasingly esoteric subjects being reviewed, it is difficult to mark out a clear trend, but there was noticeable growth in the number of reviews assessing scholarship by its incorporation of social, economic, and psychological trends, drawing on the methods and subjects of New History.[31] The growing diversity of approaches introduced added difficulties for the editors, who felt increasingly challenged to find the right reviewer to match the sources used and the historiographic approach taken.

The Dilemma of Professionalization

As a check against the disruptions in the unity of what it meant to be a historian and conduct historical work, members of the discipline struggled to define specific characteristics and skills that could clearly mark someone as a historian. The label *profession* was rarely used, and when it was, it still tended to be ambiguous as to the area of the historical enterprise it was meant to cover. J. Franklin Jameson's first published use of the term *historical profession* in the *AHR* appeared in a 1909 article discussing the deficiencies of the AHA that prompted the formation of the *Review*.[32] But his list of the organization's early failings included a lack of support for "practical activities," such as cooperation with the state and local historical societies, bibliographies of historical writings, and efforts to gather source materials—precisely the sorts of activities that he and others pressed on the association between 1895 and 1900. So even though the term was in circulation in this period, it is difficult to say that it was clearly centered on research scholarship and academia in the way it is today. And aside from a few particular instances, references to a profession of history or historical profession remained fairly rare.

Within the correspondence of the association, the use of the term *profession* was also exceptionally rare, and where it does appear, it generally arose in the narrower context of teaching. In a survey of the relationship between teaching and research, for instance, Lucy Salmon observed that:

> Before entering on his profession the teacher has been a collector, when he becomes a teacher he is a distributor; at this point he often stops, but he needs to become also a producer if his work is to be really fruitful. The teacher must be a producer to prevent arrested development, to be able to train his pupils to produce, to pay the debt of gratitude he owes to his profession, to pass on with increase the inherited wealth he has received from those who have gone before him.[33]

Regardless of any ambiguity in the labels, the notions now generally located under the label of a historical profession were gaining added currency. Where historians today refer to members of the historical profession, in this period they tended to refer to *historical scholars* and *historical students*, rather than to more pedestrian *professionals*. Jameson, for instance, used these terms regularly when addressing the common interests of the discipline, whether seeking financial support for research aids (such as the *Writings on History* project) or summoning historians to use their skills to serve the nation's military interests in 1917.[34] And within the pages of the *AHR* more generally, these terms served to center discussions about the emerging history profession. Scholars and scholarship were represented as the core of their activity. The term *scholar* served as a key benchmark in the book reviews of the *AHR*, pointing back to elements of the ideology of scientific history articulated by Herbert Baxter Adams and his contemporaries—the exhaustive gathering of fresh materials, the painstaking assembly of information, clarity and impartiality of analysis, and provision of a clear trail back into the sources that others might follow.[35] These elements remained a fundamental part of the identity of history scholars in this period, regardless of the growing separation from other historians on the subjects and methods of their research. And even though many relatively conservative historians (including Jameson) felt ambivalent about the new approaches proposed under the New History label, key proponents of the idea (including Robinson, Becker, and Beard) joined the *AHR*'s editorial board between 1910 and 1925.

Persistent concerns about the quality of history writing fed into these discussions, with renewed attention to the training of historians. A number of the authors suggested that the root problem lay in the scientific focus on document gathering and dissemination above all else. Historian and publisher William Roscoe Thayer compared the problem in history to the professionalization process in law schools: "If a law school should teach its students nothing more than to run down the titles to deeds, or to draw a will, it could hardly be more restricted than those American history departments have been which make the tracking of original sources the beginning and end of history."[36] To assess the issue, in 1920 the AHA organized a committee to study the problem of scholarly writing in history, which focused a significant amount of its attention on doctoral programs and the scholarly culture. One member lamented, "Scholars write for each other, not for the public. They are afraid of each other; for they have, what the nonprofessional 'historian' has not, a professional reputation as historical scientists at stake, and to them the most minute discrepancy in fact is of far more importance than unreadability."[37] The committee concluded that the scientific work of historical research should not come at the expense of the literary qualities needed for good writing, and concluded that courses need to be put in place that "treat of history not as pure science but as literature."[38]

Other historians, working out in the states, noted a separate line of difficulty, as "very few competent research students will turn their attention to local history." According to Benjamin Shambaugh at the State Historical Society of Iowa, "by far the most productive and satisfactory method of carrying monographic studies is through research associates employed by the historical society."[39] For a number of societies, this became an important branch of their larger projects (and an important area of employment for historians with graduate training).[40] Local history would become a more active area of interest and research in the mid to late twenties, with the ascent of social history, but for the moment, graduate-trained historians were perceived as largely only interested in topics of national significance and often left such work to writers with more of an antiquarian or genealogical interest.

Building the AHA into a Professional Association

Nevertheless, growth in the size and complexity of employment in academia, and the growing facility to disseminate research scholarship, prompted a new focus on the content as well as the form of research scholarship and new attention to the role the AHA might serve in promoting scholarly ideals. Some members pressed the AHA to serve a policing function for the discipline. As early as 1910, Albert Bushnell Hart argued forcefully that "it is the duty of a studious and sober body like the American Historical Association to dwell upon the strictly scientific character of history, to emphasize the fixed principles of research, to warn the world against the consequences of unsound study and scientific research."[41] A few years later he reiterated the point, with an observation that "from two professions, divinity and authorship, is expected not only the truth, but originality."[42]

Regardless of the growing ambiguity about what it meant to do research and how to judge it, the association increasingly moved into a position to provide such work with more active support. In 1921, William K. Boyd, a professor of history at Trinity College in North Carolina, petitioned the AHA to establish a Committee on Research—the first committee of its type in the association—aimed at "stimulating historical investigation, especially in those educational institutions which do not maintain a graduate school."[43] A similar proposal offered in 1912 had failed.[44] But indicative of its growing recognition of the AHA's role in supporting history scholarship, this time the AHA Council quickly approved the proposal. The new committee was directed to press colleges and universities to develop the institutional apparatus necessary to support research and "encourage instructors in history to utilize such facilities."[45]

The twin dilemmas laid out in the report—the lack of institutional support at many colleges and the apparent failure of some faculty to conduct research—animated the work of the committee and ever larger portions of the association over the next two decades. At least initially, the perceived failings of some faculty were described in fairly benign terms. In his original proposal, Boyd suggested that young faculty members at these institutions just needed the encouragement of a little "external stimulus."[46] The early work of the committee followed this positive approach, conducting a brief survey of support for research at various institutions in the South and Midwest and sponsoring gatherings at the annual meeting to discuss how faculty in teaching positions could continue their research despite a lack of local support. But by 1925, Boyd reported growing frustration at their lack of progress.[47]

In subsequent years, the committee and the association as a body became more assertive about the professional necessity of ongoing research production by historians employed in academia. By the end of 1925, the direct support of history scholarship had emerged as a critical feature in the association's work. The organization's efforts remained in some disarray, but the institutional pieces that shaped the association's involvement in these issues over the next fifteen years had taken shape. In the process, the AHA began to articulate a more explicit role for itself in husbanding resources to facilitate and encourage the production of articles and monographs. The shift in focus reinforced some of the emerging barriers between academia (but particularly faculty at research universities) and the other spheres of the historical enterprise, by establishing alternative support networks for research scholarship.

In the midst of the larger intellectual and structural changes taking place in the discipline, the leadership of the AHA increasingly reflected the emerging professional ideal of the research scholar, rather than the other aspects of the historical enterprise. Historians credentialed with PhDs and employed in academia became a disproportionate segment of the members in elected and appointed positions. While the history PhD quickly became an important criterion for committee service in the AHA, there continued to be room for history workers with other degrees and other types of training throughout this period. Among the general membership, the proportion with PhDs grew at a fairly even pace—rising between 15 and 20 percent every five years, except for a brief uptick between 1915 and 1920, when the five-year growth rate jumped to almost 33 percent.

This coincided with a sharp increase in the representation of historians with PhDs in the leadership of the association over the same span. After holding fairly steadily at a bit less than half of the members with elective or appointive positions, the proportion with doctorates earned in the United States rose rapidly between 1910 and 1925. At the end of that span, 75 percent of the leaders in the association held PhDs, which was essentially where it remained until 1940 (fig. 4.4).

Throughout this period the association was pulled in a number of competing directions by different interests in the historical enterprise—representing them all to varying degrees but representing none to the complete satisfaction of any particular group. The period between 1910 and 1920 was relatively prosperous for the AHA, and the association nearly doubled the number of committees engaged in various projects, trying to attend to different aspects of the historical enterprise. But the organization suffered a number of distractions in this period that

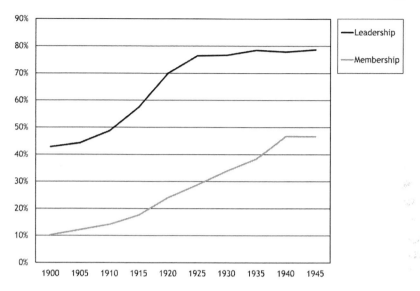

FIGURE 4.4. Proportion of AHA leadership and general membership with domestic history PhDs, 1900–1945
Source: Data from comparison of published AHA membership rosters to doctorates listed in Kuehl, *Dissertations in History*. Note that AHA "Leadership" included all elected members of the council and appointed members of committees.

prevented it from clearly representing any of the different interests in the discipline.

Perceptions of the organization's conservatism, the relatively limited number of members invited to participate in the association's work, and some peculiarities in the relationship between the *AHR* editorial board and the council combined to feed a fairly large insurrection against the leadership of the association in 1915. The ensuing flap exposed a number of divisions between northern academics (described by some as a "big university trust") and historians living in other regions and employed in other areas of the historical enterprise.[48] After the head of one history organization (Dunbar Rowland of the Mississippi Department of Archives and History) voiced anger in the *Nation* at being excluded from a position in the AHA, the council recognized that it contained a disproportionate number of academics. In an effort to address the point without conceding to the attacks from Rowland, the AHA leadership brought Frederic Bancroft (a historian at the US State Department) onto the council. Once there, however, Bancroft became convinced of the validity of accusations that a "ring" was running the association in its own self-interest, and he joined Rowland's campaign.

The particulars of the case against the "ring"—detailed in a series of pamphlets and a running argument in the pages of the *Nation*—seem remarkably picayune in retrospect. They involved obscure details about the actual ownership of the *AHR* (which had not been formally transferred from the editorial board to the association in 1898) and oversight of spending for editorial board meetings. But the related correspondence suggests that the real fuel for the dissent was the relatively closed circle of members serving on the committees and council of the association and the status anxieties of those who felt excluded—a convergence of issues channeled through a progressive idiom. The perception of a narrowing in the leadership of the AHA was not without foundation. From 1885 to 1900, an average of almost 6 percent of the membership served in one committee or another of the association. Between 1910 and 1915, however, the participation rate fell to barely 3.1 percent of the association's membership, even though the number of committees had increased over the same span.

The sense of narrowness and exclusion was exacerbated by a growing tendency to promote members from the northern tier of states into leadership positions.[49] While the regional composition of the membership had not changed substantially, the number of historians from the South seeking offices in the AHA had grown. So it is no surprise that historians of the South generally led the revolt. Rowland and Bancroft, who both wrote on southern history, were joined by other southern historians, such as Ulrich B. Phillips and William E. Dodd. While the southerners led the way, correspondence in the files of the MVHA indicates that academics and leaders of historical societies and archives in the Midwest shared many of the same concerns.[50]

The insurrection ended after some modest reforms to the governance structure and as a result of the far larger concerns caused by the First World War. The most profound effect within the organization was that it helped reinforce the shift toward privileging academics for leadership posts in the association. There was a clear generational division on this point in the period leading up to the revolt. Reflecting the growing sentiment of younger historians, Max Farrand, an assistant professor at Yale, advised one council member that "there are several men in academic life whom many members of the Association think should be honored, and until this is done I am afraid that the appointment of so-called outsiders would only increase the feeling that worthy men have been neglected."[51] Speaking for the older generation of historians, Hart rejected the notion, observing that "I do not like the idea growing up in the association that no one else is qualified."[52]

The reforms implemented after the revolt substantially widened the range of members involved in the work of the association. The proportion of the membership serving on the various committees and activities rose back up over 5 percent well into the 1930s. But Jameson was quick to note that by becoming more democratic, the elected leadership of the organization became less representative of the entire historical enterprise: "In the days when the Council always talked over the nominations with the chairman of the Nominating Committee . . . we used to try to make sure that the non-professorial element was recognized." Jameson reported that under the new rules, senior faculty members had a distinct advantage because "the professor inevitably has more friends and acquaintances among the younger element—former pupils and the like— than the isolated or amateur worker."[53]

More visibly, the reforms resulted in the establishment of a unified secretariat. Instead of the decades-long division between an academic as "Secretary to the Council" and a nonacademic as the day-to-day "Secretary" of the organization, the council gathered them into a single position, and appointed John Spencer Bassett of Smith College to the position.[54] Bassett was an academic, but the catalogue of reasons for his appointment attests to the breadth of the constituencies the council still hoped to reach—in part as a result of the lessons learned from the insurrection. His principal sponsor, Victor Paltsits of the New York Public Library, summarized his qualifications in this regard:

> You have been connected with the education of young men in the South [at Trinity College in North Carolina]; you are now connected with the education of young women in the North; you have been editor of a periodical that made you widely known for progressive ideas and ideals; you have written a textbook type of history putting you in touch with the needs of high school teachers of history and the problems they confront; you have written for the advanced student of history and are now to edit the source-material.[55]

Regardless of Bassett's potential virtues in reaching out to various constituencies, the decline in the number of members without PhDs accelerated after the insurrection—from 86 percent of the membership in

1911 to 72 percent in 1925. Whether this was due to the bad press following the accusations of financial malfeasance, or other changes in the
work of the AHA, cannot be clearly determined.

Signs of Growing Diversity in the Historical Enterprise

Despite the growing number of members with PhDs, however, the proportion of members employed in academia actually fell slightly between
1910 and 1925. As of 1911, approximately 44 percent of the total membership was employed in academia (fig. 4.5). Another large segment of the
membership was still employed in teaching history, but it was engaged in
precollegiate teaching, either as classroom educators or through training
in teachers colleges. Outside of the educational fields, another 16 percent
of the membership identified themselves as working in some other area
of the historical enterprise—in library or archival work, publishing (as
authors, editors, or publishers), or some other historical work at the local, state, or national levels. While two-thirds of the members with history PhDs were employed in academia, a significant proportion of the

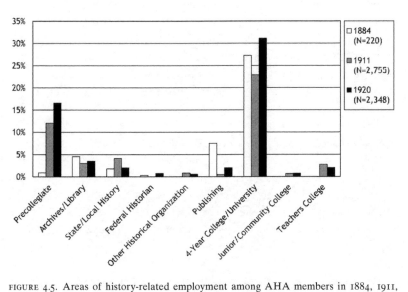

FIGURE 4.5. Areas of history-related employment among AHA members in 1884, 1911,
and 1920
Note: This tabulation includes only those who provided information on their current employment and does not show those who were not employed in history-related work.

membership was employed in other activities. The largest proportion of nonacademic PhDs held jobs in high schools, with the remainder spread out across almost every employment category.

By the next survey of the membership in 1920, employees at four-year colleges and universities comprised less than 40 percent of the members responding to the survey, and only 31.8 percent could be identified specifically as history faculty. (Another 4.2 percent of the membership identified themselves as specialists in another discipline—including languages and sociology, as well as professional fields such as law and education—and 2.6 percent of the respondents reported they were students.) Those employed in some aspect of precollegiate teaching (either as teachers and administrators or as faculty at teachers colleges) still comprised more than 20 percent of the membership. Other types of history-related employment accounted for 14 percent of the membership. Notably, there had been a significant amount of erosion in the proportion of members working in some aspect of state and local history, as they began to gravitate into other networks of professional activity (such as the American Association of Museums, established in 1906). But they still represented a significant portion of the total membership. And as the large number of members in nonhistory employment (31 percent) suggests, in 1920 the AHA still elicited a strong avocational interest from the general public, regardless of their level of participation in the actual work of the association.

This period also appears to mark the one relatively brief moment before the 1970s when women were welcomed in the association. They rose from about 18 percent of the membership in the 1907 roster to almost 26 percent in 1925—their highest point until very recently. In contrast to their apparent neglect of regional concerns, members of the council seemed actively concerned in this period about assuring that there was at least one woman on each committee of the association.[56] As a result, in 1915 Lucy Salmon of Vassar College was the first woman elected to the council. And the representation of women on AHA committees rose modestly but steadily to a high point of 9.5 percent in 1930.

At the same time, the association had begun to embody many of the centrifugal forces pulling constituencies in the historical enterprise away from each other. By December 1925, the association's meeting had up to three concurrent sessions as the fragmentation in the discipline proceeded apace. It no longer held joint meetings with other scholarly disciplines (the last such joint meeting, with the American Political Science

Association, was held in 1923), due both to the growing size of the organizations and to a greater sense of hostility toward the other disciplines sparked by growing disputes over the school curricula.

This was a rather ironic outcome for a period that started with calls from Robinson and others for increased interdisciplinary communication. Instead of reaching across disciplinary lines, by 1925 the association's "joint meetings" were increasingly only with smaller pieces of the history discipline such as the MVHA, Agricultural History Society, American Catholic Historical Association, Bibliographic Society of America, and History of Science Society. While Jameson's summary of the meeting generally welcomed the other societies, he abhorred other, more tangible signs of hyperspecialization in the discipline. He noted with particular regret that "much of the program was devoted to subjects of limited range. In consequence of this, there could be little real discussion of the papers, few auditors having the temerity to dissent publicly from the views of one who has apparently made himself master of a small, or perhaps obscure, portion of history."[57] This sense of ambivalence about growing hyperspecialization arose even among those working to enclose their own areas of the discipline. Joseph Schafer, shortly before his election as president of the Agricultural History Society, expressed some regret that "I have always been doubtful about subdividing history. I am pretty well convinced that what history needs in order to attain its maximum influence is emphasis upon its inclusiveness—rather than upon its exclusiveness."[58]

Alongside the troubling signs of fragmentation (troubling at least to the older members of the organization), the meeting was also marked by the announcement of a new effort by the association to raise funds for "research"—though the specific definition of that term was rather vague. For purposes of external discussions, the organization emphasized the tools and materials of research. But within the organization, the emphasis for fundraising was primarily on increasing support for research scholarship. At a luncheon dedicated to the question, the association put Guy Stanton Ford and Arthur Schlesinger forward to cast the need for funds in terms of the New History movement, where they emphasized "the new forms which historical research is taking on and must increasingly take on in the future, by reason of the advances made by other sciences and the complex demands which such advances in economic, social, and psychological knowledge make upon the historian."[59]

By 1925, the leaders of the association were actively seeking an accommodation with new approaches to the discipline and trying to adjust to growing historiographic diversity by establishing narrower (but higher) standards for work in academia. The internal boundaries of academia still remained somewhat ambiguous, as the elite in the discipline tended to describe an academic ideal of research scholarship without regard to the types of institutions that employed many historians—though there were signs of growing concern about the effects of employment in teaching-oriented colleges and universities.

Likewise the definition of research remained somewhat ambiguous as well, as some in the discipline still easily applied the term to the scholarly gathering of primary source materials and related tools for the work of other scholars. But these expectations relied heavily on the nostalgia of older members (such as Jameson, Salmon, and Turner), who still tried to combine a wide array of scholarly activities and teaching. Toward the end of her life, Lucy Salmon testified to this older tradition, with a reminder that "history takes on protean forms and often our greatest historians have not written history at all."[60] But as her generation started to pass from the scene in the mid-1920s, the narrower focus on research scholarship was moving forward as a focus of the organization's energies.

CHAPTER FIVE

Placing the Tools and Materials of Research in "Other Hands"

In comparison to the slow shift in organizational attention to research scholarship between 1910 and 1925, the association started off the period with a keen interest in the work of other historical institutions but then let it slowly drain away. Initially, the Historical Manuscripts and Public Archives Commissions and the Conferences of Historical Societies and Archivists enjoyed substantial support from the members and leaders of the organization, and the association continued to develop more topic-focused committees (such as the Committee on the Bibliography of Travel) to address specific subjects. But throughout this period, subtle changes in professional resources and networks began to strain the relationship between academics and the specialists employed in other areas of the historical enterprise.

Developments took place on two levels. Within the association, institutional problems—particularly a scarcity of funds during and immediately following World War I—shifted the distribution of resources within the organization. At the same time, changes in the different areas of history work started to pull these constituencies apart. As Thwaites, Leland, and others refined the work of the historical organizations outside of academia, they helped to expand their institutional missions, increase the range of employment opportunities, and knit together rudimentary professional criteria and systems of qualification. As a result, these efforts helped to enclose workers in this area in a new set of networks and more particular types of institutional arrangements. While not self-consciously professionalized, by 1925 they were clearly moving toward an institutional apparatus that set them on that path.

Opening Up New Areas of History Employment

One of the crucial changes for anyone interested in this area of employment was the marked growth in opportunities for someone with an advanced degree. At the start of this period, the positions available were seen as both limited and highly problematic. In 1912, one historian seeking a position outside of academia complained that positions at "historical societies that are worth while are exceedingly rare."[1] And to make matters worse, employment in many historical organizations still suffered from the lack of strong civil service protections. Victor Paltsits, the historian of New York, for instance, lost his position in favor of a patronage candidate in 1912.[2] And Milo M. Quaife, Thwaites's successor as head of the Wisconsin Historical Society (WHS), lost his post eight years later, largely because he refused to mail a rare book to a politically connected citizen in the state.[3] Alongside the lack of civil service protections, throughout this period the heads of the WHS regularly pressed for better salaries for their staff to assure that they could rise above mere "amateur" status.[4]

But by 1925, the societies were increasingly viewed as a legitimate area of employment for history graduate students, even if the opportunities to produce research scholarship were often delimited by a specific set of civil service rules and expectations. By 1922, Margaret Cross Norton observed, "I believe I am singularly fortunate among beginning archivists in coming to work with the preliminary propaganda in favor of an archives already done."[5] Clarence Alvord, the historian of Illinois, noted that employment in this area generally encouraged a more systematic set of policies and relations than academia. He observed that "my experience has led me to this conclusion, that a well organized office under proper leadership is far better than cooperation among historians who are not closely connected."[6]

Part of the change was a recognition that the archives held value to a wide variety of constituencies in a democratic environment, most notably, with the extension of genealogy into an area of general popular interest.[7] But the various institutions included in discussions about state and local historical organizations still varied substantially one from another. At WHS, Quaife expended considerable effort trying to clarify some of the differences, particularly between the societies incorporated with a quasi-private role (including the societies in Wisconsin, Kansas,

Iowa, Minnesota, and Missouri) that had to rely on membership dues for a substantial portion of their funding. He distinguished these from organizations established with a purely public role (such as the Alabama Department of Archives and History), and argued that the former tended to reflect a variety of odd historical circumstances, which prevented a clear and rational organization of activities—but most particularly in the administration of the state's archives.[8]

Despite the variations in structure and funding, at a social level, archivists and the staff at historical societies also started to develop very specific bodies of professional knowledge, as well as networks of relationships and resources that would form the basis for a separate identity. A vital step in this differentiation process was the development of clearer networks of financial support. The archives and historical societies grew increasingly dependent on governmental support to sustain their operations, just as the academics at many colleges and universities began to look to their home institutions and other external funding agencies to support their research.[9] This added material and institutional differences to the shifting balance of relations between history workers employed inside and out of academia.

In addition to changes in material support, the period between 1910 and 1917 also marked a fundamental change in archival practices. The AHA's Public Archives Commission and Conference of Archivists produced a series of reports that provided some of the core professionalization literature for a generation to come. Waldo Leland's survey of "fundamental principles in relation to archives" and Victor Paltsits's outline of a "'Manual of Archival Economy' for the use of American archivists," both published in the AHA's report for 1912, provided a nascent sense of identity and professional coherence.[10] Drawing on European models, Leland offered a clear articulation of the protoprofessional impulse among archivists, observing that "one of the things most essential to our ultimate success is to come to an understanding among ourselves respecting the object of our efforts, our method of work, and even our common languages."[11] At the same time, even as these programmatic statements were clearly cast to an audience focused on historical research, the leaders of the effort made it clear that their responsibilities encompassed a wider array of constituencies—requiring value judgments about what to keep and what to share that would not always be driven by the interests of historians.[12] The professional impulses of archivists at the time seemed almost entirely prospective, but Paltsits characterized the 1912

meeting as "a landmark" that "brought forth the first systematic suggestions for scientific archival practice in this country."[13]

The leaders of the AHA and the societies recognized the close connection between these two areas of the historical enterprise. Due in part
to the growing focus on professionalization around archival activities,
the leaders of the association became increasingly attentive to the alignment of archival work and the interests of the historical societies. At
least at the outset, there was significant overlap in the personnel participating in the two conferences. In 1912, Leland pleaded with Haskins to
avoid scheduling them against each other at the meeting, noting that a
"great many people desire to attend both and holding them simultane-
ously would pretty nearly kill them."[14]

But by 1913, even a distinguished society such as Wisconsin felt it was
falling behind in the development of new archival policies and procedures. Thwaites conceded that "thus far we have not done much in that
direction owing to the fact that we have been so crowded."[15] Where Wisconsin suffered from constraints of space to store such materials, some
of the other societies voiced concerns about the lack of funds and local expertise to do proper gathering and cataloging work.[16] Meanwhile,
in the eastern states, running down the coast from Maine to Virginia,
the absence of any formal connection between the historical societies
and their state governments meant that the archiving of state records remained haphazard at best.[17]

Regardless of the concerns within the historical organizations, the
scholarly community was increasingly vocal in its appreciation of their
work. Jameson, for instance, publicly repented some of his earlier criticisms of the societies, observing that "twenty-five years ago the publications of most of our historical societies seemed, at least to impatient
young minds, hopelessly provincial and unscholarly. But we were then
just at the beginning of a new period in all our historical work." While
still lamenting their tendency to focus on local over national perspectives, he praised them for bringing a higher level of training and "work-
manship" to their efforts.[18] His comments reflect a growing awareness
and appreciation of the societies' efforts to adopt the ideals of scientific
history that had become common among historians in academia.

In addition to wrestling with archival policies, the historical societies also had to adjust to significant technological changes. Shortly after
1910, the larger historical societies began to purchase Photostat machines to preserve some materials and to allow for exchanges of materi-

als with other institutions. Not to be confused with the photocopiers of today, the original Photostat machines filled a small room, required specially trained operators, and used relatively expensive supplies. But the machines could take documents of almost any size and make a picture (in a rather cumbersome two-stage process) that could be distributed to scholars and other institutions. The correspondence between the leaders of the Wisconsin Historical Society and specialists in the use of the machines is fairly voluminous over the next decade, as they struggled to perfect the technology and the skills of the relevant staff, and work out procedures (and prices) for sharing the results.[19]

The introduction of the Photostat machine marked a significant change for the societies and archival organizations, transforming them from relatively isolated warehouses of materials into organizations that had a kind of historical currency that could be exchanged with other archives or converted into a source of revenue from history researchers.[20] Many of the societies had already developed the necessary institutional apparatus to share books and printed materials in their collections, but this significantly expanded the range of material relationships.[21] The "News and Notes" section of the *American Historical Review* charted the acquisition of these machines at historical organizations over the next two decades with some enthusiasm, starting with a report from the Library of Congress in 1912 reporting that it could "supply photographic copies of manuscripts, maps, rare printed pieces, etc., at a very cheap rate."[22] By 1918, such reports became increasingly common in the *Review*.

A group of societies and archives in the West quickly took advantage of this new tool to start purchasing copies of materials from the federal government that were true representations of original documents about their states. In 1915, a group of societies in five states (Michigan, Wisconsin, Minnesota, Iowa, and Illinois) commissioned a historian in Washington, DC, to identify and then arrange copies of documents related to their states.[23] And the societies also began to develop networks to exchange and purchase Photostat copies of documents and newspapers that existed at one of their peers. Quaife noted a fundamental change in behavior among the societies, which had previously been crushed by "the absence of a sufficiently strong get-together spirit" and "the lack on the part of any public institution of the necessary photostatic equipment." In its place, he detected a new spirit of collaboration emerging among the historical organizations.[24]

Searching for a "Get-Together Spirit"

Building on this emerging enthusiasm for cooperation, the leaders of the historical organizations reorganized the Conference of Historical Societies in 1916, making it a "semi-independent organization" within the AHA funded by society memberships.[25] Despite the additional funding, there was little change in the actual work of the conference, which continued to work primarily through exchanges of information both at the AHA meeting and through the publication of a small annual report.[26]

Meanwhile, the MVHA, which remained deeply rooted in the historical societies of the Mississippi Valley, offered a more localized model for the historical societies by focusing a considerable amount of its attention on the intersection between historical society materials and the schools.[27] Members of the committees placed a heavy emphasis on the way the materials of research could add vitality to history teaching, while also noting that engaging students in local history could serve the interests of the societies and the discipline as a whole).

Unfortunately, the momentum for many of these efforts was halted by financial and political exigencies during World War I. As Milo Quaife reported, "A large proportion of our men have gone into war service of one kind or another," which ranged from work in local munitions factories to military and advisory posts in Washington or overseas. This drained the organizations of trained staff and leadership, while also curtailing revenues for many projects.[28]

Under the auspices of the National Board for Historical Service, the leaders of the AHA did try to stimulate the historical societies to develop ideas and collaborative approaches to gathering and collecting materials for future histories of American participation in the war. The chair of the committee assigned the task, Solon Buck, hoped it would "arouse a certain rivalry among the states and be a means of giving circulation to ideas about what to do and how to do it."[29] At the same time, this wider area of history work also gained growing interest and attention from the general public. Clarence Alvord's efforts to gather and collate materials in Illinois, for instance, attracted the attention of the *New York Times*.[30]

Aside from war-related activities, the AHA curtailed most of its other work, including all committees related to the societies and archives.[31] Citing the exigencies of the war, the Conference of Historical Societies suspended efforts to solicit dues, and the AHA also suspended the work of the Manuscripts and Archives Commissions.[32] Even after the war, many of the leaders of the association (including Leland) continued to focus on reconstruction efforts in Europe, so it was not until 1921 that the AHA began to revitalize its efforts in this area of the historical enterprise. It was only then that a group of the association's leading members pressed for the restoration of the Archives and Manuscripts Commissions and also promoted the work of the Conference of Historical Societies, emphasizing the "importance of maintaining cordial, sustained, and effective relations" with the societies. To help finance the revival of the commissions and conferences, and to provide adequate space for the publication of their materials, the committee recommended permanently dropping the publication of works of interpretive scholarship from the annual report—noting that such work had ample outlets in the *AHR* and elsewhere.[33]

This led to a brief revitalization of the commissions, but after barely a year their work was stymied by another shortfall in association funding. As a result of further declines in membership and rising paper and printing costs for the *Review*, the association suffered a large deficit and had to resort to voluntary contributions to cover operating expenses.[34] At the same time, federal support for the annual publication of the report was substantially reduced, curtailing the available space and delaying the publication of a number of reports from the various conferences and commissions.[35]

As a result, the *AHR* became the only regular public voice for the association through the 1920s. This firmly cemented interpretive scholarship as the center of the association's work and effectively deprived committees focused on other kinds of activity of a voice—and of a purpose—outside of the annual meeting. So once again the work of the Manuscripts Commission was halted, and the Public Archives Commission was told it could proceed but only on a voluntary basis. Paltsits, then serving at the New York Public Library and as chair of the Archives Commission, condemned the council's action, lamenting that "the commission was suspended at a critical time, and all the while left without a penny, when its work for archives might have yielded a national service not less than that of other national agencies during the war and since the peace." Jameson, responding for the council, expressed sympathy but maintained that "like so many other excellent things in this world, it depends upon the state of the pocketbook."[36]

The AHA's ability to provide leadership for the professional concerns of historical societies, archives, and related organizations diminished even further when Leland resigned from the secretary position in 1919. Even though he regularly offered advice over the next two decades, his attentions were diverted to the management of the American Council of Learned Societies, a massive bibliographic project calendaring materials in French archives, and efforts to rebuild the International Committee of Historical Sciences after the war.[37] His successors—John Spencer Bassett from Smith College, Dexter Perkins of the University of Rochester, and Conyers Read of the University of Pennsylvania—were increasingly oriented to academic interests and less able to provide substantive leadership for other areas of the historical enterprise. As a result, there was little central guidance on these issues.

Jameson continued to encourage attention to these subjects, and the Conferences of Archivists and Historical Societies annually sent proposals to the council for consideration, but their proposals tended to languish and the activities tended to drift. Julian Boyd observed a decade later that the "difficult problems of organizing state historical work and of affecting inter-society cooperation either remain largely in the status they were in when the conference first addressed itself to them, or else have been modified largely by the initiative of state and regional societies."[38] This erased the vital work of Thwaites, Shambaugh, and others within the association but fairly reflected an extended period of inertia in the work of the AHA.

The opportunities for such initiatives to work their way onto the council agenda were further diminished by a growing differentiation in the personnel participating in the association's work. Within a number of the committees dedicated to historical work outside of academia, there was a clearer separation in the roles assigned to different members, reflecting growing specialization in professional practice. Bibliographic work, for instance, had become so specialized that members of the library community began displacing academic historians on bibliographic projects such as the *Guide to Historical Literature* and *Writings on American History*. Similarly, the other committees working on the materials of research were increasingly comprised of archivists, librarians, and the staff at historical societies, as the academics gradually withdrew to positions on committees related to research and its assessment (such as book prize committees and the editorial board of the *AHR*).

Specialization and New Lines of Fragmentation

Part of the change was due to the growing gap between the skills expected of someone engaged in this sort of work, and the abilities and interests of many academic historians. Justin H. Smith, chairman of the Historical Manuscripts Commission, noted the growing challenge of finding historians to take up such projects, and observed that it "requires abilities and attainments of a fairly high order; competent persons are seldom ready to spend their time on work usually classed as drudgery."[39] Meanwhile, the war—and the effort to preserve materials from different parties in the war—created new employment opportunities outside the AHA for specialists interested in articulating the needs and attributes of an archival profession, including the first substantive primer on archival administration.[40]

The Conferences of Archivists and Historical Societies became increasingly differentiated as well. Academics occasionally participated in the two conferences, but staff at archives and historical societies performed most of the actual work. A good measure of this can be seen in the authorship of reports for the Public Archives Commission. Before 1910, two-thirds of the reports were written by faculty at colleges and universities. Between 1910 and 1928, less than 20 percent of the authors of reports were employed in academia.[41] Similarly, the proportion of academics speaking at the Conference of Archivists fell from 80 percent of the papers delivered at the first conference to none of the featured speakers at the 1927 meeting. The Conference of Historical Societies was a more distinct body almost from the beginning. But here again, the proportion of academics speaking at the conference fell significantly. At the first conference, half the speakers had at least a part-time affiliation with a university department. At the 1925 meeting, however, all but two of the twelve members who spoke at the conference were employed full time at a society. Structurally the lines of interaction and communication taking place within the AHA were clearly withering.

While the trends are clear, it is hard to discern the specific push and pull factors that lead to the sense of separation. From the summaries of discussions at the two conferences, it is clear that their conversations became increasingly technical and focused on specific problems common to staff at archives and societies—conversations about the status of particular records, the arrangement of materials, and the coordination of collection practices.[42] Meanwhile, efforts to bridge the divide between academics and staff in the historical organizations became increasingly difficult. In one case, the head of the Conference of Historical Societies invited a professor specializing in local history, who agreed but conceded that he had "only a vague notion of the subject." In an effort to redress his ignorance, he circulated a survey to society heads that framed his concerns by asking, "What have you done for the *scholar* . . . ?" (emphasis in original).[43]

As the association's meetings differentiated into multiple overlapping sessions on specialized topics, academics clearly gravitated toward the work of their scholarly peers and paid diminishing attention to discussions about the professional details of other areas of the historical enterprise. As a result, the conversations of specialists in the societies and archives were increasingly enclosed within the conferences, and the lack of viable publishing outlets within the association provided very little opportunity for their discussions to filter out to more general attention in the historical enterprise.

These issues were coming to a head in the mid-1920s as the nonacademic activities were starved for AHA-sponsored outlets for their work. To address the problem, the association initiated a fundraising campaign intended to benefit the entire historical enterprise. Establishing funding priorities, however, and articulating who needed support and why, opened up a wide-ranging discussion about the AHA's roles and responsibilities to different constituencies. The broad focus of the AHA's campaign was on support for "American history and history in America," which seemed broad enough to encompass both academic interests and the emerging interests of other professionals in the historical enterprise.[44]

Early descriptions of the project focused on supporting the tools and materials of research and revitalizing the work of the Historical Manuscripts and Public Archives Commissions.[45] But over the course of extensive debates and discussions about how to define the projects to be supported, a significant gap opened up between the immediate concerns of academics and the activities represented by other areas of the historical enterprise. A number of academics working to develop the project promoted the idea of using funds from the campaign to directly fund scholarly publication, in the form of a planning body that could coordinate and promote new areas of research, and direct support to new cooperative research projects.[46] But a number of members working outside of academia strongly objected to this narrowed notion of the proper work of the AHA, and a marketing firm hired to consult on the project agreed that simply supporting research scholarship would be a hard sell to potential contributors.[47]

With that in mind, in 1926 the association turned to a senior politician turned history writer, Albert J. Beveridge (a former senator from Indiana), to serve as the public face of the campaign, and asked Solon J. Buck (the superintendent of the Minnesota Historical Society) to serve as executive secretary of the project. After an initial presentation that promoted supporting the AHA's efforts "to get serious historical work before the world," the focus shifted to support for the tools and materials of research.[48] The final plan still placed academic scholarship projects at the top of the list of priorities, but most of the proposed projects addressed work outside of academia.[49] As the consultants predicted, these aspects of the campaign were more appealing to potential donors and the general public and gained prominence in the *New York Times* and other national media.[50]

This effort was to mark the first clear point where the interests of academics fell into explicit competition with those working in a variety of historical organizations. Largely starved of resources within the AHA, and given few opportunities for places on the association's meeting program or agenda, by 1926 staff members at societies and archives realized they would need to look elsewhere for representation, as the increasingly diverse constituencies in this area of the historical enterprise turned their thoughts to bolstering their own distinct—and professionalized—interests.

CHAPTER SIX

History Teaching Finds Its Own Voice

Much like the renewed attention to the archives and societies at the start of this period, the association started the decade with a burst of support for precollegiate teaching, but over the next fifteen years, academics gradually became alienated from the professional aspects of this area of work. In contrast to the relative simplicity of the conditions that gave rise to the Committee of Seven's report, the students, schools, and other participants in the educational system were becoming much more diverse. And the academic members of the discipline were also dividing into separate, and often opposed, camps on a number of fundamental issues related to teaching. As a result, the leadership of the American Historical Association became increasingly annoyed and frustrated at the growing complexity of the issues.

A Renewed Concern for Pedagogy

In late 1910, there were signs that the association intended to step up to a new level of leadership for history teaching. Most notably, the AHA Council leapt at the opportunity to revive and adopt *History Teacher's Magazine*, which had suspended operations earlier in the fall. In response to a plea from the magazine's editor, the council decided to subsidize the *Magazine*'s production in exchange for discounted subscriptions for AHA members.[1] For a time this subsidy even included payments to authors for their contributions, following a similar practice at the *Review*.[2]

The opportunity arrived in a rare moment when the council was feeling rather flush with funds, so it focused most of its attention on sorting out the potential for overlapping coverage between the *AHR* and the *Magazine* rather than the actual costs to the association. In an effort to coordinate the content of the AHA's two journals, the two editors agreed that the *AHR* would "set forth and appraise the ideals and achievements of historical scholarship" while the *Magazine* would "set forth and appraise the ideals and achievements of classroom instruction in history."[3] McKinley was quite grateful for the association's support, and he was joined by others involved in the training and preparation of teachers who strongly commended the association's effort.[4]

The AHA tangibly benefited from the arrangement in the short run. The *Magazine* provided significantly more coverage of AHA activities than it had previously—offering long articles on pedagogical discussions at the association's meetings, for instance, and playing up the work of various committees on the subject. As a result, the AHA moved into a visibly more important role for teachers at all levels—in many ways, much larger than the association's other organized efforts on teaching issues truly merited. And as a result, the number of members employed directly or indirectly in precollegiate teaching almost doubled between 1911 and 1920 (fig. 4.5).

Despite the official connection to the AHA, the *Magazine* still offered ample coverage of other organizations—publishing reports from regional history and teachers' associations, as well as other disciplinary associations in the social sciences. The *Magazine* even provided one of the first outlets for the National Education Association's Committee on Social Studies in Secondary Education between 1914 and 1917—which defined the social studies movement in ways that deeply offended many members of the association and reverberated into interdisciplinary relations at the academic level.[5]

While the other history organizations were generally pulling in the same direction—demanding more room for history and pressing for better teaching methods and apparatus—they often represented very different interests on particular topical issues. The leadership of the Mississippi Valley Historical Association for instance, rooted as they were in the valley's historical societies, pushed back a bit against the nationalized view of history espoused by the AHA. They argued in favor of a more localized treatment of history in the classroom, by aligning classroom assignments with visits to local societies and museums and adding state history to high school curricula.[6] They also used the leverage of their joint meetings with the AHA to lobby for a better representation of the interests of teachers in AHA meetings.[7] The effort to graft state and regional histories into the AHA's nation-focused history curriculum in this period opened up an important fault line in the discipline's position on teaching issues.

Redefining the Professional History Teacher

Despite the rather grand gesture to support *History Teacher's Magazine*, the AHA's attention to teaching issues quickly began to drift, even though the organization continued to assign committees to study different aspects of the subject. The last notable effort before the First World War was a Committee on the Certification of High School Teachers of History, gathered at the request of history teachers at normal schools and teachers colleges.[8] This new committee, intended "to secure a better preparation on the part of teachers of history in the elementary and secondary schools," was chaired by the medievalist Dana C. Munro of Princeton University. But reflecting the AHA Council's growing defensiveness about the discipline's place in the school curriculum, the clearest aspect of the committee's charge was an admonition that they had "no authority to set up any specific standards of preparation without further action by the Council."[9]

This committee primarily sought to coordinate the efforts of other organizations on history and secondary education in terms laid out by the Committee of Seven almost twenty years before, hoping to provide sufficient time for it "to take root."[10] The committee called on the New England History Teachers' Association, the Association of History Teachers of the Middle States and Maryland, and the Northwestern Association of History Teachers, as well as the MVHA, "asking their cooperation in the appointment of committees to give each [of the four year blocks in the Committee of Seven report] a more precise definition."[11] But this narrow mandate led to a fairly weak effort from the other organizations.[12] After a decade in which the association wielded considerable influence in defining the broad outlines of history education, the rather desultory leadership from the AHA on vital issues of professional preparation for teachers was ceding much of that authority to others. Education specialists, state and local school boards, and other teacher organizations stepped in to translate the curricula into the classroom, and also to define what it meant to be a professional history teacher.

The leaders of the association failed to realize that teaching practices were becoming professionalized in ways that made training in research skills seem completely inadequate for the classroom. Lucy Salmon's notion of the professional teacher-as-researcher read at the 1916 meeting of the AHA typified the AHA Council's growing disengagement from the problems of the public school history classroom, and diminished the AHA's credibility with teachers (in high schools and also in many colleges) burdened with heavy teaching loads and no support for sabbaticals.[13] Professional educators increasingly (and quite fairly) came to view the AHA as distant and disengaged from the realities of the precollegiate classroom.[14] Despite the association's financial support to the *History Teacher's Magazine*, the development of a body of knowledge and the networks of relationships and resources necessary for the professional identity of history teachers began to develop largely outside the AHA.

The growing academic disengagement from trends in history teacher training was not limited to the AHA. In 1913, a number of regional history teachers' associations joined together under the leadership of the MVHA to propose their own training program for history teachers, but it too largely excluded preparation in pedagogy. While focusing on issues of certification, the committee (comprised almost entirely of academic faculty) cast a critical eye on training practices in the colleges and universities, but ultimately concluded that the primary problem was a failure to emphasize that "mastery of his subject is the prime necessity for the teacher."[15] The committee argued that a proper course of study should include only one course on teaching methods for every ten history courses.[16] This created a significant point of disagreement with the education community and the political overseers of the certification process, who were articulating more stringent requirements for teacher certification—in some cases, that up to a quarter of all coursework should be on pedagogy.[17]

While the AHA and other academics were dithering about policies on the training of teachers, the Association of History Teachers of the Middle States and Maryland offered a much more substantive analysis of the training necessary for a "modern" history classroom. Drawing on comparisons to European practices, they noted that "the training there is such that teaching is a profession, whereas with us it is too often a job." The Middle States report attempted to establish a middle ground between disciplinary specialization and professional practice, insisting that at a minimum "a history teacher should have done in college some specialized work and should also have some instruction in methods of teaching history."[18]

The effort to raise the bar on teacher training gained added force with the development of formal teaching requirements at the state and local levels. A dozen states had developed specific certification standards for history by 1911.[19] These requirements and recommendations from groups such as the Middle States Association point toward an emerging consensus about pedagogical training—that professional preparation increasingly had to be as teachers first and as subject specialists second. While these criteria were not incompatible, they existed in some tension with each other as specialized history classes remained in the history departments while training courses in teaching methods were generally handed over to education departments.[20]

In the period before the First World War, there were also relatively few discussions about teaching at the collegiate level. College and university faculty still actively contributed to discussions about teaching for the regional teachers' conferences and *History Teacher's Magazine*, but it was increasingly in the role of subject experts, imparting knowledge about their particular area of research, rather than imparting their expertise about how to teach that subject in a classroom. And when faculty members were not writing down to the teachers, suggesting how their particular research work could or should be brought into the nation's classrooms, they tended to write about the need for teachers to incorporate research into their own classroom preparation. There is very little evidence of self-reflection when it came to teaching practices at the college level, and when one AHA member proposed a committee on the "problems of college instruction" in 1915, the idea died rather quickly.[21]

The general failure of academic historians to keep pace with trends in the professionalization of history teachers further undermined the discipline's efforts to protect its portion of the school curricula. What success the association had in staving off the challenges of educational and social studies movements was largely due to the good advice and counsel of Henry Johnson, a history education specialist at Columbia University's Teachers College. Like Waldo Leland, Johnson failed to fit the standard profile of a professional in history. He started his career as a history teacher in Minnesota, never earned a PhD, and wrote solely on pedagogy. Nevertheless, he represented a rare combination among those advising and representing the AHA on teaching issues in this period, as someone who actively promoted better and more professional teaching practices in history, while also strongly advocating the AHA Council's defense of the Committee of Seven orthodoxy.

While conservative about the shape and structure of history in the school curriculum, Johnson dedicated himself to improving teaching methods by providing models and materials of best practices. In one of the first multimedia presentations at an AHA meeting (in 1909), Johnson developed an exhibition of "aids to visualization of history consisting of lay figures, models, casts, utensils, weapons, coats of arms, and other objects of various kinds as well as pictures, maps, stereoscopic views, lantern slides, etc.," categorized into the four blocks recommended by the Committee of Seven.[22] He also developed and disseminated syllabi and curricula for the schools, fostered in-service training and summer school programs for history teachers, and wrote a manual on history teaching that remained the standard in the field from 1915 to at least the mid-1930s.[23] The leaders of the association quickly recognized Johnson's value to their cause as someone actively working with educators who could also be relied upon to represent their views on curricular issues. As a result, they sought him out for every teaching-related committee the AHA assembled between 1910 and 1935—starting with the first advisory board for *History Teacher's Magazine.*

Looking back on these events from the present, Johnson can also serve as an important barometer of changing attitudes about the AHA's role on these issues. In almost every discussion about committee assignments and interdisciplinary relations on teaching issues, Johnson was repeatedly singled out by friends and critics alike. Depending on the subject, Johnson's assignment was often marked as either a sign of the association's hostility toward the other disciplines and the larger social studies movement or as a challenge to the AHA leadership to better understand the interests of teachers. He also marks the association's growing ambivalence about the significance of teaching issues in the historical enterprise, as the only person to serve almost continuously on AHA committees over a twenty-year span who was never elected to the AHA Council.[24]

Nevertheless, the association had considerable need for Johnson's services. By 1910, other disciplinary associations were actively promoting the interests of their own subjects into the curriculum, as faculty in the other disciplines actively sought jobs for their graduates in the schools. But history maintained a preeminent position. For a time, the AHA's continued close relations with the College Entrance Examination Board helped to block efforts to establish other disciplines in the curricula.[25] History maintained a significant presence among college entrance requirements, even though it was relatively small in comparison to the core disciplines. In 1913, 80 percent of the colleges and universities had a history requirement, but most of them required only one unit (as compared to an average of 4 in foreign languages, 2.9 in English, and 2.3 in algebra). Perhaps equally important, given disputes within the AHA about the proper balance between different geographic fields and time periods, the schools were generally indifferent to the specific history topic required.[26]

New History and the Social Studies Challenge

By 1915, history found itself challenged from within and without by the development of a movement to integrate history into other social science disciplines. The other social science disciplines had been pressing for their own space in the high school curriculum since the turn of the century, but collectively they found themselves lumped together under the umbrella term *social studies* in a fresh review of school curriculum from the NEA developed with the active support of the federal Bureau of Education.[27] The report of the Committee on Social Studies in Secondary Education cast the purpose of history in utilitarian terms, declaring that "a primary aim of instruction in American history should be to develop a vivid conception of American nationality, a strong and intelligent patriotism, and a keen sense of the responsibility of every citizen for national efficiency."[28]

Reflecting some of the growing divisions within the historical enterprise, James Harvey Robinson served as a leading member of the committee and actively promoted his New History concept as part of a fusion of the different disciplines into a unified teaching subject. He is quoted extensively in a section detailing the "tests" history would have to pass if it was "to hold its own in our schools."[29] And the committee's conclusions echo those of the larger New History agenda—drawing from and integrating the work of the other social science disciplines, and placing the past in service to the civic needs of the present. This meant dimin-

ishing the blocks of history instruction in favor of new courses for other
subjects and adjusting the temporal focus of history courses closer to the
present.

While the rise of the New History movement had little substantive effect on the new works of history scholarship produced in this period, it
decisively undermined perceptions of a unified history position around
the Committee of Seven's report. This perspective remained in the minority on the AHA Council for the next two decades, but it had a prominent constituency among some academics in the membership. More
importantly, as Robinson's rhetorical contributions to the commission
demonstrate, historians identified with New History ideas materially
aided the emerging social studies movement. When proponents of the
social studies sought to develop new curricula or promote their ideas
to politicians and the general public, they had a pool of historians they
could rely on to lend their names and affiliations as professors of history
to the effort.

The divisions in the discipline undercut the arguments from conservative historians that the social studies movement was all part of a broad
effort to cast history out of the curriculum. To the contrary, as one historian observed, it suggested that the historical enterprise lacked a clear
view of history in the curriculum: "Let us imagine the American lay-
man—the intelligent member of a school board say—asking himself this
question, What's the use of history in the schools? Where shall he look
for an authoritative answer? Judging from my own experience, if he
questions rather widely he will soon be struck by the fact that the people most likely to have answers to the question are not agreed among
themselves."[30]

Even before it was published, the social studies commission's preliminary communications prompted a number of history teachers' groups to
reassess their place in the history curriculum. As an early indicator of
this trend, in 1915, a meeting of history teachers in New York resolved
that "a course in Community Civics be recommended as a fundamental
part of the curriculum in all public high schools."[31] These events spurred
the AHA to some action. Evarts Greene expressed the grave concerns
of many council members about the social studies commission report's
proposed "radical reconstruction of the elementary and secondary
school programs in the social sciences."[32] And the association dedicated
a significant portion of its subsequent meeting to an overdue discussion
about the necessary balance between social studies subjects (history, civ-

ics, and economics) in the schools, as well as the proper balance between local and national histories in the curriculum.[33]

Despite the association's efforts, the report of the social studies committee quickly gained wide currency, as it was published as a bulletin of the US Bureau of Education and in the January 1917 issue of the *History Teacher's Magazine*, and served to drive a fresh set of educational reforms. One observer estimated that in less than a decade the social studies commission's "recommendations seem to have been exerting as much influence in the school as its rival, the reports of the American Historical Association."[34]

Forging New Connections with Teaching in the War

Although the report is generally taken as the first major step in the articulation of the social studies movement, its implementation was delayed for a time by the First World War.[35] Discussions about integrating war-related issues into the history classroom consumed much of the available energy for reform (or resistance) among historians and educational reformers. As one observer noted, "The check to plans for developing public education is counted as one of the great disasters entailed by the European war." Legislatures turned their attention from education to war and the economy, and much like the other areas of the historical enterprise, many of the best minds and best teachers were drawn off to war-related work, and funds for further experimentation became scarce.[36]

Within the history community, war enthusiasm pervaded most of the discussions about teaching for the duration. Some of the best-known names in the profession (including Jameson, Leland, and Ford) helped to form the National Board for Historical Service (NBHS), which demonstrated a rare enthusiasm on the part of the AHA to directly engage teachers and develop specific materials for the classroom. The board produced a stream of anti-German propaganda materials for the schools, "helping teachers to present to their pupils the historical background of the war and some appreciation of the historical ideals and policies of the United States."[37] *History Teacher's Magazine* became the primary publishing organ for its work, and the editors changed the magazine's name to *Historical Outlook* to reflect the changed pedagogical relationship between past and present fostered by the war.[38] Even history-related organizations with little direct involvement in the war, such as the MVHA and the Middle States Association, focused substantial amounts of the teaching-related discussions at their meetings to subjects such as "After-the-War Reorganization of History in the Elementary School" and "How the War Should Affect the Teaching of History."[39]

At one level this staved off discussions about the social studies for a time as history demonstrated its value to those pushing more present-minded concerns by serving the war effort. And by most measures, the subject remained very well entrenched in the school systems. In 1919, more than 95 percent of schools offered courses in ancient history and "American history and civics," and just over 90 percent had courses in medieval and modern European history. In comparison, all of these schools offered English and algebra courses, but less than half offered economics and barely 4 percent offered classes on sociology. But evidence of the history discipline's security was probably inflated by an absence of questions about integrated social studies courses. This was the last such survey of school subjects by the US Bureau of Education that failed to ask.[40]

Unfortunately, from the perspective of some members of the historical enterprise, the efforts of the NBHS set a precedent that the profession quickly came to regret. When the war was over, the academics generally retreated back to their campuses—chastened a bit that they had cast away some of their professional ideals in wartime enthusiasms. But teachers and educators had noticed that academics could and would engage them when it served their purposes.[41] Moreover, the academics' rationales for engaging in prowar activities and providing a useful service to the nation buttressed the utilitarian objectives of the emerging social studies movement. As one observer noted, "The war has caused the reconsideration of history and its known attributes as a subject of study, is calling for a revaluation of those attributes and is placing the emphasis where it seems to belong."[42]

The shift in attention even extended to the college level, where the correspondence among the leaders of the AHA and articles in the *Historical Outlook* show a significant increase in discussions about postsecondary teaching issues. Initially, this was just part of the larger effort to make history relevant and useful to the war effort. But after the war, history faculty noted a sharp increase in the number of students in their classrooms and speculated about a renewed interest in studying the historical antecedents of the recent conflict. At an intellectual level, this opened the door to widespread efforts to push New History ideas into the college curriculum. Between 1918 and 1920 the AHA and the regional history organizations sponsored a number of discussions calling for a fundamental rethinking of the way history was taught at the college level, trying to assess how "history courses should 'function in the present.'"[43] Based on a survey of almost two dozen departments, Arthur Schlesinger observed, "What the colleges have done in the past in the name of 'history for history's sake,' they are now willing to sacrifice for a more generous emphasis upon modern times treated from a broadly social point of view."[44] This presented a significant challenge to the more orthodox views of history teaching in the discipline, which maintained that two-thirds of the history curriculum should be allocated to the period before 1776 and to regions outside North America. In its place, historians associated with the New History movement gravitated toward the social studies movement's emphasis on more recent periods and more local concerns.

While the war was often cited as a turning point for history in the school and college curricula, school teachers and academics differed about the actual mechanism of change. Looking back over the previous decade just after the war, Albert McKinley noted four substantive changes in the material printed in the *Historical Outlook*: (1) "the expanding content and changing emphasis seen in college courses in history," (2) "uncertainty and widespread discussion of high school courses in history," (3) "the report of the Committee of Eight and its adoption with modifications in many elementary schools," and (4) "the influence of the World War upon historical activity and history teaching in all grades from the primary school to the university."[45]

The scope of McKinley's vision in this period reflects a continuing effort to encompass all levels of history teaching into a common vision of the historical enterprise. And another author in the same issue celebrated the fact that "one of the most marked changes that has taken place over the past ten years is the disappearance of much of the suspicion and antagonism that formerly existed between teachers of history in colleges and secondary schools."[46] To some extent, this can be dismissed as the type of boosterism elicited by an anniversary celebration. But the range of authors in the *Historical Outlook*, the membership rosters of organizations ranging from the AHA to the regional teachers' associations, and the speakers at the meetings of the teachers' associations all demonstrate that these kinds of connections remained quite active and vital in this period: Authors of articles in the *Historical Outlook* were still comprised largely of academics into the early 1920s. Twenty percent of the members of the AHA were high school teachers, and conversely, about 20 percent of the members in the teachers' associations were academics; and speakers at the regional teachers' association meetings were split about fifty-fifty between academic historians and educators.[47]

Citizenship, Social Studies, and Fresh Challenges to History

Beneath the numbers, however, there were ample signs of growing disarray in the historical enterprise about the discipline's place in the schools. This was most evident in the work of an association committee on "History for Education and Citizenship," which tends to be overlooked in studies of history teaching because its final report was effectively repudiated by the AHA Council.[48] But the committee itself marks an important transition point, in both its personnel and as an indicator of rising tensions between historians and the social studies movement.[49]

The leaders of the committee signal a shift in responsibility for teaching to other areas of the historical enterprise. Earlier committees on teaching were generally comprised of faculty at elite universities and private schools. This committee, however, was chaired by Joseph Schafer, who left a teaching position at the University of Oregon to lead the NBHS in Washington, DC, and then departed midway through the committee's work to head the State Historical Society of Wisconsin. Meanwhile, much of the committee's real work was done by its secretary, Daniel C. Knowlton, a high school teacher who subsequently chaired the social studies program at New York University. Both held history PhDs, and represented the more diverse picture of professional employment in the historical enterprise, but neither was typical of the personnel on previous AHA teaching committees.[50] The committee also reached out extensively to history teachers at all levels, surveying hundreds of instructors at the elementary and high school levels about their classroom practices and how they were integrating the citizenship issue into their history instruction.

The committee struggled, however, to negotiate between a number of competing views about the role of history education, as well as the changing attitudes of many in the parent organization. Internally, the committee had to negotiate between the position represented by the AHA during the war (in the form of the NBHS) and a postwar shift on the AHA Council back to its traditional view of the sacrosanct nature of the Committee of Seven's report. Meanwhile, tapping public sentiment on the citizenship issue introduced added challenges. On one side, patriotic societies clamored for history classes that promoted "Americanism"; on the other, the citizenship question also facilitated the utilitarian arguments of many in the social studies movement.[51]

Over the course of two years, the members of the committee became increasingly frustrated in their efforts to juggle the various competing interests. In their final report, the authors extensively quoted teachers about their practices, hoping to demonstrate that they were not advocating for the social studies but merely recording changes already taking place in the schools. The committee advised that "it is by no means the intention of the committee to suggest a reduction in the time usually allotted to history in high school programs. It is rather the intention . . . to increase the positive requirements in social studies for graduation as a guarantee of citizenship training."[52] But a few carefully placed assurances could not hide the fact that their recommendation for a twelfth-grade course on the "problems of American democracy" undercut one of the basic blocks of the Committee of Seven's report by flipping the balance between history and civics in the fourth year. So when the committee finally asked to publish its findings, the AHA Council refused to allow them to be printed in the AHA's official *Annual Report*, citing "the fact that a considerable difference of opinion seems to exist among members of the Association." The council did, however, agree to the report's publication in the (increasingly independent) *Historical Outlook*, and their findings and recommendations finally appeared (with dissents from two members) in 1921.[53]

The appearance of the report exposed growing cracks in the AHA's efforts to maintain a solid edifice of history education. The committee's efforts to balance all interests, and the council's decision to effectively reject it, helped to catalyze some of the strongest proponents of the social studies movement. One leader of the movement, Harold Rugg at the Teachers College of Columbia University, sharply condemned the council's behavior and cited the support of a number of New History scholars (and future AHA presidents) such as Robinson, Beard, Becker, and Ford for the social studies program.[54] Arthur Schlesinger also expressed doubts about the AHA's handling of these issues: "It seems to me that the time is past when a group of learned men can lock themselves in a room or send out a few questionnaires and then proceed to promulgate a uniform history program for the teachers of the nation."[55]

The sharply negative reaction to the council's actions prompted the association's leaders to put Henry Johnson at the head of a new effort to regain its leadership position on history education.[56] But developments outside of the association quickly sidetracked this effort. In December 1921, a number of teachers in the various social studies disciplines gathered to organize the National Council for the Social Studies (NCSS).[57] The response to the new organization was rather mixed. The AHA Council publicly voted its "sympathy with the movement," hoping to "bring about cooperation in the framing of a programme for the teaching of history and the social sciences." They even asked Johnson to "take an active part in this cooperative," and he agreed to serve as the first vice president of the NCSS.[58]

Even the *AHR* initially offered a welcoming hand to the NCSS, telling its readers,

> Its purpose is to lay the foundation for training democratic citizens; and its sponsors believe that such training can result from a carefully developed and adequately supported system of teaching in the elementary and secondary schools. Its plan looks to promoting cooperation among those who are responsible for such training, including at least the university departments which contribute knowledge of facts and principles to civic education; and the leading groups of educational leaders, such as principals, superintendents, and professors of education, who develop the methods of handling these facts.[59]

The note is remarkably expansive in its description of ongoing cooperation across the historical enterprise—engaging teachers in the schools and universities as well as the full expanse of the educational community—which suggests a wide interest on these issues on the part of the academic members of the AHA. But the distinction between those contributing "facts" and those contributing "methods" represented a large and widening gulf between the communities—with little attention to the fact that teachers increasingly found themselves with those working on methods. That was not immediately apparent, as the organization's first secretary noted with regret that "nearly all efficient and highly trained teachers in the schools were called history rather than social studies teachers." As a result, they were often relatively conservative in their outlook and "slow to join this new and 'radical movement.'"[60]

The organization faced an additional challenge, as it lacked a publication it could truly call its own. McKinley served as president and provided the *Historical Outlook* as a tangible benefit to NCSS members, but even though it offered extensive coverage of the work of the NCSS, McKinley refused to treat the social studies as an integrated field in the pages of the magazine or allocate significant space to the other subjects.[61] To make matters worse, after the organization's first year some members of the AHA Council grew ambivalent and tried to reassert the discipline's central role in the larger school curriculum. While they were willing to promote classes for other social science fields, the association's leaders were not willing to cede the history discipline's preeminent position.[62]

Despite the tensions this generated, the association did briefly benefit from an alliance with the education community in response to a series of virulent attacks on history textbooks by politicians and patriotic organizations. The sharpest criticism focused on the representation of specific nations—particularly perceived biases for or against Germany and England. The attacks included book burnings, demagogic assaults by politicians, and demands from citizens' committees that texts promote a particular viewpoint.[63] Since the texts at issue were generally issued by academic members of the association, the organization had ample cause for alarm. The leaders of the organization took the relatively rare step of passing and widely distributing a resolution condemning these activities, and warned that "the successful continuation of such an agitation must inevitably bring about a serious deterioration both of textbooks and of teaching, since self-respecting scholars and teachers will not stoop to the methods advocated."[64]

This brought the AHA Council and Bassett into close and friendly contact with many in the educational community. J. Montgomery Gambrill at the Teachers College of Columbia commended the AHA's efforts, urging the association to "throw the weight of its influence against the kind of pressure to which the teachers and the school officials are now subjected. They need moral support and some of them need a bit of education. A large portion of the public, it is unnecessary to say, is also in need of education."[65]

Unfortunately, the association's other activities sent very mixed signals, including antagonizing the heads of the NCSS by tinkering with its constitution in an effort to assure the primacy of history. Internally, members of the AHA Council repeatedly reminded committees on teaching issues that they were not authorized to make public statements or policies on the subject.[66] And even though they largely handed the *Historical Outlook* over to the NCSS to provide a house organ and material foundation for the new organization, a transparent goal was also to remove some of the magazine's expenses from the books. These actions, and the growing separation from the *Historical Outlook*, served to further diminish the AHA's role in precollegiate history education.

A significant part of the association's changing attitude can be traced to the narrowing representation of the larger historical enterprise in the leadership of the organization. The council was increasingly dominated by faculty and former students from elite universities that scrupulously maintained a distance from teacher training. A 1920 survey of "professional training for high school history teachers" at college and university history departments found that most programs had introduced specific courses on pedagogy in the previous decade. The exceptions were primarily at the same elite research universities (Harvard, Yale, and Princeton) that increasingly dominated the association's council. Even at institutions that addressed pedagogy, the transition was hardly a sign of growing engagement. According to the historian who conducted the survey, the course in methods in the other departments was generally given by someone who had taught in the secondary schools. She observes, rather tellingly, that "an instructor with experience only in college teaching can scarcely give to the student the same insight into the secondary school problem."[67]

In an effort to obtain "some definite objective information as a basis for determining the present duty of the association to the teaching of history in the schools," the AHA Council asked Edgar Dawson, a professor of history and government at Hunter College and the first secretary-treasurer of the NCSS, to survey the state of history in the school curricula and its relations to other disciplines.[68] Dawson is another of those curious figures at the emerging disciplinary fault line represented by the social studies. He received his PhD in history at the University of Leipzig, and served briefly as professor of history at the University of Delaware and Princeton, before settling into a position at Hunter College and devoting most of his writing and scholarship to political science and pedagogical issues.[69]

Drawing on information from over 2,400 schools, his findings re-inforced the anxieties of the conservative members of the AHA Council and the discipline in general. He offered three major findings—a signifi-cant overlap in staffing (in many cases, the "social studies" teacher was a history teacher), a shift in the training of new teachers to the social stud-ies model, and the compression of history into an ever smaller portion of the curricula. In a preliminary tabulation of his results, Dawson noted that principals and school superintendents planned to increase space in the curriculum for civics and economics and had a general preference for recent history over the more distant past.[70]

The most incendiary finding, however, was the compression of history in the curricula under the weight of a number of school reforms. The pri-mary effect of this was the collapse of ancient and modern European history courses into a one-year "general" or world history course, while American history was separated from civics into a separate course. This posed a significant internal problem for the AHA—where a majority of the academic members specialized in regions outside the United States—and helped feed the growing alienation of many academics in the AHA from issues in the schools.

Privately, council members worried over how to inhibit the trend. According to Dawson, one member even asked, "Why don't we let the Social Studies Council die quietly?" while he was sitting in the room.[71] Publicly, however, they commended Dawson's report to members as "in-telligent, catholic, unbiased, and sufficiently extensive, and the report a model of fair, comprehensive, and penetrating statement. So full and ex-cellent a description of the state of things will be invaluable as a basis for future improvement and progress."[72] As many on the council feared, however, members of both the history and social studies communities cited this report over the next few years as the clearest evidence of the rising status of the social studies at the expense of history.[73]

Even without Dawson's report, there were ample signs of history's waning status in the schools and college admissions. By 1922, 57 per-cent of American colleges and universities required entering freshman to have one or more credits of study in the "social sciences." And the mix of subjects under that label was changing, as nonhistory subjects grew or at least became acceptable as a substitute for history. Ancient history was the most required specific subject in the social sciences but only by 8 percent of colleges and universities. Meanwhile requirements for American history had dwindled from 8 percent of the colleges in 1913 down to just 4 percent. The author of the study rather lamely speculated that the "decrease is probably largely due to the fact that American history is now required for graduation quite commonly by the high schools of the country . . . [so] there is probably no particular need in prescribing it." But that does not account for the fact that fields almost universally required at the high school level, such as English and math, showed no decline.[74]

By 1925, the storm clouds over history education were growing quite ominous, and the Council of the AHA recognized that they needed to provide renewed leadership for these issues. But by that time the AHA, and through it most academic historians, had relinquished much of its authority in the area of history teaching at the secondary level. By failing to engage in the increasingly rigorous discussions about the professional interests of teachers, the organization was ceding its authority in this area to others more willing to work directly with teachers. As the decade reached its midpoint, the prerequisites for a professional separation between teachers and scholars were in place, and the self-styled "research men" were prepared to force the rupture.

PART III

Scattering the Historical Enterprise, 1926 to 1940

CHAPTER SEVEN

The Crisis of the "Research Men"

B y 1926 any lingering perceptions of unity in the historical enterprise were being sundered under the weight of wide-ranging social and cultural changes in the discipline. As the early generation of American history PhDs such as J. Franklin Jameson, Frederick Jackson Turner, John Spencer Bassett, and their peers began to pass from the scene, the ideal of a disciplinary jurisdiction encompassing academia, a variety of historical organizations, and teaching at all levels began to wane under the weight of differences large and small. As younger generations of academics took up leadership positions in the association, they sought to establish a clear set of professional parameters for academia that could serve as a container for their increasingly esoteric subjects of research.

After 1925, the American Historical Association visibly narrowed the jurisdictional scope of its responsibilities and took on the shape of a professional organization intended primarily for "research men"—understood as historians with the credential of a PhD and employed in academia but relatively unburdened by teaching responsibilities. At a fundamental level, the divisions among and between historians were built on a rapid expansion in the number of history faculty, new PhDs, and new scholarly publications in the discipline. This sudden growth fostered a number of divisive crises that focused the AHA's attention on the need for professional standards in one area of the historical enterprise (academia) largely to the exclusion of all the rest. Meanwhile, the leadership of the American Historical Association narrowed socially and demographically, drawing primarily from the students and faculty of a small cluster of elite universities. In the process, the AHA became the hub of a professional support network that defined the work of others employed in the historical enterprise into separate spheres of activity. Work on gathering historical materials for other scholars, for instance, was increasingly characterized as a profession of its own or at most an avocational interest for scholars. And the narrowed focus on particular research concerns left little time to engage in intellectual work on other activities, such as developing curricula or policies about history teaching. As a result, by 1940 the organization had wandered quite far from the association's earlier efforts to promote the wider historical enterprise.

Assuming a "More Positive Leadership" for History Scholarship

Starting in 1926, a fairly narrow slice of research university faculty became increasingly assertive about elevating their own interests within the work of the association. That February, the leader of the endowment campaign observed that "hitherto the American Historical Association has been mainly engaged in the preliminary and necessary work of providing equipment for the investigator. This work will still be necessary; but the time has come when it is proper for the Association, as the organ of historical scholarship throughout the country to assume a new leadership."[1] In this new direction, the organization "ought to assume a more positive leadership in stimulating and guiding research and in publishing the results."[2]

This shift in responsibilities for the association was built upon an explicit change in the definition of what it meant to be a full and participating member of the "historical profession." This was manifest in a number of new projects that elevated the ideal of a "productive" scholar, defined as someone employed in academia who published interpretive scholarship, primarily in the form of book-length monographs. Prior to 1926, the association had been relatively content to promote a positive model for research activity, by elevating high standards of scholarly quality set by the *AHR*, book prizes, and occasional exhortations from the speakers' dais at the annual meetings.

In *The Writing of History* report (written in 1924), leaders of the association challenged historians—and particularly those training the next generation of scholars—to improve the quality of their published work.[3] This marked the first substantial effort in decades to clearly articulate history research and writing as a responsibility of the association that extended outside of the *Review*. In this it followed the attitude of the

AHA's generally ineffectual Committee on Research, established in 1921 to aid scholars at institutions that failed to encourage or promote scholarly work by their faculty. But where the writing and research committees made a positive case for improving and expanding research in the discipline, a new effort in 1926 to define the "The Productivity of Doctors of History" cast the issue in starkly negative terms—as a failure of the professionalization process and a personal failure of those not actively producing new research.

The study started as an effort to establish the proper balance between the association's diverging interests in research scholarship and the development of new tools and materials of research. In the end, the committee (comprised of six faculty members from research universities) took a position strongly in favor of the former.[4] The committee surveyed five hundred history PhDs in a way that framed the issue as a professional problem from the start, asking "why graduate work in history leads to so little productive research on the part of holders of Ph.D. degrees."[5] Following from that premise, the authors concluded that barely a quarter of all working history PhDs were productive "research men," and explicitly divided the academic community into "two types of faculty men: the teacher and the 'researcher.'" The work of the latter was narrowly defined by the publication of articles and books—excluding work promoted by older historians, such as J. Franklin Jameson, that included pulling original documents out of the archives and making them available to others.

Marcus Jernegan (University of Chicago), writing on behalf of the committee, attributed the "failure to produce" to one of three causes: failures in the professionalization process (that advisers of doctorial students did not inspire sufficient zeal to conduct research and publish), failures in the historians' institutional settings (particularly at institutions that emphasized teaching over research), and a systemic failure to properly coordinate and promote scholarly work.[6] Jernegan characterized the association's role in recognizably professional terms—proposing limits on access to the PhD (through a "more thorough weeding-out process during the period of study for the degree"), improving the financial returns for those producing "worth-while research" (in the form of salaries, promotions, and additional support for research), and finally, by publicly defending the value of historical research. The report concluded, "Scholarship must be more generally recognized in the professional world and by the general public; and the scholar must be given more social recognition in one form or another."[7] The Jernegan report established a new benchmark for academic professionalism in the discipline that emphasized research scholarship—and more specifically monograph production—over other forms of work in the historical enterprise.

Privately, older historians such as Jameson expressed qualms about the implication that "the main business of young men under consideration is to produce historical print."[8] But this perspective was only rarely advanced in the discussion. Unlike many committee reports from the AHA, this study elicited an exceptionally high level of interest—both within the association and by the general public. In his annual summary of the December 1926 meeting, Jameson had to cast back thirty years to find a comparable level of enthusiasm and excitement for a committee's work in the hallways and meeting rooms of the association—comparing it to the attention elicited by the Committee of Seven's report on history teaching in 1897.[9] And the results of the survey resonated well beyond the history workers attending the meeting. Given the connection to the much-publicized endowment campaign, these assertions attracted nationwide attention, including a lengthy article in the *New York Times*.[10] All this attention served as a professionalization tool for academics at research universities, and the report became so popular that it was quickly published in the *AHR* and reprinted as a separate pamphlet.[11] Over the next decade, the findings and the benchmarks laid out in this report set the terms of discussion for graduate training in the discipline, what it meant to be an active and productive member of the profession, and the AHA's mission in the coming decades.[12]

A New Generation Enters the Discipline

Jernegan's heavy emphasis on assuring that the PhD was properly constituted as a "research degree," rather than a teaching degree (a point repeatedly reinforced in public statements from the AHA and its leaders over the next fifteen years), bolstered a substantial change in attitude about professional training at a crucial time of transition for graduate study in history. The number of new history PhDs conferred annually more than doubled—from 61 to 141 degrees—between 1925 and 1930, and then grew by another 24 percent by 1940. Viewed another way, twice as many history PhDs were conferred in the fifteen years from 1926 to 1940 (2,057) as had been conferred in the fifty-two years from 1873 to 1925 (1,021).

The comparatively rapid growth in the number of new young PhDs accelerated a significant generational change in the history faculty at American colleges and universities and employed in other areas of the historical enterprise. By 1940, history PhDs from this cohort were employed in all of the major universities and in many of the professionalizing historical societies and archives, all of whom had been instilled with the urgent sense that the PhD was definitively a research degree and that the AHA served the interests of research scholarship.[13]

At the same time, the landscape of history PhD programs was undergoing profound changes. In 1925, just five programs—at Harvard, Columbia, Berkeley, Chicago, and Wisconsin—dominated the field. They awarded well over half of the new PhDs in history, at an average rate of almost six degrees per year. By 1940, however, those schools were awarding barely a third of the new doctorates in the discipline, as the large departments faced growing competition. Some of the private universities (led by the University of Pennsylvania, Catholic University of America, and Stanford University) began to confer significantly larger numbers of degrees in this period, but so too did a number of the state universities in the Midwest and West (led by programs at Ohio, Minnesota, and Washington).

As the older programs grew larger, a number of other departments started conferring degrees, spreading doctoral studies out to other regions of the country, particularly in the South and west of the Mississippi River. The total number of programs conferring history PhDs increased by a third, and helped to fill localized needs for history faculty in regions and states that might not attract (or retain) doctoral degree recipients from the North and East. In states such as California, Georgia, Kentucky, North Dakota, and Texas, the number of employed history faculty doubled or more than doubled between 1928 and 1940. And in many of those same areas, the effort to develop professional archives departments and historical societies created added demand for new PhDs.[14]

As the number of historians receiving PhDs in this period increased rapidly, so too did the number of subfields in the discipline. There was very little change in the balance of geographical interests, as US history accounted for about 55 percent of the PhDs conferred, European history for another third, and specialists in other regions and topics (including "ancient" history) for another 13 percent. But as ever larger numbers of faculty burrowed deeper into their research topics, the topical categories across the various geographic divisions fragmented quite rapidly. This is most visible in the annual listings of dissertations in progress, which underwent a series of rapid structural changes in the late 1920s and 1930s. As the leaders of the association struggled to maintain both conceptual order and the list's functional value for anyone trying to scan the future of work in the discipline, the number of categories used to organize the listings quadrupled between 1925 and 1947 (from twenty-one to eighty-nine). The editors subdivided US history into a number of broad topical and temporal subjects (e.g., "Biographical," "Colonial and Revolutionary," and "Political"), and added a number of subcategories within the social and economic history of the United States (the largest of which was "local," but with quite a few students working on agriculture, industry, and railroads, as well). Outside of US history, the editors also added categories for specific countries in Europe, Asia, and Latin America (though Africa remained undifferentiated and subordinated into the "British empire" until 1947).[15]

The sharp increase in the number of doctoral students proved more than just a conceptual problem, as it also disrupted some of the more genteel aspects of the academic job market. The papers of Guy Stanton Ford in Minnesota, as well as the Harvard history department, for instance, show a growing volume of correspondence from colleagues hustling work for their students.[16] The level of anxiety ratcheted up sharply in the early 1930s, when the hardships of the Depression cut deeply into academic hiring. There are no statistics to show how far the academic job market fell relative to the growing ranks of new PhDs, but senior members began to complain about "unemployed PhDs crowding the halls" of AHA meetings.[17]

While the general increase in numbers of new PhDs through the Depression may seem irrational, the growth and diversification of faculty employment in a widening array of colleges encouraged history doctoral programs to confer additional doctoral degrees. Regardless of the challenges for new PhDs, the number of faculty positions actually increased substantially from 1,347 at 357 four-year institutions in 1928 to approximately 3,239 at 717 colleges and universities in 1940.[18]

The Stratification of History in Academia

Even as faculty at research universities shifted the corporate attention of the AHA to explicitly focus on their interests, history employment for PhDs was becoming increasingly stratified and diverse. In 1928, only a quarter of all four-year history faculty members were employed at the twenty-nine research-oriented institutions of the American Association of Universities. With only one exception (Johns Hopkins University), these departments had a dozen or more faculty on staff. The largest program (at Columbia University) reported thirty-two faculty members, while the departments at Yale and NYU had twenty-four each. But these larger programs had developed tiered faculty structures that supported research work by a few. Almost half of their departmental faculty were employed at the teaching-oriented rank of "instructor," which typically comprised a larger portion of the department than the rank of full professor.

At a practical level, the experiences of instructors at the larger schools were similar to the often neglected majority of academic historians in teaching-oriented institutions.[19] More than half of the history departments in the country had fewer than four history faculty members in their departments, assuring that each of them had to cover large chronological and geographical spans in their teaching (fig. 7.1). Less than one-tenth of the departments held more than nine faculty members, which seemed to be the threshold number to allow considerable specialization

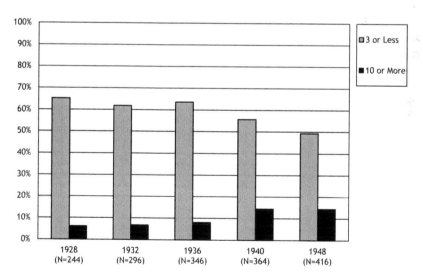

FIGURE 7.1. Number of faculty in history departments, 1928–1948
Source: Tabulation of faculty in *American Universities and Colleges* published by the American Council on Education at four-year intervals (no data collected in 1944).

and opportunities to conduct substantial research. A department with ten or more faculty generally allowed a tiered hierarchy in the department—allowing for a separation between the faculty with substantial teaching responsibilities for undergraduates and those who could teach smaller classes and graduate students.[20]

Faculty at research universities enjoyed an additional advantage in the level of support for their research. In 1932, barely one college in five provided sabbatical leaves. Even at research universities that did grant leave, the evidence suggests that sabbaticals were rarely conferred on faculty members at the rank of instructor.[21] And research grants, even those intended primarily for those "who are in actual need of such aid and unable to obtain it from other sources," also largely went to faculty at the larger research universities.[22] Despite the impediments to specialized work, 65 percent of the faculty in history departments reported they were conducting some form of research—though less than half had published a book or article in the previous five years.[23]

As the only snapshot of its kind, it is not clear whether this represented an increase in productivity spurred on by the Jernegan report. But in comparison to other academic disciplines, history was barely average in the proportion of its faculty conducting or producing research. This is a rather crude measure, given that at least some faculty at small institutions managed to be both highly productive scholars and revered teachers, but it suggests the problem inherent in treating research universities as normative for the history profession. These institutional differences simply widened the gulf between the professional lives of the relatively small numbers of research-supported professors at elite institutions and the vast majority of history faculty employed in the rest of academia.

At the same time, some of the most basic aspects of historical research were evolving in more fundamental ways, with the growing refinement of note-taking methods, such as using card systems in place of the (up to then) traditional method of taking notes in letter books or on folded sheets of paper. At the same time, the infrastructure for private research and writing began to change, as departmental secretaries effectively became a part of the research team for faculty at a number of the rising colleges and universities—typing up drafts of articles for even the most junior faculty members and assisting with smaller research inquiries. Even personal Photostat machines became a tool for historians of means.[24]

The general disengagement of research faculty at elite universities from the professional realities of historians at the majority of higher education institutions set them apart from history PhDs teaching at smaller colleges and universities (as well as teachers at the precollegiate level and even the instructors in their own departments). On behalf of the research men, Jernegan complained forthrightly that "the universities have allowed large numbers of candidates to gain the degree whose sole aim was to use it to get a 'job,' for teaching positions," even as those jobs provided a significant and growing opportunity for new history PhDs throughout this period.[25]

Changes in the way history was taught at the secondary school level reinforced the growing distance between faculty at the research universities and their colleagues at teaching-oriented institutions. While the larger departments had the size and scale necessary to allow ever greater specialization, smaller colleges and universities, particularly at public institutions, increasingly subsumed their history departments into "social science" departments or paired the subject with other disciplines. As the number of colleges and universities expanded to accommodate a growing student population with more diverse needs, the proportion of colleges with pure history departments fell fairly steadily up to 1940, declining from 67 percent of the four-year institutions in 1928 down to 53 percent (fig. 7.2). Meanwhile, the number of schools that subsumed history into a social sciences or social studies department, or paired it with a number of other social science fields (in departments of "history, geography, and political science," for instance), rose to almost 45 percent of the listed institutions. Schools with history buried in the social sciences increased from just 4 percent in 1928 to 23 percent in 1948—as changes in the secondary school curriculum echoed back up the line into the departments training teachers. Most of the growth occurred at public institutions, particularly teachers colleges, where 37 percent of the history departments had been subsumed into the social sciences by 1948 (up from just 1 percent two decades earlier).

Compartmentalizing History Scholarship

While teaching arrangements were assimilated into or with disciplines at many institutions, the fragmentation of historical research into increasingly narrow topics continued apace. The rapid growth in the number of

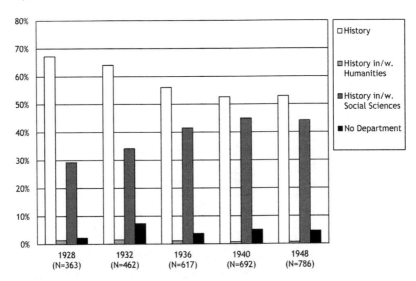

FIGURE 7.2. Distribution of history departments in four-year colleges and universities, 1928–1948
Source: Data drawn from editions of *American Universities and Colleges* published by the American Council on Education at four-year intervals (no data collected in 1944). "History in" program means it was not designated in the department name, "history with" another program means it was part of the name (e.g., a department of history, political science, and geography).

new PhD recipients, increased competition for jobs, and expanding support for research from universities and funding agencies such as the Social Science Research Council and the American Council of Learned Societies worked together to foster a sharp increase in the number of scholarly books and articles competing for attention.

The journal literature provided the clearest evidence of growing specialization. At least thirty-two new peer-reviewed history journals began publishing in this period, promoting further compartmentalization of the discipline into subfields. The new titles included journals for specialists working on specific time frames, on particular regions of the United States, and in ever-narrower subjects of topical interest.[26] Each was developed to mark out new territory for a specific subject field and to create a publishing forum for articles considered too narrow for broader journals such as the *AHR*. And far from lamenting the expansion, the editors of the *Review* welcomed them as adding "to the sum of American knowledge, and will not narrow, even if they do not succeed in broadening, the specialists' view of their subject."[27] Starting in this period, the editors of the *Review* regularly started suggesting specialized journals to authors whose articles they rejected.[28]

The rapid expansion of history publications contributed to the trend toward specialization, assuring that scholars could pursue their own particular research subjects largely in isolation from all but a few other specialists. By 1940 very few historians were working collectively across the entire discipline, and the reports on the AHA's annual meeting tended to emphasize both the vastness of the scale of the meetings and the near impossibility of tracking any specific trends in particular subfields.[29]

The increasing specialization of the work being produced forced a number of adjustments in the gatekeeping mechanisms for the profession. In the early 1930s the *AHR* stopped paying for articles, due in part to financial exigency but also in recognition (drawn from the example of the newer journals in the discipline) that academics would provide content for free to gain recognition in an increasingly competitive profession.[30] And reflecting the dispersion of research into highly esoteric subjects, the journal also began to move toward a system of more specialized peer review for articles. By the mid-1930s members of the Board of Editors were no longer serving as the primary reviewers of article submissions, as the *AHR* editors realized that board members could not adequately assess whether articles were "fresh," "original," and of "real importance."[31] The editors began seeking out specialists on particular subject areas instead, who could offer a more critical assessment about the methods, tools, and existing secondary literature on the subject. They also instituted a more substantive form of assessment through the use of blind peer review (where the author would not know the reviewer).

Despite the effort to impose a more professionalized selection process, however, some authors still remained above such rules. The editor of the *Journal of Modern History*, for instance, could still accept an article from one senior member of the profession without passing through review, simply because "we get so few articles from the aristocrats of the profession that when we do we seize on them avidly."[32] But the correspondence from even the small journals indicates that, the few aristocrats notwithstanding, all of the history journals were implementing policies for specialized review of articles prior to publication.[33]

To make room for the growing volumes of scholarly content, the publication of primary documents, news items, and bibliographic materials began to wither away. For the *AHR*, this change was elevated to a principle in a 1939 directive to "publish only such articles as throw light upon what had been dark before, or suggest new and fruitful fields of historical study, or advance significant new historical interpretations."[34] This move was reinforced later that year, when a group of historians petitioned the journal's editors to "encourage the publication of interpretive articles as distinguished from those of factual presentation based on specialized research, articles dealing with concepts and methods used in other areas of knowledge, [and] articles of a bibliographic character."[35] These assertions mark an effective repudiation of the broader intentions of the *Review*'s founders, clearly elevating novel interpretation over novel information. Following this shift, the smaller history journals, most of which modeled themselves on the *AHR*, sought additional interpretive work and also let their sections of primary documents generally fade away by 1940.

While articles were highly valued, the book increasingly became the gold standard among academics in the discipline. Unlike the book publishing industry as a whole—which fell off by about 20 percent as the country slid into depression—history remained strong in the 1930s, and the number of new books in the field continued to grow. The industry published an average of 590 new history books every year between 1930 and 1940, peaking at 934 titles in 1937.[36] The relative ease with which historians could publish their books actually became a significant problem for one of the AHA's high-profile efforts to take on a new kind of role for academic scholarship. In 1926, the association developed a "revolving fund" to facilitate the publication of new research by younger scholars that might not be commercially viable.[37] While the effort started with considerable fanfare, it ended in disappointment after receiving very few submissions from American and European historians, who reported little difficulty publishing in those fields. In the end, the project had to publish a disproportionate number of titles in Chinese history, since that proved to be one of the few areas in which it was truly difficult to find a publisher.[38]

Even though many of the new history books being published were not authored by academics (which rankled many in the profession), the number of books considered worthy of review in the *AHR* nearly doubled—rising from an average of 148 titles reviewed per year between 1925 and 1930 to an average of 290 between 1940 and 1944. To adjust to this need, starting in the late 1920s, the balance of content in the *AHR* began to tilt heavily toward book reviews, shifting from about 40 percent of the content in the *Review* in the 1920s to almost 60 percent of the pages in the journal by 1940. The trend was reflected in most of the other history journals, even extending to the journals of a number of the state historical societies.[39]

The mix of publications reviewed also became increasingly oriented toward new interpretive scholarship. While the number of reviews of biographies of individual subjects and scholarly editions of primary source documents increased slightly throughout this period, reviews of works of interpretive scholarship increased more rapidly—essentially swamping the appearance of all other material reviewed in the *AHR*. As the books took over a substantial portion of the journal literature, the reviewing process became sufficiently routinized that monograph authors began to develop ways to game the system. By 1941, one *AHR* editor complained about a growing practice of preventing critical reviews "by getting everyone who knows anything about the subject to read his manuscript and then acknowledge indebtedness to all of them in the preface."[40]

The relative ease of publication also fed private concerns from faculty at some elite research universities about the quality of some of the material making it into print. Even before the problems of the revolving fund for publication became evident, a separate proposal to find additional funds to support publication by younger historians elicited a number of sharply negative responses from members of the AHA Council.[41] Contrary to Jernegan's blanket concerns about "unproductive" historians, Samuel Eliot Morison (of Harvard University) warned rather darkly that using AHA funds to develop collaborative publishing programs would "simply help fourth-rate people do third-rate work."[42] And Carlton Russell Fish (a professor at the University of Wisconsin) predicted that additional support would only "deaden the much more important work of individuals rather than stimulate those who might otherwise do nothing."[43] Picking up a similar theme, Stringfellow Barr (University of Virginia), complained that "we have no canons, or none worth writing home about. So we construct the Tower of Babel instead, using Ph.D. theses for bricks."[44] These observations ran contrary to the implicit assumption in the Jernegan report that a great deal of scholarship was being lost to other activities (particularly teaching) or general laziness among some members of the profession. The opinions of Morison, Fish, and Barr indicate that some senior members of the profession were content to let a significant amount of "third-rate" work never see publication—and helped to drive efforts to develop new methods of peer review and higher standards of assessment.

Adjusting to Change in the Discipline

The disruptive effects of rapid growth and differentiation were overlaid with the intellectual disruptions caused by wider historiographical changes—most evident in the spread of New History ideas under a variety of new (and perhaps more accurate) labels. By the late 1920s, the term oriented numerous discussions about the state of historical research and writing outside the discipline. Much of the discussion revolved around whether following New History principles and including new topics and subjects (often abstracted as the "common man") served to make history more vital and real—not just on its own merits but also in engaging the interests of the general public. Although they were not speaking directly to each other, in 1929 Francis Hackett, an editor and author, and Wilbur Abbott, a member of the faculty at Harvard, offered extended treatises characterizing New History as the future for professional history writing—but differed sharply about whether it saved such work from a general lifelessness (Hackett) or simply made it unreadable (Abbott).[45]

Within the discipline, however, the term was losing some of its salience just as the underlying concepts were being realized in new scholarly work. The publication of the first volumes in the collaborative History of American Life series, edited by Arthur Schlesinger (recently appointed to Harvard) and Dixon Ryan Fox (of Columbia University), for instance, marked a new effort to synthesize a history of the United States reflecting these newer methods. In contrast to the earlier American Nation series, edited by Albert Bushnell Hart, which heavily emphasized its scientific methods and political history, the new series forthrightly sought to synthesize a history of the nation from more recent approaches to the past. But in place of the broader term of *New History*, the editors used *social history* to describe the goals of the series.[46]

Regardless of the label, however, faculty recognized that adopting the new methods of social, cultural, and economic history presented a significant problem for the training of new members of the profession. Schlesinger acknowledged that trying to incorporate all the ancillary disciplines into a student's preparation (including other social science disciplines, as well as psychology and statistics) would mean that "the historian of the future is evidently a creature not to be envied, and the doctoral examinations of the next generation may well be 'weltering fields of the tombless dead.'"[47] This led to a rethinking of doctoral programs at a number of schools, including American University and the University of Minnesota, and presumably others. Putting Schlesinger's point more positively, the department at American University promoted reforms in its program that would "open up many subjects in the past which historians have neglected because they have not been trained to think and observe in these terms."[48]

One of the clearest indicators of the disruptive effects of the rapid demographic and intellectual changes taking place in this period was a surge in the amount of self-reflection in the discipline, as evidenced by a sharp increase in the number of new books on the history and practice of historical writing. Three new histories of the discipline appeared between 1925 and 1937—the first book-length histories since J. Franklin Jameson's *History of Historical Writing* in 1891—as well as three new manuals on historical methods.[49] Each of them staked out different areas of the discipline, but collectively they represented a wider effort to come to terms with a discipline that seemed to be diverging into a loose coalition of topics and methods.

The disparities among the methods manuals point to growing differences over even the most fundamental aspects of historical research. In comparison to earlier methods handbooks by American historians, a new manual by Homer Hockett placed much greater emphasis on handling large quantities of material over the fine reading of a few documents. Where the earlier authors devoted most of their books to the necessary techniques and ancillary sciences for closely analyzing documents for their accuracy and provenance, Hockett allocated a substantial portion of his book to the problems of sifting through a large secondary literature.[50] New manuals by Allen Johnson and Allan Nevins were more theoretical, offering themselves as more of a starting point for considering the vast array of potential issues, topics, and sources that historians had to handle. Johnson, for instance, assessed the limits of available evidence on any subject and promoted greater attention to psychological considerations in the analysis of historical trends and events. The new methods manuals also suggest an important shift in the setting for historical research. Where the implied work space in the earlier handbooks was a home study—little different from the gentlemen historians—the

newer manuals allude to a more institutional space for professional research, in libraries or departmental offices.[51]

The histories of the discipline were marked by similar changes. Michael Kraus (City College of New York) and students of Jernegan placed
an emphasis on continuity in an American tradition of historical writing
(in Kraus's case extending back to the Pilgrims, while the Jernegan *festschrift* only reached back to George Bancroft). Harry Elmer Barnes (a
student of James Harvey Robinson), on the other hand, structured his
history in terms of the disruptions caused by New History methods and
ideals—casting a jaundiced eye on traditional methods extending from
the ancient Greeks to his contemporaries.

The manuals and histories reflect larger clusters of thinking about
work and trends in the history profession, but historians associated with
the New History movement still seemed to set the terms for discussion.
As scholarship in this mode began to emerge, it became a more general
subject of discussion. Barnes actively proselytized for the concept and
seemed to play the largest part in bringing the term to the attention of
the general public and scholars in other disciplines.[52] While his energetic work on behalf of the concept helped to bring the term into more
general use, his pugilistic personal style made him anathema to many
historians.[53]

The new histories and methods books published in this period also
point to the arrival of a new and definitive sense of professionalism in
the discipline for good or ill. Kraus and Barnes, for instance, often in-
voke "professional historians" as something fairly novel but nevertheless
representing the highest standards of rigor in the writing of history. In
his manual, on the other hand, Nevins tried to develop a sense of conviv-
iality with lay readers by assuring them that the book was "written by an
amateur of history in the hope that it may assist other amateurs."[54]

The AHA Becomes the Academics' Historical Association

As a counter to the various centrifugal trends, research faculty turned to
the AHA to limit the effects of rapid expansion and growth in the discipline. Under Schlesinger's direction, in 1930 almost forty members of
the association (all from research universities) assessed "the fundamental needs and opportunities of the profession."[55] Focused on the broad
categories of specialization considered significant to the association at

the time—ancient, medieval, and modern European history, and eastern and western perspectives on American history—the assembled historians sought to fuse questions about the professional needs of the discipline with the technical needs and questions of the New (now social) History movement. (They cited the neglect or needs of social history ten times in their relatively short summary of findings, even as they acknowledged that the ancient and medieval historians did not share their concerns.) In the end, they concluded that the discipline suffered from systems of support and professional training suited to the previous century, not the 1930s. They reasserted the idea that the AHA should serve as a professional association for the interests of historical research, by promoting the economic interests of the discipline, coordinating research work, and encouraging other specialists (viewed explicitly as outsiders in the process) to gather and collect materials for the emerging areas of research.[56] This report helped to establish a clear trajectory to the work of the association as it entered the 1930s, reflecting the efforts of research faculty to use the AHA to impose some order on the academic segment of the historical enterprise and promote their economic and intellectual interests.

Clearly, this narrowed focus of attention excluded most of the historical enterprise, not to mention a sizeable number of the historians in academia. But this simply reflected demographic changes in the organization, which increasingly mirrored the research-oriented faculty and elite research institutions it was being called to serve. Between 1925 and 1940, the top leadership of the association narrowed from a group of academics representing a cross-section of colleges and universities to an organization heavily dominated by historians at or from a handful of elite universities (principally Harvard). Meanwhile, the evolving structure and personnel of the other committees of the association tended to reinforce fragmentation in the historical enterprise rather than building bridges among them. Committees related to research (including the editorial board of the *AHR* and the book prize and publications committees) were populated with scholars from the same narrow range of institutions as the association's council. In contrast, committees on the tools and materials of research and teaching were filled primarily with specialists who were brought in from outside the academy to contribute their expertise.[57]

More generally, the representation of members employed in other areas of the historical enterprise fell off sharply. By 1940, the association's

membership was comprised of a large plurality of academics, a significant segment of members with only an avocational interest in history,
and a small shrinking population of those employed in history-related
work outside of academia—a very poor representation of the historical
enterprise in its totality.

At the start of this period the association seemed ready to assume a
renewed leadership for the historical enterprise. By 1930 the AHA had
regained most of the members lost before and during the First World
War, and its treasury had been greatly enhanced by the endowment campaign and related publicity. But the organization was severely weakened
in the late 1920s by a series of misfortunes. Organizationally, the association suffered a particular blow when John Spencer Bassett was killed in
an auto accident in 1928. His ability to build bridges to a wide range of
constituencies in the historical enterprise had helped to ameliorate many
of the incipient tensions among the different constituencies in the organization, and his death deprived the association of a leader who might
have negotiated some of the growing rifts in this period.

In his place, the council appointed the benign but rather ineffectual
Dexter Perkins (University of Rochester), who led the organization for
the next three years. The correspondence suggests that, while he was
well liked on the council and among many members, he was exceptionally passive as an administrator at a particularly difficult time for the association. The Carnegie Institution in Washington cut off its financial
support in 1928, and the association (like its members) suffered heavily in the economic downturn of the 1930s. Many of the funds gathered
in the association's endowment campaign of the mid-1920s were lost in
the stock market crash, and the membership fell 22 percent in five years.
As a result, instead of working energetically on behalf of the historical
enterprise, the AHA spent a significant portion of its organizational efforts in the early 1930s seeking funds just to sustain its operations.

In an effort to revitalize the organization's leadership, while also
moving in the direction laid out by Jernegan and Schlesinger, the AHA
Council decided in 1932 to appoint a high-profile salaried executive secretary. In contrast to the broad array of skills and networks in the discipline that made Bassett seem so attractive when he had been appointed
in 1920, the council hired Conyers Read (University of Pennsylvania) for
his acumen in scholarship and business. Despite considerable need, and
Read's apparent willingness to take the post, members of the council still
worried that he was "too valuable and too much a productive scholar

to sacrifice himself on the purely administrative duties."[58] Despite these concerns, Read assumed the position in 1933, with an explicit mandate to "promote historical scholarship in America through the agencies of the Association."[59] He also introduced a more hierarchical view of academic institutions by actively promoting faculty from elite academic institutions and their students to positions on committees at the AHA.

Read's autocratic style and rather casual contempt for other areas of the historical enterprise exacerbated the tensions already pulling the different constituencies in the association apart.[60] He focused most of his attention on supporting academic scholarship, while also promoting better relations between history and the general public through a nationally broadcast radio program and failed efforts to create a popular magazine for history.[61] Aside from his pet projects, the AHA became consumed with conserving resources and shedding much of its direct involvement in other areas of the historical enterprise.

One consequence of the administrative disarray and the financial hardships of the early 1930s was that many members who viewed their participation as a marginal or unnecessary expense—which was increasingly those without PhDs and academic appointments—simply dropped their memberships.[62] This helped to consolidate (or perhaps just to confirm) the preeminent role of the academic members of the association. When the association surveyed its members about their areas of employment in 1940, academics were clearly ascendant once again in the general membership as history workers in the rest of the historical enterprise fell significantly (fig. 7.3).[63]

By 1940, academics comprised 42 percent of the total membership roster. In real terms, the number of identified faculty at four-year colleges and universities doubled between 1920 and 1940 (from 681 to 1,293). While the number was growing, it was significantly less than the total number of history faculty in 1940 (estimated at 3,239 in that year's *American Colleges and Universities*). The difference reflected a general shift toward the elite universities in the Northeast, which comprised a substantial portion of the academic members of the association in this period. This was reinforced by trends in the leadership of the organization, where PhDs from Ivy League institutions increasingly held elected and appointed positions. As the measure of what it meant to be a historian became increasingly difficult to judge by older metrics, leaders of the association looked to simpler measures of quality. Read and others tended to draw on narrower networks of association, typically those

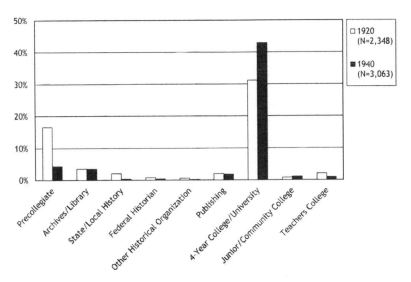

FIGURE 7.3. History-related workplaces of AHA members, 1920 and 1940 (nonhistory employed not shown)
Source: Tabulation of AHA members listed with employment information. Membership information published in *AHA Annual Report, 1920* and *AHR* (1940).

built up during graduate school. By 1930, more than half of the association's committee members with PhDs had earned their degrees in an Ivy League school, even though those schools awarded just 44 percent of the PhDs awarded over the previous thirty years (and had conferred a declining portion since the turn of the century). The disparity was even more pronounced on the association's governing council after 1935—where Ivy League PhDs comprised 80 percent of those holding elected positions in 1940. Before 1925 the association's leadership had been much more diverse, drawing more heavily from the rising universities (though particularly from Johns Hopkins University).

As the size of the profession grew past any one person's ability to know, the networks of relationships seemed to narrow. Although there had been complaints about this problem going back to the turn of the century, it was really in the late 1920s that this became a tangible point of concern. Between 1925 and 1945, members employed outside of academia declined from almost 25 percent to 19 percent of the members on the council and committees of the association. The proportion of members directly involved in precollegiate teaching and history work outside of academia declined substantially. The proportion of precollegiate educators fell from 17 percent of the total membership in 1920 to just 7 percent in 1940. In real terms, their numbers dropped by almost 66 percent, from 389 to just 131. And others doing history work in areas outside of academia (but particularly the historical societies and archives) also declined as they developed separate professional networks in the 1930s. Aside from faculty and students in academia, the balance of the membership was increasingly comprised of those with only an avocational interest in the discipline.

At the same time, there was a perceptible shift in the employment patterns of those drawn into the work of the association, as members working in areas of precollegiate teaching were largely phased out along with committees dedicated to their work. Outside of the teaching fields, the AHA developed advisory committees on archives and bibliographic work consisting almost entirely of professionals from those areas of employment. But the committees were relatively isolated from the other activities of the organization—serving in more of a consulting role than as an intrinsic part of the work of the association.

While the leadership of the AHA was never a perfect representation of the larger historical enterprise, it was really only in this period, when the association began to turn a substantial portion of its corporate efforts toward shaping and promoting the interests of research scholarship, that those working in other aspects of the historical enterprise turned away from the association and sought organizations dedicated to their own professional concerns.

CHAPTER EIGHT

Handing Tools and Materials Over to Others

After 1926, the differences between the various areas of the historical enterprise began to harden into clearly distinct and sharply defined categories. Members of the AHA based in archives and historical societies, for instance, began to identify themselves as working in a discrete professional sphere, while defining the academics into a separate category where their relationship was essentially transactional. At the same time, the academics began to identify archivists and the staff at historical societies as discrete professional groups, representing a unique and separate set of skills and interests. As their discrete networks and conversations about their own practices began to go their own way, the various members of the historical enterprise started to formally separate into new and distinct professional organizations of their own.

Social History Adds to the Burden of History Work

Regardless of the preferred label, the expansion of historical research to encompass new topics and methods sharpened a number of the differences between the "research men" and other areas of the historical enterprise. Arthur Schlesinger observed in 1929 that integrating social history into the professional apparatus of academic research required gathering and collecting new types of materials. But his observations marked a clear sense of separation from work on the "equipment of research." He concluded that this division was necessary because the two types of work—scholarship on the one hand, development of the tools and materials of research on the other—had reached such a level of technical difficulty that they each required much greater specialization.[1] But for those still trying to straddle the realms of scholarship and the gathering of historical information, this was met with considerable alarm. The elderly J. Franklin Jameson (who was then serving as head of the Manuscripts Division at the Library of Congress) became increasingly annoyed at efforts to focus on newer subjects in the collection of materials, and also to divert AHA funds from gathering materials.[2]

In the end, their differences played out over the types of material to be gathered. Schlesinger pressed actively for more expansive coverage, noting that "since the social historian is interested in everything relating to the past of American civilization, he wants everything collected and preserved."[3] But Jameson became increasingly insistent that the AHA's support for documentary editing and collections projects should continue to focus on political subjects. He maintained that

> I have always thought it much more difficult to document social history in a solid and authoritative manner than political or constitutional, because in the latter there are fundamental and authoritative documents the whole series of which can be printed, whereas the materials for social history are often so voluminous, so diverse, and so scrappy, that inevitably a selection has to be made; and all collections of selected material are open to the suspicion or the possibility of bias in the selection. They have not therefore the same standing, relative to the drawing of conclusions, that collections of constitutional and political material most commonly have.[4]

In subsequent discussions, however, Jameson found himself increasingly isolated on these issues, as other members of council questioned the basic premise of the discussion and argued that there was little value in publishing *any* manuscript materials. One member noted that the increased specialization of research projects forced scholars into the archives for growing portions of their research, and made it less likely that any published collection would find a significant audience.[5] The study from Schlesinger's Committee on the Planning of Research brought these differences into sharper relief. In an exchange with Schlesinger about the direction of the committee, Jameson expressed deep reservations that "the planning which this committee is to conduct is not planning for the work of individuals, but for the organized and corporate work of the Association." He insisted that the committee's work should be focused on "the provision of instruments of research or the making of volumes of original material, source books."[6]

While Jameson was speaking up for embracing a wider range of historical work, his letter also made it clear that this was still conditioned by a narrower view of the material that should be included in that work. He offered a specific proposal for a sourcebook on the development of "economic democracy," but the material he specified consisted largely of legislative and judicial acts and statutes.[7] The final report by Schlesinger's committee reflected the social historians' more expansive view of what should be gathered, calling for attention to a range of other materials such as newspapers and motion pictures, as well as the "great variety of business and social data, especially the papers of obscure persons and organizations."[8]

In the end, the committee attempted to split the difference—devoting a large section to the "Enlargement, Improvement and Preservation of Materials," but emphasizing the need to gather materials for the new types of history, and describing such work as largely external to the work of scholarship. "The amassing of data for social, economic and cultural history," they observed, "should be systematized and coördinated; institutional coöperation upon a regional basis should be encouraged; and the American Historical Association should be responsible for leadership and advice in this respect."[9] The authors envisioned a role for scholars in guiding such projects but clearly supposed that the actual work would be performed by organizations and specialists outside of academia.

The sense of a clear and sharp division between academics and staff at historical organizations was clearly growing from the other side as well. In 1925, the head of the Conference of Historical Societies invited two college professors to the meeting with the goal of "challenging the historical societies"—particularly on their collection policies for "general history."[10] And more fundamentally, the leaders of the societies were acutely conscious of the fact that technology was fundamentally changing the way they operated, including their ability to gather and distribute materials—most noticeably with the introduction of the microfilm machine.[11] As one group of society leaders noted in 1930, "innovations in applying technology to scholarship were not concluded when typewriter and filing system invaded the professor's study and the photostat installed itself in the library basement." Throughout they emphasize the enormous challenges of attempting to gather the growing variety of materials scholars were seeking for research, while keeping pace with the expanding capacities and added costs of new technologies.[12]

The technological changes varied widely but generally included the introduction of new classification systems and card indexes for records and (starting in the early 1930s) microfilm for preservation and distribution.[13] Each of these changes had significant staffing implications, as new types of jobs opened up that were increasingly specialized and narrowly focused on specific sets of tasks. The employment records for the Wisconsin Historical Society show increasingly technical sets of questions for potential hires and assessments by quantifiable measures—demonstrating both growing specialization and the expanding influence of civil service rules.[14] Gradually the highly professionalized staffs of these organizations were working in their own specialized spheres.

Even though the council of the association increasingly identified its interests with the "productive scholars" described in Marcus Jernegan's report, they did make a few modest efforts to provide opportunities and leadership to other aspects of the historical enterprise. In 1928, the Conference of Historical Societies joined the archivists in formally expressing their discontent at the lack of a voice in the organization, and the council responded with one final effort to provide them with a substantial opportunity to participate in the work of the association.[15] In 1931, the council revived the Public Archives Commission—now comprised entirely of archivists and administrators at state historical societies—and asked them to prepare a guide for public officials about the preservation of local archives. The resulting report, published the following year, provided specific policy guidance, and demonstrated some fresh vitality on the committee.[16] The commission also resumed its previous activities of surveying archival activities at the state level and produced a report on South Carolina in 1933.[17]

But as the academics began to define their interests more narrowly— and mark out internal territories that separated one academic historian from another—staff members at other types of institutions became increasingly invisible to the leaders of the major history organizations. This led to a host of small and petty slights to historians working outside of academia. An effort to attract new members to the Mississippi Valley Historical Association in 1930 was targeted specifically at "history teachers," without any mention of others in the historical enterprise.[18] A few years later, Read sent out a survey about new scholarship in the discipline, but only sent it to faculty at research universities (eliciting an angry letter from Joseph Schafer at the Wisconsin Historical Society, who continued to publish quite regularly).[19] By a series of such turns, the main history organizations left little doubt that staff members at the historical organizations were considered outsiders.

From Conference to Society of American Archivists

By the early thirties, the archival community had the most advanced professional identity among the historical organizations. The most notable (and oft-cited) statement of independence was set out by Margaret Cross Norton in 1930. Speaking as head of the Archives Department at the Illinois State Library and a former member of the Public Archives Commission, she warned, "Unless the archivist can forget more or less temporarily his personal enthusiasm for history and work for building up of a real archives department functioning as an efficiency proposition in state administration, he is neglecting both his duty as a historian and as a public official."[20] This marked an important shift in the professional self-definition of the archivists—from someone charged with caring for the historical record to someone managing public records for multiple uses and users. As a number of subsequent historians of the archival profession have observed, this had an "incisive effect on the thinking of American archivists," facilitating an expansion and clarification of their professional identities apart from the field of history.[21]

By 1935, a majority of the states had established archival policies and institutions for their records (fig. 8.1), and most of the rest relied on less formal collection activities by state historical societies. Within the organizations, increasingly staff members were working in their own specialized spheres. And the apparatus around employment was more professionalized as well, as civil service rules over employment increasingly defined their situations and status.[22]

Even if the AHA leadership had wanted to provide a forum in the annual reports for the archivists and societies, the organization was limited by a rising deficit and cutbacks in federal support due to the Depression. So once again, efforts to develop and disseminate new projects, such as the revived Public Archives Commission, were prevented from publishing by the lack of any vehicle except the *AHR*. As a result, the drift away from the activities and interests represented by other areas of the his-

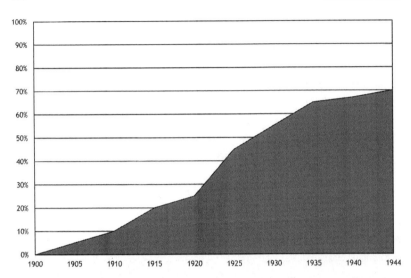

FIGURE 8.1. Proportion of states with archival programs for public records, 1915–1944
Source: Based on a tabulation of historical information published in Posner, *American State Archives.*

torical enterprise continued unabated. Perhaps detecting this drift, Leland suggested that it would "be a great advantage" to bring Solon Buck
(chief of publications at the newly established National Archives) onto
the Council of the AHA, because "the welfare of the Archives must for
a long time be one of the principal preoccupations of the Council of the
Association."[23]

In another bid to reclaim some leadership on these issues, the council assigned another committee to revisit the subject of the AHA's relationship to documentary editing and public archives. Instead of providing clear guidance, however, they merely reemphasized the growing
professional divisions between academics and others in the historical enterprise. The committee metaphorically described a clear line of separation—"The historian is the man in front of the desk, seeking expe-
ditious service. The archivist or custodian is the man behind the desk.
Each has an interest in every phase of the whole problem of archives, but
the primary interests and problems of the two are different." This laid
out the separation in fairly explicit terms, with the AHA viewed as an
outsider in the archival process, whose "chief interest is in their location,
and their availability through descriptive guides and publication." With

that in mind, the authors floated the idea of a separate organization of archivists, even though they doubted whether there was a sufficient core of potential members. The committee paternalistically advised that "if these groups under nurture of the American Historical Association become sufficiently self-conscious and strong to lead a more independent existence, the Association should manifest a sympathetic and cooperative interest."[24]

The foundation for this self-consciousness was provided by the formal establishment of the National Archives in 1934, which provided the core leadership and the resources necessary to bring the organization to fruition.[25] Solon Buck, who was among the first hires to the archives, was a central figure in this effort. Even after his appointment as treasurer and AHA Council member, he remained convinced of the need for a separate organization for archivists. His correspondence indicates little hostility toward the academics running the association, just the positive need for an association to represent the emerging professional needs of the archival community. Conversely, there is little evidence in the correspondence of the other leaders of the AHA that the academics were particularly troubled about the archivists forming their own organization.

The abstract goals of the new organization were framed almost exclusively in professional terms—to improve and coordinate the practices of those serving as archivists, and to provide a professional apparatus that could demonstrate their value to their superiors in the federal, state, and local governments. Margaret Cross Norton celebrated the idea of a separate organization, observing that the lack of publications for their work made it "difficult to make our political chiefs see that our work is professional and should entail professional appointees when there is no body of literature to which we can point to prove that we are professional."[26] At the AHA's 1935 meeting, members of the Conference of Archivists agreed to separate from the AHA and form an association that could support this emerging professional identity and provide tangible support for their work.

Buck spent the next year elaborating a plan for the new organization, which came together as the Society of American Archivists (SAA) the following December.[27] This proposal demonstrated the wide range of professional interests that the AHA had not been able to satisfy—laying out an extensive institutional apparatus for the organization, including a journal editor and eleven committees ranging from "international relations" to a "committee on terminology, to formulate definitions for technical terms used in archival economy and to promote uniformity in the usage of such terms."[28] The only substantive debate about the structure of the new organization arose over whether there should be professional criteria for membership. A small segment pressed unsuccessfully for a very narrow requirement for actual employment in an archives. But in the end, the organization's constitution limited membership "to those who are or have been engaged in the custody or administration of archives or historical manuscripts or who, because of special experience or other qualifications, are recognized as competent in archival economy."[29]

It is not clear how a narrow professional limit on membership might have affected the development of the SAA, but there was considerable overlap between the initial roster of SAA members and the AHA and MVHA. More than half of the founding members of the SAA in 1937 were members of the other organizations as well. Lester Cappon estimated that most of the founding members of the Society of American Archivists also had advanced degrees in history, observing that "none of the archivists had been trained as such, for no opportunity existed." It would take a number of decades before professional archival training developed into departments separate from history.[30]

Despite the separate professional organization, there still remained some ambiguity about the archivists' identity as a discrete profession. The Council of the AHA formally welcomed the new organization and ceded the work and activities of the Public Archives Commission to the SAA.[31] But the SAA in turn asked Samuel Flagg Bemis (a professor of history at Yale University) to draft a report on the training of archivists in United States. Not surprisingly, perhaps, he maintained that a history PhD should be the core credential for a "first class" archivist.[32] And the SAA's publications committee contemplated "a manual on archival economy for American archivists," but ultimately concluded in 1939 that "the time is probably not yet ripe for the preparation of such a manual."[33] Given the widely disparate organizations employing archivists—ranging from public institutions to the poorest of historical societies—the archival community struggled to develop a clear sense of commonality into the 1960s.[34] While their sense of internal coherence still suffered from the disparate character of the institutions they served in (and the colleges and universities that trained them), the establishment of the SAA marked a clear sense of separation from the scholars who were perceived primarily as the users of their materials.

The Societies Build a New Home

The historical societies also became more assertive about establishing a professional identity of their own in this period. Writing in 1934, Julian P. Boyd (a history PhD serving as librarian at the Historical Society of Pennsylvania) described the growing alienation of historical societies from the AHA over the previous two decades, though he commended some recent improvements as the result of "increased interest taken in these agencies by members of departments of history in American colleges and universities."[35] But like the archivists, he identified a new spirit of professionalism among society staff members in the development of scientific practices in the societies. At the same time, as localities and particular identity groups took a greater interest in promoting their own pasts, this was a period of rapid expansion for institutions that served history at the state and local levels that paralleled the growth in institutions of higher education and archives. As tabulated by the Conference of Historical Societies (and the succeeding association), the number of historical societies grew from 313 in 1926 to 1,378 just eighteen years later (fig. 2.1).

For their part, the state and local historical societies were developing professional resources of their own and publication outlets to reflect their own interests. One mark of this is the growing number of journals dedicated to the history of particular states during this period. By 1926, historical societies in a dozen states had journals dedicated to their subject. These journals were comprised of news about the society, genealogical notes, and scholarly articles, reflecting a desire to encompass a wide variety of historical practices and interests. These provided additional vehicles for the dissemination of historical knowledge and an additional set of resources from the state and local history perspectives. As Ian Tyrrell noted, these developments cut in two directions. There was a measure of convergence taking place in the historical enterprise, as many of those taking over the state and local historical societies were credentialed history PhDs with a "scientific" view of history scholarship. But here again, there was a shift in identity as they "developed new loyalties to the state scene and chafed at the attitudes of nationally oriented academic historians."[36]

Even though the archival profession was the first to formally move out of the AHA, the historical societies were the first to actually consider the move. As chair of the Conference of Historical Societies, Herbert Kellar (McCormick Historical Association) proposed a "thorough survey of the present status of historical agencies to make recommendations regarding the formation of a national organization" as early as 1934.[37] But Christopher Coleman from the Indiana Historical Society forestalled a decision. He conceded that the AHA "was composed of, and controlled predominantly by, a university constituency, and that the state and local historical agencies were composed, for the most part, and manned by nonuniversity constituents." Nevertheless, he argued that despite the differences, the association's limited funds, and the organization's growing tendency to direct those funds to faculty at universities, the societies were better off working within the association to help "maintain recognized standards of historical work."[38] As a result, the issue of a separate organization was deferred for three years.

Part of the cause for the delay was the wide array of historical organizations brought together under the auspices of the conference, which still represented a fairly diverse set of institutional characteristics. Collectively they represented a range of employees engaged in a wide variety of historical practices—including document editing and archiving, historical interpretation in museums and other public spaces, and other forms of outreach to the general public. It is not clear how many people were actually employed in the societies, but the leaders of those institutions increasingly saw themselves as representing a new and distinct profession. In his survey of work in the societies, Boyd particularly cited the "younger generation of trained scholars now engaged in this field" as a measure of the growing professional standing of the societies on their own—a standing that seemed poorly served within the narrow confines of the AHA. The core of his article seems intended to show that a number of young history PhDs were running these organizations in a highly professional manner and still producing as scholars, but that their interests increasingly led them away from the AHA.[39]

Given the passive neglect of the parent organization, C. C. Crittenden of the North Carolina Historical Commission revived the movement for a separate organization after he was selected to chair the conference in 1938. Shortly after he assumed the post, Crittenden asked other members whether the time had come for "a better coordinated, more closely knit organization," noting that "what can be accomplished along such lines is clearly shown by the . . . formation of the Society of American Archivists."[40] Even though a majority of the former chairs of the conference expressed reservations, the general membership of the conference voted to press ahead with the idea.[41] Drawing on the advice and experience of many of the same people who led the formation of the SAA (particularly Buck), members of the conference spent the next year working through issues of policy, resources, and centralization—problems that had been greatly simplified for the SAA by the role of the National Archives. Just as the Conference of Historical Societies had wrestled throughout its existence with the variety of institutions brought together under its banner, the members of the conference wrestled at length with the identity and function of a new organization. As one member conceded, "The several hundred historical societies have many different interests which make effective cooperation difficult." And here again, members debated whether to limit membership "to people professionally engaged in the work."[42]

Despite concerns about the great diversity of institutional forms and interests among the historical societies, they concluded in 1939 that they had enough in common to proceed with a new organization to be called the American Association for State and Local History. In addition to developing a comprehensive program for cooperative projects between the societies, the founders proposed a broad plan for working with the general public and officials at the state and local levels.[43] The sponsors of the new association did not define themselves against any particular deficiency of the AHA, but rather defined their interests positively and as complementary to the other interests of the organization. Like the archivists, they defined themselves as a separate profession within the larger disciplinary boundaries of history; a profession drawing on a wide range of skills and speaking to a segment of the population with more localized historical interests.

After the Divide

Despite the separation of the two primary groups working on the tools and materials of history, the AHA continued to engage in a variety of smaller projects throughout this period. But they were relatively modest affairs and increasingly driven by particular endowments and the interests of their funders.[44] In contrast, the Society of American Archivists spent a considerable amount of time discussing how further developments in technology were changing access to historical materials and whether it made activities like the AHA's old Historical Manuscripts Commission obsolete. The SAA set up its own committee for the publication of archival materials to provide information about where they were, how they should be cared for, and how they should be edited for source collections. Citing "recent progress of microcopying, near-printing, and other cheap methods of reproduction," the chair of the committee noted that "formerly it was printing or nothing. Now, however, these cheaper methods make it unnecessary to print many documentary materials which nevertheless ought to be reproduced. Should we not aim more than formerly to print only materials that will have a wide general interest?"[45]

Solon Buck agreed about the transformative effect of the technology on the kind of work documentary editors should do, and suggested that the SAA's time could be better spent on developing a list of documentary projects in production, observing that it could be comparable for its field to the listings of research projects in history then published by the AHA.[46] The staff at the *AHR* came to a similar conclusion about the futility of scattered publication of primary sources, recognizing that the traditional "Documents" section had become an anachronism that should be omitted to provide "more space for major articles."[47] Technological changes thus further altered the relationship between academics and specialists working with the source materials.

By 1941, professional practices in this area of the historical enterprise had differentiated to the point that archivists, historical societies, and academics clearly recognized each other as representing entirely different professional interests and differing jurisdictions. The coming of the war sharpened the lines between the different areas of the historical enterprise, as the professional activities of all three organizations were refocused on war-related projects. The AHA focused most of its organizational activities on advisory projects for the War Department and the SAA on "emergency" recordkeeping. The work of the American Association for State and Local History focused on gathering local material about the national crisis and producing a modest handbook of the societies.[48] The members and officers of the three organizations continued to consult regularly—both during and after the war—but each of the organizations found their own "useful purpose" during the conflict that served as a clear expression of their separate professional identities.

CHAPTER NINE

Teaching Goes Its Own Way, 1925–1940

The professional divergence between the "research men" and those who defined themselves as teachers followed a similar, but more acrimonious, trajectory. By 1925, as the professional literature and networks became more distinct and the number of competing voices from the education community and the other teaching disciplines grew, the "research men" began to withdraw from discussions and simply declined to engage with them. At the same time, those who taught history in the schools increasingly identified with other teachers as a professional category.

Recognizing this, the AHA took up its largest effort yet to define the role of history in the classroom and the professional employment of teachers for decades to come, in the form of an extensive Commission on the Social Studies. But the effort was beset by problems from the start and ultimately convinced association leaders to largely cede this area of the historical enterprise to the education community, just as they had relinquished other areas to professionalizing archivists and historical societies.

Searching for a Full and Fair Assessment of History in the Schools

As early as 1924, the AHA Council resolved to try to regain some of the association's lost authority over the issue of history in the schools, but the growing distance between the association's leadership and changing practices in precollegiate teaching made it almost impossible to find someone to lead the effort. Of two possible candidates, John Spencer Bassett reported that members of council viewed one with suspicion because he was "thought to be inclined to compromise in favor of civics," while the other candidate was viewed skeptically because his supporters seemed to be "leaning toward the National Council for Social Studies." For their part, neither candidate was particularly enthusiastic about taking on a committee that seemed to lack clear support from the association.[1]

Oddly enough (given his previous lack of interest in these issues), in mid-1924 Waldo Leland encouraged the council to take up a new and more vigorous effort to engage with the social studies. As secretary of the American Council of Learned Societies, Leland found himself at the intersection of a number of different disciplines. From that perch, he was struck by the level of engagement with teaching issues in the languages, which seemed much more secure in the curriculum. In a letter to Bassett, he enthused that the Modern Language Association (MLA) had developed a survey of the curriculum that was "completely objective," which "does not try to prove that the study of modern languages are worthwhile, but tries to find out what really are the advantages of such study, and what objects should be sought in the teaching of foreign languages." He concluded that the "only way" for the AHA to resolve similar issues about history's place in the curricula was to "go to the very root of the matter and be willing to ask the question, is history worthwhile, and if so, how is it worth while? and what valuable elements in education can be supplied by history which cannot be supplied by anything else." He issued a stark warning that if the AHA Council failed to address these issues in a more honest and forthright manner than it had, "nobody outside the Historical Association is going to be interested or impressed."[2]

Leland put Bassett in touch with Max Farrand, a former member of the AHA Council teaching at Yale, who had recently become director of a small educational foundation called the Commonwealth Fund. The fund had supported the modern languages project, and Farrand was enthusiastic about supporting a similar project for history. But his support was conditional. He considered himself a "progressive" on educational issues and insisted on assurances that the AHA was open to a full and fair consideration of "the relation of History to the other social studies." He insisted that "if we temporarily yield our traditional position of superiority—but what the other studies are apt to call supremacy or even domination—we would be in a stronger position than ever, . . . and if we cannot maintain that position as a result of scientific inquiry, we ought to drop to our proper level."[3]

Bassett and the AHA Council acceded to his conditions and agreed to a study of the relationship between history and the related disciplines on "scientific" and "objective" lines. Unfortunately, their willingness to take up the task was not met by a similar willingness from senior historians to actively join the effort. Perhaps the clearest evidence of the growing separation of academia from precollegiate teaching is the association's long and agonizing efforts to find a senior faculty member to chair the new teaching committee. Arthur Schlesinger, who had served on a number of teaching-related committees over the previous decade, declined to serve even temporarily as chair, lamenting, "The fact is that for the past three or four years I have been trying hard to develop a genuine interest in the problem of history teaching in the schools—but I have not succeeded! I regret this, for I believe that it is perhaps the most important question that faces our profession."[4] Similarly, Charles M. Andrews of Yale, then serving as president of the association, refused to assist. Bassett conceded, "I appreciate your lack of sympathy on the whole subject. As a research man you have my complete support. I agree with you thoroughly that our Association has run too much into work like this but the remedy, it seems to me, is to get plans devised for bringing it back on the right track."[5] This perception that "research men" need not trouble themselves with teaching issues helped to energize critics of the discipline's place in the schools. Edgar Dawson, then serving as secretary of the NCSS, warned rather starkly that "if the American Historical Association does not look out for history as a means of education, it would seem that no one else is under obligation to do so. Certainly there is no one else who both can and will."[6]

Dawson laid out his growing frustration with the attitude of many historians a few years later. He insisted that he was perfectly content to treat "history" and "social studies" as interchangeable labels—as long as history was defined in the terms articulated by AHA presidents James Harvey Robinson and Edward P. Cheyney, or "the dean of history teachers," Henry Johnson.[7] He noted with regret, however, that "if the average historian insists on giving a narrow and visionless definition of his subject, some of the members of the teaching profession must find another term to describe the work they are doing in this field."[8] Even if the AHA Council did not consist of "average historians" by most measures, it certainly clung to a narrow definition of the field. At least part of its attitude seems to be generational. At the time, the council was still largely comprised of historians who entered the profession around the time of the Committee of Seven report, so it is not surprising that most still held an older view of history teaching, even as a few members (most notably James Harvey Robinson) remained quite open to repositioning history in the curriculum.

As he struggled to find someone to lead the effort, Bassett complained that one candidate's "view would easily satisfy the Council, which is generally conservative. I am not sure that it would satisfy the more modern school."[9] Bassett expressed frustration with the "divided opinion in the Association. Some of us are quite conservative and wish to follow the old lines [laid out by the Committee of Seven]. Some others are modern and wish to accept a different kind of material for entrance to college and also for the freshman course. It is a subject we ought to thrash out."[10]

Ultimately the council settled on August C. Krey, a medievalist at the University of Minnesota. Even though he was not particularly distinguished as a scholar, Krey seemed the perfect choice, as someone who taught high school history while earning his PhD and subsequently aided the National Board for Historical Service during the war.[11] In Krey they finally happened upon someone with the energy and enthusiasm to push the issue forward while drawing support for the different interests on these issues. Dawson endorsed Krey as someone with "positive, but not ossified, views on history and its place in the school. . . . He is more conservative than I am; but he is reasonable and well informed."[12] Krey accepted the post with considerable reluctance, however, repeatedly stating his anxieties about taking on a position that was so politically fraught.[13]

After studying the issues for a year, he strongly encouraged the council to take up an extended multidisciplinary survey along lines first recommended by Leland and Farrand; one that looked deeply at all areas of history in the schools, including curricula, teaching methods, teacher training, and testing. Krey offered little comfort to the conservatives on the council, observing that the "conditions of the country as a whole have changed considerably" since the Committee of Seven report. He catalogued a long list of societal changes that transformed the fundamental purpose and function of the schools (including the population shift from rural to urban, women seeking careers outside the home, increased geographic mobility, the nation's growing involvement in world affairs, and that secondary education was "no longer preparation for college but for life"). He concluded that the "science of education, then almost nonexis-

tent in this country, has become an important profession with a vast ac-
cumulation of literature and a very respectable group of scholars," and
the association needed to adjust its thinking to fit these new realities.[14]

With some reluctance, the council agreed to form an "Investigation
on History and Other Social Studies in the Schools," but Bassett was the
only elected member of the council initially willing to serve on the committee. After further review of the issues, the committee returned to the
council and asked quite pointedly whether it was

> willing to sponsor an investigation whose end shall be a systematic program
> of social education for the fourteen grades of the public schools, understand-
> ing: 1. That such an investigation and program will involve all of the social
> subjects. 2. That the resultant program may make serious changes in the con-
> tent of history now offered in the schools.[15]

The council again reaffirmed its support of the project, though there is
no evidence that it seriously engaged with the issues laid out by Krey and
the committee.

An Independent Identity for School Teachers

Unfortunately, it took the better part of three years to secure proper
funding for the investigation (from the Carnegie Corporation of New
York), during which time the NCSS grew more independent from the
AHA.[16] In 1925, the NCSS reconstituted itself as a "department" of the
National Education Association, and asserted that within the schools,
the various social studies disciplines "including history, economics, sociology, and government, if offered, shall be organized in one department,
unless the school is so large that separate departments are required for
one or more of these studies."[17] The AHA also diminished its public
connection to the *Historical Outlook*, even though it continued to support the publication financially and still appointed some members of the
editorial board. But at the AHA Council's insistence, the description of
the relationship on the magazine's cover was changed to read that it was
"published with the endorsement of the American Historical Association." Bassett stressed, however, that this was "not to be taken as lessen-
ing to any extent the cordial approval felt by the Council for that excellent journal."[18]

Regardless of the council's "cordial approval," in both quantitative and qualitative terms, history was increasingly subsumed into the social studies in the *Historical Outlook*. After 1925, the authors publishing articles in the *Outlook* became increasingly distinct from the membership of the association. The number of academics writing in the magazine (at least academics not affiliated with education departments or teachers colleges) was perceptibly smaller, while historians from research universities disappeared almost entirely from the *Outlook*'s pages. Moreover, the topical content of the magazine began to change. A diminishing proportion of the pages focused on particular historical questions or content, displaced instead by a growing attention to pedagogical experiments written by education specialists, psychologists, and faculty in other social science disciplines. Meanwhile, even some history teachers were beginning to identify the merits of forming history into a larger department with the other social sciences.[19] And former friends of the discipline also started to cut their ties with the AHA's official position, most notably Daniel Knowlton, the disaffected former secretary of the AHA's Committee on History Education and Citizenship, who called for explicit reductions to history's role in the curriculum.[20]

Regardless of the association's efforts to resist change, national surveys of student enrollments demonstrated the substantial erosion of history's place in the curriculum. By 1928, less than half of high school students were taking history courses (fig. 9.1), and the mix of history courses changed significantly as well. There was a sharp increase in the proportion of students taking American history courses, while the number of students in European history courses (ancient, medieval, and modern) had all declined sharply from five years earlier.[21]

As a result of the shift in course offerings, a growing segment of history teachers was being pressed into service in other courses. By 1930, less than 12 percent of the high school teachers whose primary field was history were able to teach in just that one field. The rest were teaching in a wide range of other subjects. Almost half (45 percent) taught courses in English, another 10.3 percent taught mathematics, and 8.9 percent taught at least one course in foreign languages.[22] This was hardly news, at the time. Krey cited anecdotal evidence along the same lines, in 1925, and used it as a critical selling point to the council in arguing the need to set aside narrow and idealistic notions of what it meant to be a "history teacher."[23]

But by this time many teachers at the precollegiate and collegiate

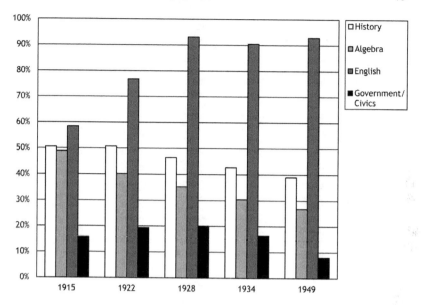

FIGURE 9.1. Proportion of public high school students enrolled in courses in select fields, 1915–1949
Source: Jenssen and Herlihy, *Offerings and Registrations*, 28 (table 1); and Smith, *Offerings and Enrollments, 1948–49*, 28 (table 1).

levels had grown weary of waiting for the association to provide real leadership on the issues. One junior college teacher observed that

> the typical college professor of the typical learned societies are themselves too far removed from the life of the adolescent to understand him; and they are too afraid that the robes of their academic dignity may have some of the glamour rubbed off if they sit at the same conference table with high school teachers, argue the matter, and give the latter some credit for knowledge.[24]

Investigating History and the Social Studies

The association did little to allay these concerns when it finally appointed a Commission on Social Studies that consisted only of academics, education professors, and school administrators. So by the time the commission truly got underway (in 1928), the lines of professional differences were already hardening against any recommendations the AHA might offer. Nevertheless, this commission was to be one of the largest undertakings in the association's 125-year history, encompassing more than twenty commission members and staff, working with a host of associated organizations on five broad areas of activity: objectives for the social studies, content, placement of content in grades, methods of instruction, and preparation of teachers and training.[25]

The membership can hardly indicate the relative scale of the project in the larger work of the AHA. The $250,000 the Carnegie Corporation provided for the commission was eight times the entire annual operating budget of the association in 1928. And at its peak in 1932, the commission had eight employees working on salary and more than twenty people serving on one of its committees—as many paid staff as all the other association activities (including the *AHR*) combined and comprising almost a third of all the personnel working on AHA committees.

To obtain these funds the council had to agree to further compromises, however. The Carnegie Corporation insisted on a smaller proportion of historians and greater emphasis on the practical aspects of teaching, particularly student testing.[26] So from the outset, the role of history was situated in a context that prevented the historians from offering their normal assertions about the primacy of historical research. This was signaled in part by formally dropping the word *history* from the name of the commission, but it was also marked more tangibly on the leadership team for the project, in which historians comprised only a third of the members.[27] The commission started its work with a host of surveys on teaching practices, the development of new tests to measure student knowledge and work in the field, and a series of narrower studies on best practices in particular subject fields.

While Krey provided the operational direction for the commission, Charles Beard provided much of its intellectual direction, both as a member and ultimately as president of the association when the commission completed its work in 1934. Like his friend and colleague James Harvey Robinson, Beard was an early and committed advocate of the New History, and he brought a similar enthusiasm for close relations between the social science disciplines to discussions about the social studies—indeed, in some documents he was counted among the representatives for political science.[28]

Early on, Beard drafted a statement outlining the broad objectives of the commission, laying out an ideological argument for the social studies that in many ways was the commission's most enduring contribution.[29]

Beard's statement situated the study of history and the other subjects into his progressive worldview—proposing a "seamless web" in which the perspective of the present and the needs of the future shaped the teaching of each subject. Initially, his draft elicited a mixed reception from other members of the commission who felt it was too general and too far removed from the realities of the classroom.[30] Nevertheless, as the commission struggled to find its bearings after two years of producing narrow and highly technical reports for each other, the members finally decided to publish Beard's statement (with some revisions) simply to offer some public signs of life.

Unfortunately, Beard's statement, like much of the commission's subsequent work, was widely criticized, because it seemed too theoretical and abstract to have much application to the real work of teachers—as some on the commission had already predicted. Worse still, the publication of Beard's statement marked the unraveling of Krey's original plan, which envisioned a series of consensus reports published as products of the entire commission. By 1930, the commission had fallen into disarray—a poor model of the ideal type of collective behavior the commission set as its model outcome for social studies education.[31] Instead of speaking with the authority and assent of the full commission, the divergent specialized interests could not reach a consensus on even the simplest issues. As a result, much of the commission's work (including a series of lengthy and wide-ranging surveys assessing changing enrollment patterns, teaching practices and networks, and new tests and measurements for the classroom) never saw the light of day. And the commission ultimately decided to publish all but one of its reports as authored by individual experts.

The commission was undercut by three distinct problems. First, the project was developed in the prosperity of the late 1920s but came to a close in the very different circumstances of the Depression. As a result, the impetus for the social studies, and more specifically teaching that spoke to the social and economic crisis of the day, hardly needed the commission's efforts to justify them. And while the Beardian emphasis on developing a social-minded temperament aligned well with the early New Deal, very few school systems had the resources in the 1930s to turn these ideals into actionable plans in the schools.

Second, the same lack of agreement that prevented the commission from producing consensus reports (even the one compromise report, published in a slender volume of "Conclusions and Recommendations,"

appeared with three of the sixteen members dissenting) undercut any aspirations that the work produced by the commission represented a definitive statement on the subject.[32] Commission member Frank Ballou
(superintendent of the Washington, DC, schools) offered a fairly devastating critique of the final report, arguing that it was "destructively critical of current educational practices which the Commission did not adequately investigate and dispassionately appraise; on the other hand, the
report does not present a reasonable definite, constructive program for
the improvement of instruction in the social studies."[33]

Finally, the widely dispersed system of authorities over the schools
made it impossible for any broad national program for history or social
studies curricula to find much traction—a fact Krey tacitly acknowledged
by following his work on the commission with a volume on *A Regional
Program for the Social Studies*.[34] As a number of analysts observed at
the time and since, the highly localized system of authorities in precollegiate education presented daunting challenges to any reform effort.

Whatever the intended goals of the commission's early sponsors on
the council, by 1934 there was ample evidence that it had done little to
stem the diminution of history in the schools. Just as the commission was
concluding its work, barely 43 percent of all high school students were
enrolled in history courses (fig. 9.1). Even the proportion of high school
students taking American history had declined slightly since 1928, from
17.9 percent to 17.4 percent of the students enrolled. Meanwhile the
European history fields continued to shrink, with just 6.7 percent taking ancient history and 6.2 percent taking medieval and modern history
courses. World history was the only field to show a real increase, from
6.1 percent in 1928 to 11.9 percent of students in 1934.[35]

By all accounts the long-term effect of the commission was quite limited, which is why it tends to receive very little attention in the historiography about history teaching despite the relative scale of the undertaking. But it did have three discernable affects. First, it added the AHA's
prestige to efforts to legitimate the social studies as an umbrella for a
number of school subjects (of which history was only one). The National
Council for Social Studies marked the commission's recommendations
as a vital starting point for fresh experimentation with social studies
courses and curricula.[36] Second, the wide-ranging investigation gathered
information on the state of the art in the schools and laid out a coherent
rationale for the development of new social studies courses, which provided essential source material for further work. And finally, the diffi

culties surrounding the commission largely convinced the AHA's Council to cede precollegiate education to other organizations and interested parties, particularly the National Council for the Social Studies.

As a tangible expression of the AHA's separation from teaching issues, in 1934 Krey and Beard convinced the AHA Council to use the funds left over from the commission's work (about $10,000) to subsidize the *Historical Outlook* (to be renamed *Social Studies*) and the National Council for the Social Studies.[37] But the shift was deeply contentious and exposed many of the raw feelings between the history scholars and the teaching community. Even though the NCSS had suffered a sharp decline in membership as a result of the Depression, and the leaders of the association were willing to underwrite the costs, the leaders of the NCSS were deeply suspicious of the academics' motives and intentions.[38] Dawson observed that "the [NCSS] has soft-pedaled and marked time for as long as it ought to do so," and added that "it is difficult [to see] how the agents of any organization of specialists . . . should expect the teachers of the social studies to be content in a side-show tent under the patronage of an association of scholars who are primarily devoted to research and specialized scholarship."[39] The correspondence around the move shows this reflected a common feeling among the leaders of the social studies council, where the sense of separation between the research men and the teachers was sharp and fraught with mistrust, and the leaders of the two organizations argued extensively over the proper shape of the magazine reconceived as a house journal for the NCSS.[40]

In the end, Beard agreed to serve as the chair of the editorial board of the magazine, and reported that "*The Social Studies* is the official organ of the National Council for the Social Studies and . . . serves as a valuable connecting link between the [American Historical] Association and the National Council." But, he acknowledged, "There can be no doubt at all that *The Social Studies* is serving a very useful purpose, particularly to the secondary school teachers in the field of the social studies. It is very definitely addressed to quite a different clientele from that of *The American Historical Review*."[41]

This marked a critical turning point for the two organizations, as the magazine explicitly expanded its focus to serve as a professional outlet for the social studies in the schools. This quickly became evident in both the content and the authors writing for the journal. The content increasingly embraced all the social studies subjects (including articles specifically on teaching geography and political science, for instance), and a declining number of articles dealt specifically with history (barely 8 percent between 1934 and 1937). A better reflection of the changing professional networks evolving around the journal can be found in those authoring articles. The number of authors who were professors in departments of history in four-year colleges and universities had been declining steadily since the early 1920s. But after 1934 they were largely displaced by professors at teachers colleges and in departments of education, or teachers and heads of high school social studies departments.

The regional associations of history teachers generally followed the same trajectory, by revising their missions and their names. In 1935, the Middle States Association of History Teachers voted to insert "and Social Studies" into its name. It also followed *Social Studies* in greatly extending the material covered at its meetings to include the full range of social studies fields and subsumed history into the mix. Just seven years later the membership voted to drop "History" from its name altogether and formally affiliated with the NCSS.[42]

The separation became even more pronounced in 1937, when Albert McKinley's heirs seized ownership of *Social Studies* and forced the AHA and the NCSS to start an entirely new magazine called *Social Education*.[43] It is not clear what effect this had on the subscriber base of the two organizations, but the two magazines quickly established very distinct identities. *Social Studies* magazine focused almost exclusively on elementary and high school social studies teachers, while *Social Education* continued to make at least some effort to serve as a bridge between school teachers, education specialists, and academics in the social science disciplines.[44] Not surprisingly, almost none of the authors in *Social Studies* after the split were members of the AHA, but a small and significant portion of the editorial board and authors of *Social Education* were. Despite the continued link, the temper and tone of the articles exhibited increasing independence from the AHA, bordering at times on hostility. This was particularly evident in a series of sharp exchanges of letters between Conyers Read and educators who questioned the large role historians still seemed to play in setting the criteria for college entrance examinations.[45] Erling Hunt, the editor of the magazine at the time, noted with regret that the conversation "revived and aggravated" a "recent tradition of ill-feeling between some of the college men in history and the social sciences and some of the secondary school and teachers' college men who are prominent in the [NCSS]."[46]

For the next two years, there was very little contact between the AHA offices and the NCSS, except on minor functional matters. By 1939, the NCSS moved decisively into a position of clear independence. It established a central office in Washington with its own executive director, and the AHA formally ceded *Social Education* over to it (though the AHA continued to provide a modest financial subsidy until 1955). Some of the conversations surrounding these shifts reflect the growing perception of the organization as a professional operation. Addressing the membership in 1940, Ruth West, the president of the NCSS, advised that the organization "can help us, and does so, with timely publications; but it can do even more by giving us opportunities to meet and know each other, to talk over common problems together, to bring us the best minds in or out of the profession to counsel us, and to help us learn something of the values and technics of cooperation." She added that the "freedom of teaching and learning which we prize so dearly will be far less likely to suffer if our professional organization commands respect of laymen and teacher alike."[47]

By the time the AHA's Commission on the Social Studies finished its work, social studies teachers had taken on a distinct and separate professional identity, and the AHA did little to win them back. By turning *Social Education* over to the NCSS, the AHA helped to clearly establish the separate professional network that some on the AHA's Council had feared back in the 1920s. By the mid-1930s, those concerns had largely disappeared. The academic members of the council were content to let the NCSS serve as the professional association for history teaching, even if it meant the subject was largely subsumed into the social studies. As Ruth West's comments attest, by 1940 the professional fragmentation of the historical enterprise was complete.

Conclusion

With the fracturing of large areas of history work into separate professional organizations in the late 1930s, the historical enterprise as defined here ceased to exist. From that point on, the various professions of history set off on distinct trajectories—firming up their own networks and identities in increasing isolation from each other, while embarking on separate processes of specialization and technical refinement of their own. Each of the groups still interacted, and often even collaborated on issues of common concern, but after 1940 it is hard to find anyone actively trying to articulate a common vision of the historical enterprise that embraced all areas of work in the discipline.

The war provided a sharp breaking point for any lingering memories of a more unified vision of the field. Much like during World War I, those in the different areas of history work spent a significant part of the war focused on applying their professional skills to the larger effort. The academics focused on creating useful information and history content, the historical societies tried to capture the experience of the war in their respective communities, and the teaching community set about explaining the war and its antecedents to students. Following the war, an extensive generational change swept across all areas of the historical enterprise, as the GI Bill helped thousands of new young history workers enter a professional world largely remade by the institutions and attitudes described here.

Within a decade, the number of new history PhDs conferred annually had more than doubled, and these new professionals were assimilated into a culture where the divisions in the historical enterprise were largely taken for granted. While the leaders of the association maintained a paternal interest in the other areas of the historical enterprise, most of their energies were focused rather narrowly on new developments within academia, as the academics were increasingly dividing amongst themselves, even within departments.[1]

Outside the AHA, the organizations that represented other areas of professional history work generally thrived over the same span. Teaching in the schools experienced dramatic growth as the baby boom generation entered the system, and many of the financial concerns voiced by leaders of the National Council for Social Studies in the 1930s eased rather quickly with a sharp increase in the number of new teachers and specialists entering the field. By the mid-1950s, NCSS membership numbers had surpassed the AHA, and it was on a sufficiently firm financial footing to assume full ownership of *Social Studies*.

Meanwhile, the nation's history organizations enjoyed similar gains. Bureaucratic growth at the state and national levels substantially increased the need for archival curation. And with the National Archives to serve as an institutional hub, the Society of American Archivists also experienced steady growth in both membership and resources.[2] The historical societies were not quite so fortunate, as their varied revenue streams prospered or withered depending on their particular local situations and the quality of their leadership.[3] As a result, the American Association for State and Local History was comparatively slow in its development in the years immediately following the war. Nevertheless, by the early 1960s, all the organizations were relatively prosperous and focused closely on the increasingly specialized needs and interests of their own communities.

The formal separation of the historical enterprise into distinct professional spheres by 1940 did not necessarily reflect a clean break between the different types of activity. Training for employment as secondary-school teachers and archivists, for instance, often remained within history departments, and as in the past, many PhDs crossed the line from doctoral studies into the larger area of history work outside of academia.[4] But with the institutional breakup into separate spheres of activity, the graduates from these programs were generally defined out of the "history profession"—a term that by 1940 was used almost exclusively to refer to the authors of academic monographs and articles. In this respect, the AHA reflected a larger consensus among the major disciplinary societies in the humanities and social sciences, all of whom took their principal mission as service to research scholars in academia.[5]

As part of the redefinition, academic historians actively ceded school issues, archival activity, and local historical work to the "true experts" in these fields of activity—especially in areas where the issues fell within a specific area of professional expertise and were not a matter of scholarly content or interpretation.[6] The AHA generally deferred to the other organizations as the proper authorities on the areas of professional work they represented. In 1942, for instance, Allan Nevins kicked off a significant controversy over the "Americanness" of history teaching in the schools. Instead of engaging the issue head on, the association's executive secretary at the time, Guy Stanton Ford, let the controversy boil on in public, while offering only private (and slightly bemused) encouragement to his counterpart at the National Council for Social Studies. Ultimately, the association agreed to join a multiorganizational study of the issues but let the NCSS spearhead the effort (and do most of the work).[7]

Likewise in other areas of history work, the association continued to operate primarily through joint committees—either explicitly with the other organizations, or indirectly, by drawing in specialists on other types of historical work. On subjects ranging from teaching to archives to publishing, the activities were placed on the same level—as separate spheres of work with their own professional codes and best practices. The role of the academics on such committees was largely to oversee the process in the interests of scholarship and historical content.

Looking ahead to 1970, one of the most striking changes in the correspondence and reports among historians is the pervasiveness of the term *historical profession* and *professional*. Discussions on almost any subject invoked the term repeatedly and with an ease that had not been evident in similar materials before World War II.[8] This is not surprising given a surge in the number of studies of professionalization in the early 1960s, which provided a fresh vocabulary for this sort of self-reflection.[9] But in the late 1960s and 1970s, academics began to actively rethink what had been lost in the separation of research scholarship from other areas of historical activity. Without ceding the privileged position of academia, many in the association concluded that they had paid too high a price in separating from branches of the historical enterprise that lay outside of academia. A significant number even cast the perceived problems in apocalyptic terms—as potentially leading to the demise of the discipline—a point made rather plainly in the title of Joan Hoff's article, "Is the Historical Profession an Endangered Species?"[10] In this history was not alone. The historiography of the various disciplinary organizations is fairly consistent in identifying a similar array of challenges that promoted discord starting around 1968: the development of new methodological innovations in the disciplines; the political radicalism associated with the politics of the 1960s; the social challenges of integrating a large demographic bubble of younger members, women, and minorities into the mainstream of the disciplinary organizations; and a crisis in the availability of academic jobs.[11] Much as in the years after 1911, the agitation in the discipline was charged by challenges from a broad array of historiographical changes under the banner of the "new." And yet again, the older generation reacted with defensiveness, precisely at a time when real leadership was needed on professional issues.

After five years in which the number of jobs was half the number of new PhDs conferred, the AHA became more attentive to areas of history work that had long since branched off from the organization and (quite belatedly) began to highlight "alternative careers" in those areas for historians in both its newsletter and at its annual meeting.[12] This shift in attitude reflected fundamental changes in the job situation for doctoral degree recipients, as about half of all history PhDs were finding employment outside of academia (at a time when the field was conferring well over a thousand degrees a year). The effort to establish a positive and constructive framework for these careers, not as alternatives but as legitimate choices in and of themselves, ultimately led to the development of a number of new institutional networks that helped to frame a new identity group—the "public historian."[13]

The exact contour of the fields and topics that fit under the label was (as it remains) rather nebulous, since public history was fundamentally a loose coalition of historical practices brought together by what it was not—academic employment.[14] In an early manifesto for the movement, Robert Kelley observed, "In its simplest meaning, Public History refers to the employment of historians and the historical method outside of academia: in government, private corporations, the media, historical societies and museums, even in private practice."[15] Various journal articles and primers trying to define this new field at the time included all of those areas described here as working on the "tools and materials" of research—including archivists, librarians and bibliographers, documentary editors, and staff at state and local historical societies. But the concept also incorporated a number of new practices as well. Some were older areas of employment that had received little interest or attention from historians in the early twentieth century, such as historic preservation and the work of museums. Others developed out of new career opportunities that had opened up, including positions in the federal government (as a growing number of historians were attached to departments and agencies) and some in private practice (as contractors or part of larger research groups).[16]

But this identity was intended to be more than a mere catchall banner for those employed outside of academia. Many of the early descriptions of what united public historians made a positive case that inverted some of the doom-and-gloom arguments of the academics around this time. Many academics felt they were fading into irrelevance because public interest and attention were turning to other subjects, and their students were moving into more practical areas of study (such as business school). The leaders in the public history movement held up their work as the answer to such defeatism. By actively working with and engaging the public in new and significant ways, they maintained that they could revitalize perceptions of the discipline. They looked to the AHA's central role in the history of the discipline, and the narrowed professional focus that it had taken on, to buttress their own roles and their own areas of activity. There had been some of this in the period before 1940, but by this time the separation had become so entrenched that they readily borrowed from stereotypes of the "cloistered academic" in defining their own identity.[17]

Thirty years later, the history discipline seems to be at a similar crossroads, with a recent burst of self-reflection framed in very familiar terms—grappling with a challenging job market, new technologies, and changing pedagogical methods. Under the pressures of new media and recurring crises in academic employment, aspiring historians are challenged to adopt a new openness to the general public and history work outside of academia.[18] These questions are not new for the discipline, but too often the discussions treat divisions that now exist in the professional life of the discipline in isolation—either without any consideration of the historical background for the separation, or in a way that casts all the blame on the academic community. The relationship between the different spheres of historical activity takes on an added salience today. In times of crisis for the scattered remnants of the historical enterprise we need to think clearly about the many assumptions that divide one area of the historical enterprise from the other—when the job market for history PhDs is in a state of chronic difficulty, when scholarly work is challenged to integrate new technologies, when many of the country's historical organizations face financial cutbacks and constraints, and as history teaching in the colleges and schools faces new pressures to conform to quantitative forms of assessment. It is too late to try to reconstruct a unified vision of the historical enterprise, but there is still time to bring the sundered pieces back together in more active conversation and collaboration with each other.

Observing the origins of the various areas of history work together in parallel can help to clarify when and why the lines of communication withered, while fostering a renewed sensitivity to the labels we use in the discipline, the personnel who make it run, and when and why many of the barriers between different branches were established. Over the course of sixty years, the twin processes of specialization and professionalization in the historical enterprise pushed the different areas of history work apart, and they have continued to separate and divide into ever smaller entities.[19] Professionals employed in the many and varied areas of history today live in a world fundamentally shaped by the choices made in the period before 1940.

The effects of this fragmentation are often regrettable, but the balance sheet for the historical enterprise does not consist only of debits and losses. The professionalization of the various forms of history work enriched our understanding of the past in any number of ways, as the historical materials are better cared for and disseminated, and the methods of history teaching are considerably improved. Even the professionalization (and to some extent enclosure) of academic history allows vast amounts of new historical information to be unearthed every year, as large quantities of specialized work, spurred on by tenure and promotion requirements, pour out in monographs and journal articles that serve as the raw material for new interpretations and new syntheses.

As with any community of activity, the benefits of professionalization are often matched with causes for complaint. In academia, for instance, the structures that help channel and focus scholarly research can also serve as a brake on the adoption of new approaches and tools.[20] There are numerous examples of similar complaints in the professional literature today for history teachers, archivists, and public historians where innovation is often juxtaposed with "excellence."[21]

It remains to be seen where today's challenges will take the discipline. But as we look forward and consider how and where new technologies and new approaches to history work might find a home in the discipline, it may help to see that sometimes they can revitalize areas of history work that seem moribund; while at others, new sets of practices can only achieve their full potential if they break off and establish separate canons and institutional arrangements of their own. Ideally, reexamining how the historical enterprise separated and divided over the first sixty years of professionalization provides a better vantage point for assessing how similar changes might affect our work in the future.

Appendix

Data for a Social Perspective on History

To provide a perspective that looks beyond the big names in the discipline, this study places a significant amount of evidentiary weight on a database of 15,156 names drawn from published and unpublished membership lists of the AHA and the Mississippi Valley Historical Association as well as published lists of dissertations in progress and PhDs conferred in the United States.

American Historical Association Membership

Data on the AHA membership were drawn from published lists for 1885, 1889, 1894, 1896, 1900, 1907, 1911, 1920, 1925, 1933, 1940, and 1947. The membership lists were typically compiled in June or September of the year in question, since the standard anniversary date for renewal was September 1. The information from each directory or membership list was scanned in, proofed for errors, and parsed into discrete fields of information. The information was then manually aligned with the other listings using last name, first name, and address. In particularly close calls—particularly where initials were used in lieu of first and middle names—other biographical sources were consulted.

To fill in two of the longer gaps, membership lists for 1915 and 1930 were reconstructed from hand-annotated versions of the 1911 and 1925 membership directories maintained by staff in the AHA's central office. The annotated 1911 list is contained in box 3 of the AHA Papers at the Library of Congress. The 1925 directory is located in the box "AHA

Membership Lists: 1925, 1933" at the AHA headquarters office in Washington, DC. The standard for both dates was September 1 of the year in question, so anyone annotated as having resigned or died prior to the date is not included, and anyone indicated as having joined or resigned after that date was included. The annotations in the 1925 directory stopped in September 1930, making a membership list for that year fairly easy to reconstruct. But the annotations for the 1911 directory end in 1920, so some members who joined between 1916 and 1919 are included in the tabulation, creating some modest inflation of these numbers.

Additional biographical information was gathered for the 580 members who served in elective and appointed positions at the association from 1884 to 1950 (5.4 percent of the AHA members recorded in the published directories). Biographical information including date of birth and death, degrees received, and employment were gathered from the Library of Congress catalog, US Census records, and other biographical directories as needed.

Mississippi Valley Historical Association Membership

Data on the MVHA membership were drawn from a published membership list from 1924 and printed lists of members contained in the MVHA's Papers for 1907, 1911, 1918, and 1934. Regrettably, no membership lists or rosters could be found for the period between 1935 and 1946. These lists were supplemented with additional information on elective and appointed positions listed in the MVHA's annual reports for the period 1907 to 1924 and from the minutes of the MVHA Executive Board available at the Organization of American Historians office in Bloomington, Indiana, for the period 1924 to 1945.

History Dissertations

The membership lists were aligned with a database of information about doctoral students and dissertations conferred during this period. This information was compiled from listings in the annual dissertations-in-progress list published first by the Carnegie Institution of Washington (1904–1928) and subsequently by the American Historical Association (ending in 1946). Given the duration of doctoral study, lists were only used at two to three year intervals (all years ending in 5 or 0 for which lists were available, and a middle year (with digits ending in 2 or 3, and 7 or 8—depending on their availability at the Library of Congress). This list was then manually merged with a database of PhDs conferred, scanned from Warren F. Kuehl's *Dissertations in History* (Lexington: University of Kentucky Press, 1965) and supplemented by information in a retrospective listing of history PhDs published by the American Historical Association at http://www.historians.org/pubs/dissertations/index.cfm. The initial list of dissertations completed extended to 1960, but for purposes of tabulation, anyone who received a degree after 1949 and had not become a member of the AHA by 1947 was deleted.

After scanning and proofing, the dissertations-in-progress lists and the dissertations completed lists were aligned mechanically and manually by name, address, dissertation title, and topic. *The Directory of American Scholars* for 1942 and 1951, the Library of Congress card catalog, and Archive Grid were also used to identify cases where there was a close variation in the name.

Notes

Introduction

1. J. Franklin Jameson, John Bach McMaster, and Edward Channing, *The Present State of Historical Writing* (Worcester, MA: Davis Press, 1910).

2. Joan Hoff Wilson, "Is the Historical Profession an 'Endangered Species?'" *Public Historian* 2, no. 2 (Winter 1980): 4–21.

3. See, for instance, Peter Charles Hoffer, *Past Imperfect: Facts, Fictions, and Fraud in the Writing of American History* (New York: PublicAffairs, 2004); Robert Orrill and Linn Shapiro, "From Bold Beginnings to an Uncertain Future: The Discipline of History and History Education," *American Historical Review* 110 (June 2005): 727–51 (hereafter cited as *AHR*); and Patricia Mooney-Melvin, "Professional Historians and Destiny's Gate," *Public Historian* 17 (September 1995): 9–25. In contrast, recent studies by Julie Des Jardins and Ian Tyrrell point past the conundrum of the professionalization paradigm. While their studies are still largely fixed in their categories, they are more careful about distinguishing academics from the entire field and more inclusive of those practicing history outside of academia. Ian Tyrrell, *Historians in Public: The Practice of American History, 1890–1970* (Chicago: University of Chicago Press, 2005); Julie Des Jardins, *Women and the Historical Enterprise in America, 1880–1945* (Chapel Hill: University of North Carolina Press, 2003).

4. In addition to the work of Tyrrell and Des Jardins noted above, I have drawn lines of analysis and general inspiration from Edward T. Linenthal and Tom Engelhardt, *History Wars: The Enola Gay and Other Battles for the American Past* (New York: Holt Paperbacks, 1996); Gary Nash, Charlotte Crabtree, and Ross Dunn, *History on Trial: Culture Wars and the Teaching of the Past* (New York: Alfred A. Knopf, 1998); James B. Gardner and Peter S. LaPaglia, eds., *Public History: Essays from the Field* (Malabar, FL: Krieger, 1999); Ron Theodore Robin, *Scandals and Scoundrels: Seven Cases That Shook the Academy* (Berkeley: University of California Press, 2004); Richard S. Kirken-

dall, ed., *The Organization of American Historians and the Writing and Teaching of American History* (New York: Oxford University Press, 2011); Francis X. Blouin, *Processing the Past: Contesting Authority in History and the Archives* (New York: Oxford University Press, 2011). Kate Theimer, ed., *A Different Kind of Web: New Connections between Archives and Our Users* (Chicago: Society of American Archivists, 2011); and the essays collected in Roy Rosenzweig, *Clio Wired: The Future of the Past in the Digital Age* (New York: Columbia University Press, 2011). My thinking on a number of crucial points was also sharpened by reading James M. Banner Jr.'s *Being a Historian: An Introduction to the Professional World of History* (New York: Cambridge University Press, 2012) while it was still in manuscript.

5. This term was used in the period under study to describe larger cooperative history projects in a manner that seems well suited to this purpose, but I owe particular credit to Julie Des Jardins for recovering the term. See Des Jardins, *Women and the Historical Enterprise*. For examples of other uses of the term see Pierre Caron, "A French Co-operative Historical Enterprise," *AHR* 13 (April 1908): 501–9; Charles M. Andrews, "These Forty Years," *AHR* 30 (January 1925): 249; and "Historical News," *AHR* 45 (April 1940): 758.

6. See, for instance, John Higham, *History: Professional Scholarship in America* (1965; repr., Baltimore: Johns Hopkins University Press, 1989); Peter Novick, *That Noble Dream: The "Objectivity Question" and the American Historical Profession* (New York: Cambridge University Press, 1988), 47ff; and Theodore Hamerow, *Reflections on History and Historians* (Madison: University of Wisconsin Press, 1987), 39ff.

7. These are the standard categories for a profession, excluding a fourth category of "control" over work. This seems particularly important in some definitions of professionalism and often serves as a critical wedge between academics and others in the historical enterprise, who are perceived to be more constrained by their institutional settings. As I hope to show, these distinctions tend to be overstated and a mask for a measure of self-seeking individualism at the elite universities.

8. See Robert B. Townsend, "The Ecology of the History Job: Shifting Realities in a Fluid Market," *Perspectives* (December 2011), http://www.historians .org/perspectives/issues/2011/1112/The-Ecology-of-the-History-Job-Shifting-Realities-in-a-Fluid-Market.cfm.

9. This is discussed in summary in Henry Johnson, *Teaching of History in Elementary and Secondary Schools with Application to Allied Studies*, rev. ed. (New York: Macmillan, 1940), but for some specific examples where a concern with presecondary teaching elicited an effort to articulate disciplinary ideals, see Edward Channing and Albert Bushnell Hart, *Guide to the Study of American History* (Boston: Ginn, 1896), 2–3; Fred Morrow Fling, *Outline of Historical Method* (Lincoln, NE: J. H. Miller, 1899), 5–7; and more generally in the

Committee of Seven report, prepared by seven historians employed at colleges but who felt obliged to note that "of the seven persons composing the committee only one is a teacher in a secondary school; three others, however, have been secondary-school teachers, while others have been actively interested for years in the general problems under consideration." "The Study of History in Schools: Report to the American Historical Association by the Committee of Seven," in *Annual Report of the American Historical Association, 1898* (Washington, DC: Government Printing Office, 1899), 429 (hereafter *AHA Annual Report*).

10. Nash, Crabtree, and Ross, *History on Trial*, 36–46; and Orrill and Shapiro, "From Bold Beginnings to an Uncertain Future," allude to this issue but tend to focus blame solely on differences over the content of the curriculum. This is viewed from the opposite perspective in David Jenness, *Making Sense of Social Studies* (New York: Macmillan, 1990), 69–111.

11. A fine example of this is Rebecca Conard, *Benjamin Shambaugh and the Intellectual Foundations of Public History* (Iowa City: University of Iowa Press, 2002).

12. See, for instance, the essays in the special issue on "Historians and the Public(s)" in *Perspectives* (May 2000): 15ff, as well as Linenthal and Engelhardt, *History Wars*; and Nash, Crabtree, and Ross, *History on Trial*.

13. In the transitional period after the war, the two most influential works buttressing this academic-as-professional perspective seem to be Richard Hofstadter and Walter P. Metzger, *The Development of Academic Freedom in the United States* (New York: Columbia University Press, 1955) and Laurence R. Veysey, *The Emergence of the American University* (Chicago: University of Chicago Press, 1965). They are cited by most of the works discussed here (though curiously not by Higham).

14. In political science, Albert Somit and Stephen Tannenhaus bracket these issues structurally, first by laying out the standard terms for "professional" membership in the discipline and then offering a separate thread in their narrative for the "extra-scientific responsibilities of the profession." Somit and Tanenhaus, *The Development of American Political Science: From Burgess to Behavioralism*, rev. ed. (New York: Irvington, 1982), 42–48, 80–85, 134–41, and 195–202. Works on the development of sociology, for instance, make a similar move in separating the "scholars" from the social reformers and survey specialists that provided the initial impetus to sociology and have remained deeply interconnected with academic departments. Andrew Abbott, *Department and Discipline: Chicago Sociology at One Hundred* (Chicago: University of Chicago Press, 1999) and Stephen P. Turner and Jonathan H. Turner, *The Impossible Science: An Institutional Analysis of American Sociology* (Newbury Park, CA: Sage, 1990).

15. Novick, *Noble Dream*, 47–49.

16. For a more detailed treatment of the literature on the disciplines and the role scholarly associations play in them, see chapter 2 of Robert B. Townsend,

"Making History: Scholarship and Professionalization in the Discipline" (PhD diss., George Mason University, 2009).

17. This study relies heavily on the theoretical work laid out in Andrew Delano Abbott, *The System of Professions: An Essay on the Division of Expert Labor* (Chicago: University of Chicago Press, 1988) to fill in some of the challenges posed in Charles Rosenberg, "Toward an Ecology of Knowledge: On Discipline, Context, and History," in *Organization of Knowledge in Modern America, 1860–1920*, ed. Alexandra Oleson and John Voss (Baltimore: Johns Hopkins University Press, 1979), 440–55.

18. This is a point reinforced by Stephan Fuchs, *The Professional Quest for Truth: A Social Theory of Science and Knowledge* (Albany: State University of New York Press, 1992), 168–75 and 182–86.

19. This phrase is drawn from the original call for an association that was sent out in the summer of 1884 and appeared in a variety of publications, for example, "An American Historical Association in Contemplation," *Magazine of American History* 12 (August 1884): 188.

Chapter One

1. "A New Historical Movement," *Nation*, September 18, 1884.

2. Stanley G. Hall, ed., *Methods of Teaching History* (Boston: D. C. Heath, 1889) includes essays from both Ely and Burgess, for instance.

3. Estimates based on membership rosters of the AHA and memoranda from Adams to the President and Executive Committee of the Johns Hopkins University (offering "A Plea for the Organization of the Department of History and Political Science"), May 29, 1886, in Herbert Baxter Adams, *Historical Scholarship in the United States, 1876–1901: As Revealed in the Correspondence of Herbert B. Adams* (Westport, CT: Greenwood Press, 1970), 83–84. Estimated count for 1910 based on membership roster of the American Historical Association for 1907 and 1911 and other correspondence in the AHA Papers.

4. Data drawn from George J. Stigler, *Employment and Compensation in Education* (New York: National Bureau of Economic Research, 1950), 29, table 17.

5. On the expansion and diversity of higher education in this period, see Christopher J. Lucas, *American Higher Education: A History* (New York: Palgrave Macmillan, 2006), 144–71; and Roger L. Geiger, "Research, Graduate Education, and the Ecology of American Universities: An Interpretive History," in *History of Higher Education*, ed. Lester F. Goodchild and Harold S. Wechsler (New York: Pearson Custom Publishing, 1997), 275–78.

6. Frank Malloy Anderson to Albert Bushnell Hart, May 6, 1905, box UA V 454.8, file "College Division," Harvard History Department Records, Harvard University Archives, Boston, MA (hereafter Harvard History Department Re-

cords). He noted that his classmate Dana Munro "remarked at Chicago that he obtained his position about the time that he had expected to get his doctorate and thereafter cared nothing about the doctorate. I feel just the other way. As I had to begin teaching before I had a chance to take the doctorate I was anxious to get my professorship first. I wanted to feel that the honor came because I deserved it rather than because I had a degree."

7. Huger Bacot Jr. reports that "the situation here seems unfortunate. The authorities are thoroughly satisfied with me and my work, but maintain that the holder of the chair of History must have a Ph.D." Huger Bacot Jr. to William Ferguson, April 3, 1919, box UA V 454.8, file "Babcock to Burbank," Harvard History Department Records.

8. See, for instance, Frederic Bancroft to Herbert Baxter Adams, June 16, 1894, in Adams, *Historical Scholarship in the United States*, 237–38.

9. Herbert Baxter Adams, *Methods of Historical Study* (Baltimore: N. Murray, 1884); Adams, *The Study of History in American Colleges and Universities* (Washington, DC: Government Printing Office, 1887); and Edward Channing and Albert Bushnell Hart, *Guide to the Study of American History* (Boston: Ginn, 1896).

10. H. Morse Stephens, "Some Living American Historians," *World's Work* 4 (July 1902): 2325.

11. Adams, *Methods of Historical Study*, 91.

12. Maurice Bloomfield, review of *The Story of Vedic India*, by Zenaide A. Ragozin, *American Historical Review* 1 (October 1895): 104 (hereafter cited as *AHR*).

13. Charles Francis Adams, "The Sifted Grain and the Sifters," *AHR* 6 (January 1901): 199. James Ford Rhodes succinctly observed that "the influence of Darwin and the support and proof which he gives to the doctrine of evolution furnish a training of thought" in "Concerning the Writing of History," in *Annual Report of the American Historical Association for the Year 1900* (Washington, DC: Government Printing Office, 1902), 58 (hereafter cited as *AHA Annual Report*).

14. Cf. John Higham, *History: Professional Scholarship in America* (Baltimore: Johns Hopkins University Press, 1989), 174; and Merle Curti, *Growth of American Thought* (New Brunswick, NJ: Transaction, 1981), 552–54.

15. This was emphasized in a number of monographs by Herbert Baxter Adams's students, such as Charles H. Levermore, "The Republic of New Haven: A History of Municipal Evolution," *Johns Hopkins University Studies in History and Political Science* 1 (Baltimore: Johns Hopkins University Press, 1886) and Frank W. Blackmar, "Spanish Institutions of the Southwest," *Johns Hopkins University Studies in History and Political Science* 10 (Baltimore: Johns Hopkins University Press, 1891), 147–49, 219.

16. Albert Bushnell Hart, *National Ideals Historically Traced, 1607–1907* (New York: Harper & Brothers, 1907), xiv.

17. See, for instance, Simeon E. Baldwin, "Religion Still the Key to History," *AHR* 12 (January 1907): 228.

18. James Harvey Robinson, "Newer Ways of Historians," *AHR* 35 (January 1930): 246.

19. John Spencer Bassett, *The Middle Group of American Historians* (New York: Macmillan, 1917), 204–6.

20. Indicative of the growing emphasis on archival research, in a critical letter to Reuben Thwaites about his volume on the colonies, Stephen B. Weeks (a professor at Trinity College in North Carolina) concedes that his difficulties must be due in part because "it is impossible for you to base your work always on original authorities." Weeks to Thwaites, November 25, 1891, box 1, file "RGT Correspondence 1891–1902," Reuben Gold Thwaites Papers, Wisconsin Historical Society, Madison, WI (henceforth designated Thwaites Papers).

21. Albert Bushnell Hart, "American School of Historians," *International Monthly* (September 1900): 307–8.

22. J. Franklin Jameson, *History of Historical Writing in America* (New York: Greenwood Press, 1969), 124–32.

23. Johann Gustav Droysen, *Outline of the Principles of History*, trans. Benjamin Andrews (Boston: Ginn, 1893), viii.

24. "History as an Art," *Nation*, December 30, 1909, 643. See also "Historical Writing in America," *Outlook*, September 20, 1902, 150–52; and "Naturalistic History," *Nation*, May 9, 1907, 427–28.

25. The German historian Gabrielle Lingelbach, after comparing the methods developing in Germany, France, and United States in the late nineteenth century, makes a compelling argument that these methods of training were often developed indigenously and with significant variations in *Klio macht Karriere: Die Institutionalisierung der Geschichtswissenschaft in Frankreich und den USA in der zweiten Hälfte des 19. Jahrhunderts* (Göttingen, Ger.: Vandenhoeck & Ruprecht, 2003) and "The Historical Discipline into the United States: Following the German Model?" in *Across Cultural Borders: Historiography in Global Perspective*, ed. Eckhardt Fuchs and Benedikt Stuchtey (Lanham, MD: Rowman & Littlefield, 2002). While her evidence and argument are rather compelling, it seems like hairsplitting given that the scientific historians gave full and regular credit to specifically German methods.

26. Adams, *Methods of Historical Study*, 22.

27. Tabulated from listings in Warren F. Kuehl, *Dissertations in History: An Index to Dissertations Completed in History Departments of the U.S. and Canadian Universities, 1937–1960* (Lexington: University Press of Kentucky, 1960). Adams, *Methods of Historical Study*, 5 and 98–99. These characteristics are generally echoed in Frank Hugh Foster, *The Seminary Method of Original Study in the Historical Sciences, Illustrated from Church History* (New York: Charles Scribner's Sons, 1888), 102–8.

28. Adams, *Study of History*, 22.

29. Henry E. Shepherd (College of Charleston) to Herbert B. Adams, October 31, 1884, box 4 "Secretary File Correspondence. 1884–1893," file "Secretary's Correspondence, 1884, P-W," American Historical Association Papers, Manuscript Division, Library of Congress, Washington, DC (hereafter cited as AHA Papers).

30. Jameson, *History of Historical Writing*, 129.

31. Ephraim Emerton, "The Requirements for the Historical Doctorate in America," in *AHA Annual Report, 1893*, 79–80. Some programs, including those at Harvard, Hopkins, and the University of Michigan had introduced these requirements by the late 1880s. See also Adams, *Study of History*, 113.

32. Data tabulated from Kuehl, *Dissertations in History*.

33. Included in Adams, *Study of History* and Hall, ed., *Methods of Teaching History*.

34. *Annual Report of the President and Treasurer of Harvard College 1900–01* (Cambridge, MA: Harvard College, 1890); Charles A. Andrews to A. Howard Clarke, February 11, 1900, box 7 "Secretary File, Correspondence, 1900–1903," file "Secretary Files—1900 A," AHA Papers; and Charles Homer Haskins to Clarence Bowen, May 12, 1906, box 219 "Treasurer's File—Corres. 1905–07," file "Corres. 1906 (1/2)," AHA Papers. This was sufficiently common that J. Franklin Jameson included published dissertations in a section in his annual *List of Doctoral Dissertations in History now in Progress at the Chief American Universities* (published privately from 1901 to 1904, by the Dept. of Historical Research, Carnegie Institution of Washington, 1905 to 1936, and by the AHA, 1938 to present).

35. Charles Kendall Adams took a number of departments to task in 1890 for their lack of similar publishing programs. He noted, for instance, that "at Harvard, where so much excellent work appears to be done, no provision as yet has been made for the systematic publication of the results that are achieved." Adams, "Recent Historical Work in the Colleges and Universities of Europe and America," *Papers*, vol. IV, no. 1 (1890), 39–65.

36. "Johns Hopkins University Studies," *Publishers Weekly*, December 16, 1882, 887–88.

37. George F. Howard (Univ. of Nebraska) to Adams, May 30, 1893, in Adams, *Historical Scholarship in the United States*, 65.

38. Minutes of March 8, 1892, meeting, p. 24, box UA V 454.5, minute volume "Record of the Proceedings of the Department of History and Roman Law in Harvard College," Harvard History Department Records.

39. The monographs in the Johns Hopkins series, for instance, generally ran between eighty and one hundred pages. Similarly, when the AHA initiated a Justin Winsor Prize to publish new monographs (often dissertations), the publications ran to only one hundred to two hundred pages, see e.g., David Muzzey, *The Spiritual Franciscans* (Washington, DC: AHA, 1907).

40. Channing and Hart, *Guide to the Study of American History*, 220.

41. Reuben G. Thwaites, for instance, had a lengthy exchange with Albert Bushnell Hart, editor of a series of history monographs, about the proper structure and form of the bibliographic and footnote apparatus for the series. Hart to Thwaites, January 13, 1904, box 2 "Wis MSS VJ," file "VJ Thwaites 1904 Jan," Thwaites Papers.

42. Adams outlines his plans and discusses the financial needs for such a program in a letter to Justin Winsor, January 9, 1885, from the Justin Winsor Papers, Massachusetts Historical Society, vol. 5, p. 30A (photocopy in AHA headquarters office, Washington, DC).

43. Herbert Baxter Adams to Clarence Bowen, June 22, 1887, box 212, file "Correspondence 1884–1889 (2)," AHA Papers; and H. B. Adams to Clarence Bowen, December 6, 1889, box 4 "Secretary File Correspondence. 1884–1893," file "Secretary Correspondence, 1889, A," AHA Papers. See related correspondence in Adams, *Historical Scholarship in the United States*, 111–27.

44. G. Brown Goode to Herbert Baxter Adams, ca. January 1890, box 463, file "Relations with Smithsonian," AHA Papers.

45. The original underwriters for the *AHR* were George B. Adams (Yale Univ.), Albert Bushnell Hart (Harvard Univ.), Harry P. Judson (Univ. of Chicago), John Bach McMaster (Univ. of Pennsylvania), William M. Sloane (Princeton Univ.), and H. Morse Stephens of (Cornell Univ.), who also comprised the first Board of Editors for the *Review*. See "Proceedings of the Conference," April 6, 1895, box 2, file *"American Historical Review,"* 1895, Hart Papers, Harvard University Archives, Boston, MA (hereafter cited as Hart Papers). (Because Hart was secretary of the board in its early years, the Hart Papers seem to have the most complete records for the *Review* in this period, since some material was apparently kept confidential from Jameson.)

46. H. B. Adams to A. H. Clark, October 30, 1895, box 5 "Secretary File Correspondence. 1893–1896," file "Secretary Correspondence, 1895, A-B," AHA Papers.

47. "Memorandum of Agreement Between the Board and the Managing Editor [J. Franklin Jameson]," May 24, 1895, appended to "Minutes of Board of Editors Third Meeting," May 25, 1895, box 2 "American Historical Association *American Historical Review*, 1895–1915," HUG 4448.22 "A. B. Hart, Special Topics," Hart Papers.

48. Cf. minutes of editorial board meetings in box 2, file *"American Historical Review,"* 1895," Hart Papers.

49. Albert Bushnell Hart to Clarence Bowen, November 2, 1900, box 216, file "Treasurer's Correspondence 1900," AHA Papers.

50. J. Franklin Jameson to William M. Sloane [and Frederick Jackson Turner], January 4, 1910, box 276, files "S 1910" and "T 1910," AHA Papers.

51. Frederick Jackson Turner, "Western State-Making in the Revolutionary Era," *AHR* 1(October 1895): 70–87.

52. Augustus H. Shearer, "American Historical Periodicals," in *AHA Annual Report, 1916*, 472.

53. Notably, however, the librarian of the university noted particular strain on use of the history reading rooms by lower-level ("elementary") and advanced students, requiring a larger space. *Annual Reports of the President and the Treasurer of Harvard College, 1900–01* (Cambridge, MA: Harvard College, 1902), 200–201. In 1900, the library contained 3,051 books, which was smaller than just three other disciplines (classics, English languages and literature, and engineering). Two decades later, the history collection had doubled to 6,729 volumes, with another 657 volumes in the graduate history collection (the previous division had been between a general history collection and a US history collection). Meanwhile, the classics and engineering libraries had grown comparatively little. *Reports of the President and the Treasurer of Harvard College, 1919–20* (Cambridge, MA: Harvard College, 1921), 193.

54. A number of the books reviewed works by nonscholars that the editors and reviewers considered at least interesting enough to inspire additional scientific research, see, for instance, Simeon E. Baldwin's review of *John Adams, the Statesman of the American Revolution*, by (Judge) Mellen Chamberlain, *AHR* 4 (January 1899): 367–69.

55. Charles Kendall Adams, *A Manual of Historical Literature* (New York: Harper & Brothers, 1882)—the description of the intended audience is found on the title page. Members of the AHA revisited the idea of doing a similar bibliography, cf. "Report of the Committee on a Manual of Historical Literature for the year 1920," box 458, AHA Papers, which still makes reference to Adams's earlier work as the model (in attachment titled "Manual of Historical Literature"). Due to the growth in the literature, it took a committee of the AHA more than twelve years to accomplish what Adams had done in barely one.

56. In a proposal for a "cooperative history," Albert Bushnell Hart observed that "the literature of American history has so extended both primary and secondary, and the field has become so confused, that it is hardly possible for any one writer to prepare in a life time an elaborate history of the United States from the foundation to the present day." Albert Bushnell Hart to Wisconsin Historical Society, January 2, 1902, box 1, file "RGT Correspondence 1891–1902," Thwaites Papers.

57. J. Franklin Jameson, John Bach McMaster, and Edward Channing, *Present State of Historical Writing* (Worcester, MA: Davis Press, 1910), 11.

58. Jameson, McMaster, and Channing, *Present State of Historical Writing*.

59. J. Franklin Jameson, "The Influence of Universities on Historical Writing," *University Record* 6 (January 1902): 298–99. Jameson goes on to note, "In

all lands professors control the historical societies, direct the journals, and fill the historical libraries with their particular type of composition."

60. David D. Van Tassel, who surveyed the papers of a number of the founding members, gives particular credit to Moses Coit Tyler (Cornell Univ.) and Charles Kendall Adams (Univ. of Michigan), with Adams responsible for much of the organizational work. Van Tassel, "History of the American Historical Association," (unpublished manuscript, AHA, Washington, DC, 1980), 21–36. See also Thomas L. Haskell, *Emergence of Professional Social Science: The American Social Science Association and the Nineteenth-Century Crisis of Authority* (Baltimore: Johns Hopkins University Press, 2000), 169–72.

61. "Secretary's Report," in *AHA Papers* (Washington, DC: AHA, 1885), 5–6.

62. For background here, I rely on Haskell, *Emergence of Professional Social Science*. Assessment of connections between AHA leaders and ASSA taken from the list of "Publications of the American Social Science Association" in the *Journal of Social Science* 38 (December 1900): xxxvi–xli.

63. Van Tassel, "History of the American Historical Association," 21–46; and Haskell, *Emergence of Professional Social Science*, 168–77.

64. Van Tassel, "History of the American Historical Association," 10–11.

65. Ephraim Emerton, "The Practical Method in Higher Historical Instruction," in Hall, *Methods of Teaching History*, 49.

66. For a different perspective on development of the history discipline seen in regional terms, see Bethany Leigh Johnson, "Regionalism, Race, and the Meaning of the Southern Past: Professional History in the American South, 1896–1961," (PhD diss., Rice University, 2001) and Steven B. Weeks, "The Promotion of Historical Studies in the South," *Publications of the Southern Historical Association* 1 (1897): 22–27.

67. On Adams's selection in sectional terms, see David Van Tassel, "American Historical Association and the South, 1884–1913," *Journal of Southern History* 22 (November 1957): 474–75.

68. In addition to conversations with the leaders of other history organizations, I also rely on the results of an unpublished survey of national history organizations conducted by the International Congress of Historical Sciences in spring 2010. Responses in the possession of the author.

69. "AHA Congressional Charter," http://www.historians.org/info/charter.cfm.

70. Flyer on "American Historical Association" dated 1904 in box 464, folder "Printed Matter," AHA Papers.

71. Undated flyer (but from personnel listed, it can be placed sometime in 1909), "American Historical Association," in box 464, folder "Printed Matter," AHA Papers.

72. Almost a third of all history PhD recipients never joined the AHA, which

leaves an open question about why they never joined an organization nominally the principal association for historians. There is only fragmentary evidence to show that the nonmember PhDs were driven by the relatively high dues (three dollars between 1884 and 1920, which amounted to over sixty dollars per year in today's dollars), the ambiguities in the organizational mission, and the dispersion of their employment. The proportion of new history PhDs who did not join the AHA seemed to grow from 1900 to 1911 (and continued to grow through the entire period covered in this study). Note that only half of the PhD recipients—227 of 454—were still members of the AHA at this time. A significant portion of the rest (almost 10 percent) were employed in precollegiate teaching institutions.

73. Edward Eggleston to Clarence Bowen, January 2, 1889, box 4, file "Secretary Correspondence 1889 B–1," AHA Papers.

74. Cf. Henry E. Shepherd (College of Charleston) to Clarence Bowen, February 16, 1889, box 4 "Secretary File Correspondence. 1884–1893," file "Secretary Correspondence, 1889, J-W," AHA Papers.

75. J. Franklin Jameson, for instance, protested that the meetings "were extremely stupid," as there were "more nobs than usual in attendance." Jameson to John Jameson, January 5, 1889, in *An Historian's World: Selections from the Correspondence of John Franklin Jameson* (Philadelphia: American Philosophical Society, 1956), 46. In contrast, Theodore Roosevelt wrote George Trevelyan about the "preposterous little organization, which, when I was just out of Harvard and very ignorant, I joined," which he describes as full of "painstaking little pedants." Quoted in Joseph Bucklin Bishop, *Theodore Roosevelt and His Time Shown in His Own Letters* (New York: Charles Scribner's Sons, 1920), 139–40.

76. Clarke was a leader in the Southern Historical Association and other hereditary societies. Some on the council, particularly Albert Bushnell Hart, dismissed him as "not a historical scholar of eminence," quoted in George B. Adams to Clarence Bowen, December 4, 1900, box 7, file "Secretary Files—1900 A," AHA Papers.

Chapter Two

1. J. Franklin Jameson to William Rainey Harper, April 4, 1905, in *John Franklin Jameson and the Development of Humanistic Scholarship in America*, vol. 2, by J. Franklin Jameson, ed. Morey Rothberg, and Jacqueline Anne Goggin (Athens: University of Georgia Press, 1996), 302.

2. Ernst Posner makes this connection explicitly in *American State Archives* (Chicago: University of Chicago Press, 1964), 16. But the same notion recurs in slightly more oblique ways in a number of the conference and commission reports discussed in the *AHA Annual Reports* up through the 1920s.

3. This seems to be an intrinsic part of the historiography of the archival

profession, even if it does not seem to arise in the historiography of academic research, e.g., Lester J. Cappon, "The Archival Profession and the Society of American Archivists," in *Lester J. Cappon and the Relationship of History, Archives and Scholarship in the Golden Age of Archival Theory*, Archival Classics Series, ed. Richard J. Cox (Chicago: Society of American Archivists, 2004).

4. Louis Leonard Tucker, *The Massachusetts Historical Society: A Bicentennial History, 1791–1991* (Boston: Massachusetts Historical Society, 1996), 166–70.

5. Charles Francis Adams, *Historians and Historical Societies: An Address at the Opening of the Fenway Building of the Massachusetts Historical Society, April 13, 1899* (Boston: Massachusetts Historical Society, 1899), 30.

6. The society was not only physically located in connection to the university, but members of the history department faculty served on its advisory committee, its library served the university, and its rooms were used for seminars by historians such as Frederick Jackson Turner. Clifford Lee Lord, *Clio's Servant: The State Historical Society of Wisconsin, 1846–1954* (Madison: State Historical Society of Wisconsin, 1967), 87–88.

7. William O. Scroggs, "The Relation of the Chair, or Department of American History, to the Work of Historical Societies," in *Annual Report of the American Historical Association for the Year 1905* (Washington, DC: Government Printing Office, 1906), 181 (hereafter cited as *AHA Annual Report*).

8. Edward Channing and Albert Bushnell Hart, *Guide to the Study of American History* (Boston: Ginn, 1896), 221.

9. H. Morse Stephens, "Some Living American Historians," *World's Work* 4 (July 1902): 2325.

10. The text of the original "Call for a Convention," and related letters and newspaper notices are available on the AHA website at http://www.historians .org/info/AHA_History/Meeting1.htm.

11. Herbert Baxter Adams cited the *Monumenta* in an early sketch of the AHA's founding meeting, for instance, Adams to Daniel Coit Gilman, August 8, 1884, in Herbert Baxter Adams, *Historical Scholarship in the United States, 1876–1901: As Revealed in the Correspondence of Herbert B. Adams* (Westport, CT: Greenwood Press, 1970), 71; and he offered it as a subject for discussion at the first meeting, "Report of the Organization and Proceedings of the American Historical Association, at Saratoga, September 9–10, 1884," *Papers of the American Historical Association* 1 (New York : G. P. Putnam's Sons, 1885), 32. References to the *Monumenta* extend well into the twentieth century in the "News and Notes" section of the *American Historical Review* (hereafter cited as *AHR*) and even the report to the federal government on historical records, reprinted in *John Franklin Jameson and the Development of Humanistic Scholarship in America*, vol. 3, ed. Morey Rothberg and Jacqueline Anne Goggin (Athens: University of Georgia Press, 2001), 65–66.

12. "AHA Congressional Charter," http://www.historians.org/info/charter.cfm.

13. Based on a tabulation of 205 PhD recipients who received their degrees between 1885 and 1900. Data from Warren F. Kuehl, *Dissertations in History*, supplemented by information from the American Historical Association's Directory of History Dissertations at http://www.historians.org/pubs/dissertations/index.cfm.

14. Based on a survey of footnotes in original articles or papers at five-year intervals. Bibliometric analysis based on the methodology in Edward A. Goedeken and Jean-Pierre V. M. Herubel, "Trends in Historical Scholarship as Evidenced in the *American Historical Review*: 1896–1990," *Serials Review* 19, no. 2 (Summer 1993): 79–83.

15. Memo from J. Franklin Jameson to the Historical Manuscripts Commission, "Suggestions from the Chairman," February 7, 1896, box 52, file 70 "Hist. MSS Commission, 1894–1905," J. Franklin Jameson Papers, Manuscript Division, Library of Congress, Washington, DC (hereafter cited as Jameson Papers).

16. See, for instance, the first census of historical societies in 1905, which included the Daughters of the American Revolution, the New England Historic Genealogical Society, and the Confederate Memorial Literary Society. "Report of Committee on Methods of Organization and Work on the Part of State and Local Historical Societies," in *AHA Annual Report, 1905*, 254.

17. See, for instance, the published proceedings of the Massachusetts and Wisconsin Historical Societies, which annually quantified the numbers of new books, pamphlets, maps, and other ephemera acquired by their institutions.

18. William Egle to J. Franklin Jameson, December 3, 1895, box 94, file "Historical Societies, State; Local," Jameson Papers.

19. C. W. Darling, "State Historical Societies," in *AHA Annual Report, 1890*, 101–3.

20. Speaking before the AHA in 1893, Ellen Hardin Walworth voiced what was to become a recurring complaint: "The separate States have had a desire to retain all records relating to each one within its own borders, even while they were all more or less careless of the safety of the most important documents." Walworth, "The Value of National Archives," in *AHA Annual Report, 1893*, 29.

21. *AHA Annual Report, 1890*, 9–10

22. After Jameson reiterated his proposal to the council, it organized a committee that included Senator George F. Hoar to attempt to persuade Congress to take this up on the assumption that "a commission backed by the U.S. Government would have much more influence and stability." H. B. Adams to J. F. Jameson, January 2, 1895, box 52, file 70 "Hist. MSS Commission, 1894–1905," Jameson Papers.

23. A. H. Clark to H. B. Adams, November 7, 1892, box 1, file "Letterbook

1890–1901," American Historical Association Papers, Manuscript Division, Library of Congress, Washington, DC (hereafter cited as AHA Papers).

24. Herbert Baxter Adams to A. Howard Clark, December 18, 1894, box 5, file "1894 A," AHA Papers.

25. "Report of the Historical Manuscripts Commission of the American Historical Association," in *AHA Annual Report, 1896*, 467.

26. "Notes and News," *AHR* (April 1896): 588.

27. *AHA Annual Report, 1896*, 470–74.

28. *AHA Annual Report, 1896*, 467–1107. Despite the quantity published, some of the expert members of the field lamented that it could not accomplish more "in the face of indifference and even opposition." Reuben Gold Thwaites to Andrew C. McLaughlin, November 14, 1904, box 136 "Office File: 1773–1794," file "Wisconsin, State Historical Society," Jameson Papers.

29. Ledger of Council Minutes, 1901–1915, box 609, AHA Papers.

30. Charles H. Haskins to Evarts Greene, June 9, 1915, tucked into Ledger of Council Minutes, 1901–1915, box 609, AHA Papers.

31. *AHA Annual Report, 1899*, vol. 1, 24–25.

32. According to William Birdsall, the enduring division between archives and manuscripts framed by the two commissions served as an impediment in the establishment of the Society of American Archivists in the late 1930s. William F. Birdsall, "Archivists, Librarians, and Issues during the Pioneering Era of the American Archival Movement," *Journal of Library History* 14, no. 4 (Fall 1979): 461–62.

33. See Lucile M. Kane, "Manuscript Collecting," in *In Support of Clio: Essays in Memory of Herbert A. Kellar*, ed. William Best Hesseltine and Donald R. McNeil (Madison: State Historical Society of Wisconsin, 1958), 33–46; and more generally, Walter Muir Whitehill, *Independent Historical Societies: An Enquiry into Their Research and Publication Functions and Their Financial Future* (Boston: Boston Athenaeum, 1962).

34. "Report of the Public Archives Commission," in *AHA Annual Report, 1900*, vol. 2, 6–7.

35. The report on New York City is contained in "Report of the Public Archives Commission," in *AHA Annual Report, 1900*, vol. 2, 163–208, while the Philadelphia report can be found in "Report of the Public Archives Commission," in *AHA Annual Report, 1901*, 231–352.

36. Cf. Homer Carey Hockett, *Introduction to Research in American History* (New York: Macmillan, 1931), 44; and Oscar Handlin et al., *Harvard Guide to American History* (Cambridge, MA: Harvard University Press, 1954), 126.

37. See, for instance, editorials like "The Safety of Records," *Chicago Daily Tribune*, May 24, 1907, 8; "Association Preserving Archives," *Christian Science Monitor*, October 21, 1911, 39; and "Archives House is Aim," *Washington Post*, December 29, 1915, 5.

38. Lester J. Cappon, "Tardy Scholars among the Archivists," in Cox, *Lester J. Cappon and the Relationship of History*, 47. In some instances, the reports of the commission provided a negative example, when critics charged that academics produced inferior reports prompting calls for more professional surveyors. See, for instance, "Review and Notices," *Publications of the Southern History Association* 7 (January 1903): 41–44.

39. The first resolution to this effect was adopted by the membership of the AHA at its 1901 meeting. *AHA Annual Report, 1901*, 36. Victor Gondos, *J. Franklin Jameson and the Birth of the National Archives, 1906–26* (Philadelphia: University of Pennsylvania Press, 1981), 15, 18–25, 27–28.

40. "Tenth Annual Report of the Public Archives Commission," and Herman V. Ames, "Conference of Archivists, Introductory Remarks," in *AHA Annual Report, 1909*, 329–41. The commission reports on legislation passed or introduced in Arkansas, Connecticut, Maine, Texas, Arizona, and New York over the previous year, while Ames cites legislation passed in twenty-four states over the previous decade.

41. Birdsall, "Archivists, Librarians, and Issues," 464.

42. Posner, *American State Archives*, 19–21.

43. In Illinois, for instance, the state library convened an advisory commission in 1905 composed of "professors of history in six of the leading colleges and normal schools of the state," which supported and facilitated a publication program for state records that "should contain all the significant material, not elsewhere readily accessible." Solon J. Buck, "A Laboratory of State History," n.d. [ca. 1916], box 61, file M-H, series 934, Wisconsin Historical Society Papers, Wisconsin Historical Society, Madison, WI (hereafter cited as WHS Papers).

44. Rebecca Conard, *Benjamin Shambaugh and the Intellectual Foundations of Public History* (Iowa City: University of Iowa Press, 2002), 18–19 and 29. Quote from J. Franklin Jameson, "The Functions of State and Local Historical Societies with Respect to Research and Publication," in *AHA Annual Report, 1897*, 55

45. Ian Tyrrell, *Historians in Public: The Practice of American History, 1890–1970* (Chicago: University of Chicago Press, 2005), 210.

46. "It will probably be found that the suggestions made here are applicable rather to the historical societies of the older States, private endowed organizations having few or no statutory duties and public responsibilities." J. Franklin Jameson, "The Functions of State and Local Historical Societies with Respect to Research and Publication," in *AHA Annual Report, 1897*, 54. See also Reuben Gold Thwaites, "State-Supported Historical Societies and Their Functions," in *AHA Annual Report, 1897*, 63–71.

47. Thwaites to Walter B. Douglas (Missouri Historical Society), May 20, 1907, box 23, file "Mississippi to Missouri," WHS Papers. His correspondence with the New York Historical Society in file "Nec – Ny" in box 25 is at best curt,

at most trivial—a striking contrast with his fulsome exchanges with the societies in the West.

48. Memo contained in box 94, file "Historical Societies, State; Local," Jameson Papers.

49. The Papers of the Wisconsin Historical Society, for instance, includes dozens of such letters exchanged with Reuben Gold Thwaites from societies and historical commissions extending from Alabama to Washington. This begins in box 4, file "1903 January," series 934, WHS Papers, with letters to leaders in Iowa, Minnesota, Alabama, and Mississippi. Not surprisingly, given their differences in organization and outlook, I found no similar correspondence with the societies of the Northeast in the period from 1900 to 1910.

50. Salmon envisioned a relationship built on "payment of annual dues or the fees for life-membership, and with mutual duties of communication and report." "The Annual Meeting of the American Historical Association," *AHR* 3 (April 1898): 416. Quote from Henry E. Bourne to Reuben Gold Thwaites, September 15, 1903, box 1, file "RGT Correspondence 1903 Aug.–Oct," Reuben Gold Thwaites Papers, Wisconsin Historical Society, Madison, WI (henceforth designated Thwaites Papers).

51. Charles H. Haskins, "Report of the Proceedings of the Twentieth Annual Meeting of the American Historical Association," in *AHA Annual Report, 1904*, 24.

52. Thwaites to J. Franklin Jameson, October 11, 1904, box 7, file "1904 Oct.," series 934, WHS Papers.

53. Thwaites to C. M. Burton, October 15, 1904, ibid.; and Thwaites to Andrew C. McLauglin, November 2, 1904, ibid.

54. Tyrrell offers a more positive assessment of the early efforts in Ian Tyrrell, "Good Beginnings: The AHA and the First Conference of Historical Societies, 1904," *History News* 59 (Autumn 2004): 21–24.

55. Tyrrell, "Good Beginnings," 24–25.

56. Reuben G. Thwaites, Benjamin Shambaugh, and Franklin L. Riley, "Report on Methods of Organization and Work of State and Local Historical Societies," in *AHA Annual Report, 1905*, 249–325. Note that once again, the committee was structured to represent regional divisions—Thwaites for the northern and central Atlantic states and the Old Northwest, Shambaugh for "the Trans-Mississippi," and Riley for the South (252).

57. Charles Homer Haskins to Thwaites, January 11, 1905, box 8, file "American Historical Association," series 934, WHS Papers.

58. Thomas M. Owen to Reuben G. Thwaites, October 29, 1909, box 8, file "Aasterud-American Geographical," series 934, WHS Papers.

59. Henry E. Bourne to Thwaites, November 30, 1905, box 8, file "American Historical Association," series 934, WHS Papers.

60. Clarence W. Alvord to J. Franklin Jameson, October 29, 1906, box 47, file "Alvord, C. W., 1904–1907," Jameson Papers.

61. Quote from Thomas McAdory Owen to Thwaites, October 29, 1906, in box 8, file "Aasterud-American Geographical," series 934, WHS Papers. Other requests for offprints can be found in the American Historical Association file in the same box.

62. Jameson first proposed the idea of a history department in the institution in 1902 and chaired the committee that laid out the plan for the department. Jameson to Daniel Coit Gilman, February 14, 1902, in *An Historian's World: Selections from the Correspondence of John Franklin Jameson*, by J. Franklin Jameson, ed. Elizabeth Donnen and Leo Francis Stock (Philadelphia: American Philosophical Society, 1956), 79–83; and "Report of the Advisory Committee," in *Year Book 1902* (Washington, DC: Carnegie Institution of Washington, 1902), 226–31.

63. Description from *Classified List of Publications of the Carnegie Institution of Washington* (Washington, DC: Carnegie Institution of Washington, 1920), 67.

64. Claude Halstead Van Tyne and Waldo Gifford Leland, *Guide to the Archives of the Government of the United States in Washington* (Washington, DC: Carnegie Institution of Washington, 1904), vii. For appraisals of the value of this *Guide* in initiating reforms in federal recordkeeping, see T. R. Schellenberg, *The Management of Archives* (New York: Columbia University Press, 1965), 32–60; and Richard C. Berner, *Archival Theory and Practice in the United States: A Historical Analysis* (Seattle: University of Washington Press, 1983), 14–15.

65. An assessment of his accomplishments in archival theory and practices can be found in Rodney A. Ross, "Waldo Gifford Leland: Archivist by Association," *American Archivist* 46 (Summer 1983): 264–73, and assessment of his work for the international level can be found in Karl Dietrich Erdmann, Jurgen Kocka, and Wolfgang J. Mommsen, *Toward a Global Community of Historians: The International Historical Congresses and the International Committee of Historical Sciences, 1898–2000* (New York: Berghahn Books, 2005), 75–84 and 180–91.

66. Charles H. Haskins to Clarence Bowen, April 29, 1908, box 212, file "Corres. 1908 (2 of 2)," AHA Papers. Haskins recommends him, because "he has considerable acquaintance throughout the country with local antiquarians and members of historical societies, as a result of his travels for the Carnegie Institution in search of manuscript materials."

67. Thwaites to A. C. McLaughlin, November 14, 1904 box 136 "Office File: 1773–1794," file "Wisconsin, State Historical Society," Jameson Papers; and Thwaites to Jameson, October 9, 1909, ibid. In the latter, Thwaites gives Jameson a broad commission: "In case some important documents come up quite early in

your search, the best thing to do would be to have them copied and forwarded to us. My commission to you includes both research and copying—in other words, I leave it entirely up to you, feeling conscious of the fact that you will do the best thing for us possible."

68. See e.g., regarding exchanges of publications, Jessie Palmer Weber (Illinois State Historical Library) to Thwaites, March 19, 1909, box 17, file "Illinois," series 934, WHS Papers.

69. "Minutes of the Meeting of the Executive Committee of the Mississippi Valley Historical Association," December 30, 1907, box 1, "Executive Committee Minutes, 1907–1909," file 1, Organization of American Historians Papers, Ruth Lilly Special Collections and Archives at the Indiana University–Purdue University at Indianapolis University Library, Indianapolis, IN (hereafter MVHA Papers).

70. Thwaites to Clarence Alvord, July 22, 1908, box 23, file "Mississippi," series 934, WHS Papers.

71. *AHA Annual Report, 1908*, 149–53. Dunbar Rowland chaired the committee along with J. Franklin Jameson, E. B. Green, Thomas M. Owen, Benjamin Shambaugh, Reuben Thwaites, and Worthington Ford. Discussion of the outcome is in J. F. Jameson to George L. Sioussat, December 9, 1919, box 52, file 69 "AHA Conference of Historical Societies," Jameson Papers.

72. Thomas M. Owen to Jameson, March 24, 1908, box 52, file 71 "Hist. MSS Commission, 1908–1928," AHA Papers.

73. Richard J. Cox, *American Archival Analysis* (Metuchen, NJ: Scarecrow Press, 1990), 22; and William F. Birdsall, "The Two Sides of the Desk," *American Archivist* 38 (April 1975): 161–64.

74. Henry V. Ames open letter dated December 1, 1909, box 471, file "Public Archives Commission," AHA Papers.

75. Waldo G. Leland, "American Archival Problems," in *AHA Annual Report, 1909*, 342.

76. Charles M. Andrews, "The Lessons of the British Archives"; Marion Dexter Learned, "The Lessons of the German Archives"; Carl Russell Fish, "The Lessons of the Italian Archives"; William I. Hull, "The Lessons of the Dutch Archives"; William R. Shepherd, "The Lessons of the Spanish Archives"; and Amandus Johnson, "The Lessons of the Swedish Archives," in *AHA Annual Report, 1909*, 349–68.

77. Victor Hugo Paltsits, "Tragedies in New York's Public Records," in *AHA Annual Report, 1909*, 369–78. At the time, Paltsits was serving in the position of state historian of New York, but his description of the actual duties of his office were recognizably at the bridge between archivist and documentary editor—to "collect, collate, compile, edit, and prepare for publication all official records, memoranda, and data." Victor Hugo Paltsits, *The Function of the State Historian of New York* (Albany: J. B. Lyon, 1908), 4.

78. Jameson to Clarence Alvord, May 6, 1908, box 47, file "Alvord, C. W., 1908," Jameson Papers. As a way around the financial concerns, over the next two decades a number of the early leaders of this area of the historical enterprise were employed with one foot in academia and the other in a society, archive, or state history office, including Alvord, Solon Buck, and Joseph Schafer.

Chapter Three

1. Looking at surveys of course enrollments in Massachusetts, New York, and Ohio in this period, Rolla M. Tryon estimates that history only comprised between 1 and 2 percent of the courses and enrollments in the period before the Civil War. Tryon, *The Social Sciences as School Subjects*, Report of the Commission on the Social Studies 11 (New York: Charles Scribner's Sons, 1935), 15–32.

2. Homer R. Seerly, "The Essentials in United States History to Be Taught in Secondary Schools," *National Education Association Journal of Addresses and Proceedings* (1898): 77. This echoed more contemporaneously in publications such as "Our Schools," *New York Times*, May 8, 1875, 4; and Francis Newton Thorpe, *"In Justice to the Nation": American History in American Schools, Colleges, and Universities* (Philadelphia: Education, 1886).

3. Edward A. Krug, *The Shaping of the American High School, 1880–1920* (Madison: University of Wisconsin Press, 1969), 4–6, 28–29.

4. From time series in table 3 of Carl A. Jessen and Lester B. Herlihy, *Offerings and Registrations in High-School Subjects, 1933–34*, US Bureau of Education Bulletin 1938, no. 6 (Washington, DC: Government Printing Office, 1938), 54–59.

5. "Afternoon Sessions" *Boston Daily Globe*, December 30, 1875, 2. The *New York Times* made a similar observation in "The Normal College," *New York Times*, March 30, 1875, 6.

6. Charles Kendall Adams, "On Methods of Teaching History," in *Methods of Teaching History*, ed. G. Stanley Hall (Boston: D. C. Heath, 1884), 208–11.

7. Hall, *Methods of Teaching History*, ix.

8. The character of the meeting was a regular subject of discussion between Herbert Baxter Adams and AHA treasurer, Clarence Bowen, though skewed a bit because Adams was often calling on Bowen to draw in his more eminent circle of friends. See, for instance, Clarence Bowen to H. B. Adams, November 2, 1889, box 4, file "Secretary Correspondence, 1889, B-I," American Historical Association Papers, Manuscript Division, Library of Congress, Washington, DC (hereafter cited as AHA Papers); and H. B. Adams to Clarence Bowen, November 10, 1890, box 4, file "Secretary Correspondence, 1890, A," AHA Papers.

9. See, for instance, James Ingersoll Wyer, "A Bibliography of the Study and Teaching of History," in *Annual Report of the American Historical Association*

for the Year 1899 (Washington, DC: Government Printing Office, 1900), 559–612 (hereafter cited as *AHA Annual Report*), which lists only a handful of articles and books by American authors before 1893.

10. Albert Bushnell Hart, "Teacher as Professional Expert," *School Review* 1, no. 1 (January 1893): 4–14.

11. An exchange between the Harvard faculty trying to develop a list of teachers from the Harvard department encompasses "teachers" at colleges, universities, and schools as representing a full range of "professional work." Albert Bushnell Hart to Charles Gross, January 14, 1907, and attached lists, box UA V 454.8 "History Department: Correspondence and Records c. 1900–c. 1910," file "History Department—Roll of Teachers," Harvard History Department Records, Harvard University Archives, Boston, MA (hereafter Harvard History Department Records).

12. The subcommittee of the Committee of Ten on history, civil government, and political economy included four AHA presidents (Charles Kendall Adams, Albert Bushnell Hart, James Harvey Robinson, and Woodrow Wilson) and was advised by two more (Charles Homer Haskins and Frederick Jackson Turner). *The Report of the Committee of Ten on Secondary School Studies with the Reports of Conferences Arranged by the Committee* (New York: American Book, 1894). The report was originally published and distributed by the NEA and the Government Printing Office in 1893, but due to high demand it was reprinted for sale.

13. For opinions on its formative significance see, for instance, Henry Johnson, *Teaching of History in Elementary and Secondary Schools* (New York: Macmillan, 1915), 133–37; and more recently Gary Nash, Charlotte Crabtree, and Ross Dunn, *History on Trial: Culture Wars and the Teaching of the Past* (New York: Alfred A. Knopf, 1998), 34.

14. *Report of the Committee of Ten*, 162–201.

15. Intriguingly, Theodore R. Sizer suggests that Wilson and Hart "tangled over whether European or American history should be emphasized in the senior year course," presaging subsequent debates about the balance between the two. Sizer, *Secondary Schools at the Turn of the Century* (New Haven, CT: Yale University Press, 1964), 109.

16. *Report of the Committee of Ten*, 185.

17. *Report of the Committee of Ten*, 170.

18. Francis Newton Thorpe, "American History in Schools, Colleges, and Universities," in Herbert Baxter Adams, *The Study of History in American Colleges and Universities* (Washington, DC: Government Printing Office, 1887), 233, and more generally, 229–235.

19. B. A. Hinsdale, "History Teaching in Schools," *National Education Association Journal of Addresses and Proceedings* (1895): 368–70. See also B. A. Hinsdale, *How to Study and Teach History, with Particular Reference to the History of the United States* (New York: D. Appleton, 1894).

20. Thomas D. Snyder et al., *Digest of Education Statistics, 2005* (Washington, DC: Department of Education, 2006), table 54, http://nces.ed.gov/programs/digest/d05/tables/dt05_054.asp.

21. History department minutes, January 8, 1896, 80–82, minute volume "Record of the Proceedings of the Department of History and Roman Law in Harvard College," Harvard History Department Records.

22. Attachment to department minutes, March 7, 1899, p. 161, minute volume, Harvard History Department Records.

23. H. B. Adams to Clarence Bowen, March 29, 1897, box 215, file "Corres. 1897," AHA Papers.

24. "The Annual Meeting of the American Historical Association," *American Historical Review* 3 (April 1898): 412 (hereafter cited as *AHR*). Note that this discussion was preceded by a roundtable on the question: "To what extent may 'sources' profitably be used in the teaching of History below the Graduate School?" The author of the report noted with some surprise, "The most striking general feature of the transactions was the prevalence of discussions of practical topics interesting to the profession, rather than of formal contributions to knowledge" (405–6).

25. Robert Orrill and Linn Shapiro, "From Bold Beginnings to an Uncertain Future: The Discipline of History and History Education," *AHR* 110 (June 2005): 731.

26. Edgar Bruce Wesley, *Teaching the Social Studies* (Boston: D. C. Heath, 1942), 208.

27. Minutes, Conference in Cambridge, April 16–17, 1897, 1–6, box 459, file "Committee of History in High Schools 1897," AHA Papers.

28. The full text of the Committee of Seven's final report is now available on the Association's website at http://www.historians.org/pubs/archives/CommitteeofSeven/, with the section on the subjects included at http://www.historians.org/pubs/archives/CommitteeofSeven/ReportFour.cfm.

29. See, for instance, W. M. West (Faribault, Minnesota), "The Purpose and Scope of History in the High School," *National Education Association Journal of Addresses and Proceedings* (1890): 655, which argued for Greek and Roman history in year one, a topical survey of medieval and modern history in year two, "to furnish the background for English history, a year which leads naturally to a year in United States history and civics—the crown of the course." A similar case is made in E. V. Robinson, "An Ideal Course in History for Secondary Schools," *National Education Association Journal of Addresses and Proceedings* (1897): 683.

30. Minutes, Conference in Cambridge, April 16–17, 1897, 4, box 459, file "Committee of History in High Schools 1897," AHA Papers.

31. Minutes, Conference in Cambridge, April 16–17, 1897, 1–6, box 459, file "Committee of History in High Schools 1897," AHA Papers; and carried over into

the final report at http://www.historians.org/pubs/archives/CommitteeofSeven/ ReportMethods.cfm. Hart's opinion on these matters is suggested in the observation that the "object of the teacher is always to teach pupils to think about what they read or hear, rather than to force upon them the passive reception of historical matter." Edward Channing and Albert Bushnell Hart, *Guide to the Study of American History* (Boston: Ginn, 1896), 199.

32. George E. Howard (of Stanford University) noted the "conservatism of the Committees, especially in the handling of disputed questions," even if he considered it "praiseworthy" for strategic reasons, in a review published under "The Study of History in Schools," *Educational Review* 19 (March 1900): 261.

33. Frank M. Phillips, *Statistical Summary of Education, 1927–1928*, US Bureau of Education Bulletin 1930, no. 3 (Washington, DC: Government Printing Office, 1930), 15. See also Krug, *Shaping of the American High School*, 56.

34. The characteristics are drawn in part from Lotus Delta Coffman, *Social Composition of the Teaching Population* (New York: Teachers College, Columbia University, 1911), chaps. 3 and 4; Edward S. Evenden, Guy C. Gamble, and Harold G. Blue, *National Survey of the Education of Teachers* (Washington, DC: Bureau of Education, 1935), 40–73; as well as descriptive comments from administrators and specialists in speeches and articles in the NEA *Proceedings*, *Historical Outlook*, and *School Review*.

35. George W. Knight, "What the Teacher of American History Should Be and Do," *School Review* 10, no. 3 (March 1902): 208–16 (quote at p. 209).

36. Department of the Interior, *Report of Commissioner of Education for the Year Ending June 30, 1904*, vol. 2 (Washington, DC: Government Printing Office, 1906), 1284 (table 3). The survey only looked at teachers in cities with populations of more than eight thousand people.

37. In 1930, the Bureau of Education reported that barely 12 percent of high school history teachers were teaching only a single subject. Evenden, Gamble, and Blue, *National Survey of the Education of Teachers*, 68.

38. A. L. Goodrich, "History in Secondary Schools," *School Review* 7 (January 1899): 32.

39. Thomas H. Briggs, *Report of the Commissioner of Education for the Year Ended June 30, 1915*, vol. 1 (Washington, DC: Government Printing Office, 1915), 120. See also the similar results of 215 schools in Hugo H. Gold, "Methods and Content of Courses in History in the High Schools of the United States: Part I. Administration of the Curriculum and Content of Courses in History," *School Review* 25, no. 2 (February 1917): 88–100.

40. See, for instance, the assessment in *School Review* 7, no. 9 (November 1899): 570.

41. "Notes and News," *AHR* 7 (January 1902): 408. See also "Report of the AHA Committee on the Training of High School History Teachers," *History Teacher's Magazine* 4 (January 1912): 22–24.

42. See, for instance, "Report of the Committee on Courses of Study," in *Register and Reports of the Annual Meetings, May 13, 1899, and October 21, 1899* (Medford, MA: New England History Teachers' Association, 1899), 21–36. The development of the syllabi and guides is discussed more generally in "Notes and News," *AHR* 7 (October 1901): 189, and "Notes and News," *AHR* 10 (January 1905): 465. Examples of their lasting impact can still be seen in exchanges of letters with Daniel C. Knowlton for the Committee on Education for History and Citizenship (1919–20) in box 767 of the AHA Papers.

43. Charles Homer Haskins, "Report of the Conference on the First Year of College Work in History," in *AHA Annual Report, 1905*, 149.

44. Haskins, "Report of the Conference on the First Year," 149–71.

45. Charles Homer Haskins discusses some of the summer courses in development at Harvard. Haskins to A. Lawrence Lowell, November 12, 1902, file "History Department—Courses," Harvard History Department Records. H. Morse Stephens discusses extension courses at the University of California, Berkeley, and advises that many of his listeners would be teachers "who will not take examinations for credit but who will be able to teach history on its most romantic side after having listened to you with an interest in the subject at present lacking through want of knowledge." Stephens to Reuben Gold Thwaites, February 21, 1905, box 30, file "Stanford–Stevens," Wisconsin Historical Society Papers, Wisconsin Historical Society, Madison, WI (hereafter cited as WHS Papers).

46. For instance, Clarence W. Alvord discusses the merits of one man (C. E. Carter) seeking a job at the University of Illinois. Alvord advises that he should spend a few more years at a small college in Illinois, because "he needs broadening instead of specializing." Alvord to J. Franklin Jameson, June 5, 1909, box 47, file "Alvord, C. W., 1909," J. Franklin Jameson Papers, Manuscript Division, Library of Congress, Washington, DC (hereafter cited as Jameson Papers).

47. James Alton James et al., *The Study of History in the Elementary Schools* (New York: Charles Scribner's Sons, 1909).

48. Wesley, *Teaching the Social Studies*, 211. See also an address by J. Montgomery Gambrill, "Shall the Course of Study Recommended by the Committee of Eight Be Adopted in the Elementary Schools?" (Given to the Buffalo Meeting—1912), box 472 "American Historical Association Miscellany," file "Abstracts of Papers," AHA Papers.

49. James et al., *Study of History in the Elementary Schools*, x.

50. Letter from B. S. Hurlbut and petition from "Head Masters of Secondary Schools," n.d., box 472 "American Historical Association Miscellany," file "College Entrance Examination Requirements in Ancient History," AHA Papers, which reports that "the College Entrance Examination Board voted to appeal directly to the Historical Association in regard to the definition of the requirement in Ancient History, hoping thereby to secure prompter action than by organizing a commission."

51. Memo to the Committee of Five of the American Historical Association, "Recommendations by the New England Teachers' Association," n.d. [but sometime in late 1908], box 460, file "Cmte. of Five," AHA Papers. This focuses primarily on the distorting effect the college entrance exams had on shaping the teaching of ancient history, particularly the balancing of coverage against the details to be treated on the tests. The teachers' association is also opposed to combining history and civics, but raises the idea of adding "industrial history" to the curriculum. See also "Notes and News," *AHR* 13 (April 1908): 672.

52. "Proceedings of the Conference on History in Secondary Schools," in *AHA Annual Report, 1908,* 77.

53. Unfortunately the correspondence in the committee's files is largely between Charles Homer Haskins and Andrew C. McLaughlin, with Robinson appearing largely as an off-stage nuisance. See correspondence in box 243 "Executive Council Secretary Corres.; Reports; Etc., 1902–15," file "A. C. McLaughlin," AHA Papers. Robinson clearly stated his preferences for the work for the committee in an address to the Middle States Association. James Harvey Robinson, "How to Make History Teaching More Definite," *Seventh Annual Convention of the Association of History Teachers in the Middle States and Maryland, 1909,* 6–11 (available at http://hdl.handle.net/2027/inu.30000055111045).

54. These themes were already being developed by Robinson's colleague at Columbia, Charles Beard, as expressed in Beard, "A Plea for Greater Stress on the Modern Period," *Sixth Annual Convention of the Association of History Teachers in the Middle States and Maryland, 1908,* 12–15 (available at http://hdl.handle.net/2027/inu.30000055111052). Robinson and Beard also objected that history teaching should avoid excessive emphasis on factual detail, but that seems a bit of a red herring in these discussions, as it is hard to find anyone in the discipline advocating for fact cramming as a pedagogical method.

55. A. C. McLaughlin to Clarence Bowen, October 18, 1910, box 621, "Treasurer's File Corres., 1910 (1 of 2)," AHA Papers.

56. For instance, the committee is cited in advertisements such as the one for Roscoe Lewis Ashley's textbooks from MacMillan Company, *History Teacher's Magazine* 3 (March 1912): 64. See also N. Ray Hiner, "Professions in Process: Changing Relations between Historians and Educators, 1896–1911," *History of Education Quarterly* 12, no. 1 (Spring 1972): 50–52.

57. "Announcements for 1909–1910," *History Teacher's Magazine* 1 (September 1909): 1.

58. "Announcements for 1909–1910." There is a curious difference between the characterization in the first issues of the *Magazine* and the description in the *AHR* that reported the "aim of the magazine is specifically and strictly to serve the interests of teachers of history, especially those of teachers in secondary schools." "Notes and News," *AHR* 15 (October 1909): 201.

59. In a survey of the authors in the first volume of the *Magazine*, thirty-two of thirty-six authors of articles were members of the AHA. The four exceptions were teachers of civics and economics.

60. E. B. Greene to Haskins, November 4, 1911, box 243 "Executive Council Secretary Corres.; Reports; Etc., 1902–15," file *"History Teacher's Magazine,"* AHA Papers.

61. "Eleven Hundred History Teachers," *History Teacher's Magazine* 3 (September 1911): 14.

62. Albert E. McKinley, "The Future of the Magazine," *History Teacher's Magazine* 3 (September 1911): 3.

Chapter Four

1. Frederick Jackson Turner, "Social Forces in American History," *American Historical Review* 16 (January 1911): 217–33 (quote at p. 225; hereafter cited as *AHR*).

2. The paper is reprinted as "The New Allies of History," in James Harvey Robinson, *The New History: Essays Illustrating the Modern Historical Outlook* (New York: Macmillan, 1912), 70–100. Quotes are from page 71.

3. Waldo G. Leland, "The Meeting of the American Historical Association at Indianapolis," in *Annual Report of the American Historical Association for the Year 1911* (Washington, DC: Government Printing Office, 1913), 40–42 (hereafter cited as *AHA Annual Report*).

4. Marcus Jernegan at the University of Chicago discusses plans to give two graduate courses on the "social history of the colonies" in a letter to J. Franklin Jameson, November 20, 1910, box 99, file "Jernegan, M. W.," J. Franklin Jameson Papers, Manuscript Division, Library of Congress, Washington, DC (hereafter cited as Jameson Papers). Notably, the courses seem to focus on popular engagement with political issues and are not significantly colored by emerging methods from the other social science disciplines.

5. Fred Morrow Fling, *Writing of History: An Introduction to Historical Method* (New Haven, CT: Yale University Press, 1920), 16, compared to Fling, *Outline of Historical Method* (Lincoln, NE: J. H. Miller, 1899), 9.

6. For a useful comparison of how this played out in graduate study and early professional life, compare the autobiographies of two doctoral students in Columbia University: Arthur Schlesinger, who was taken with the New History ideas from the first, and Roy F. Nichols, a student of Robinson's more conservative colleague William A. Dunning, who only came to the New History as an instructor at the school. Arthur Schlesinger, *In Retrospect: The History of a Historian* (New York: Harcourt, Brace, and World, 1963), 34–37; and Roy F. Nichols, *Historian's Progress* (New York: Alfred A. Knopf, 1968), 29–47.

7. James Harvey Robinson, "History," in *Lectures on Science, Philosophy, and Art, 1907–1908* (New York: Columbia University Press, 1908), 29.

8. "Program of the Twenty-Sixth Annual Meeting of the American Historical Association and Meetings of Allied Societies," final edition, December 10, 1910. Copy in AHA headquarters office, Washington, DC.

9. "The Meeting of the American Historical Association at Buffalo and Ithaca," *AHR* 17 (April 1912): 453–76 (quote at p. 454).

10. Hart to E. B. Greene, March 25, 1910, file "Meetings at Providence," Hart Papers, Harvard University Archives, Boston, MA (hereafter cited as Hart Papers).

11. "Program of the Fortieth Annual Meeting Held in Ann Arbor, Mich., December 29–31, 1925," in *AHA Annual Report, 1925*, 54–56.

12. The factors that fed into Turner's decision—particularly the salary, support for students, and exceptional library facilities—are all discussed in Ray Allen Billington, *Frederick Jackson Turner: Historian, Scholar, Teacher* (New York: Oxford University Press, 1973), 297–302.

13. Turner to Albert Bushnell Hart, December 16, 1909, box 26, file "Turner, Frederick J.," Hart Papers.

14. Department chair to Harvard Corporation, March 4, 1910, box UA V 454.8 "History Department: Correspondence and Records c. 1900–c. 1910" (annotated as box 1 of 21), file "History Department—Appointments," Harvard History Department Records, Harvard University Archives, Boston, MA (hereafter Harvard History Department Records).

15. Payson J. Treat (then at Stanford) to Archibald Cary Coolidge, April 2, 1908, ibid.

16. J. Franklin Jameson, John Bach McMaster, and Edward Channing, *Present State of Historical Writing* (Worcester, MA: Davis Press, 1910), 15.

17. Data drawn from George J. Stigler, *Employment and Compensation in Education* (New York: National Bureau of Economic Research, 1950), 29 (table 17); and National Center for Education Statistics, *Digest of Education Statistics: 2007* (Washington, DC: Department of Education, 2008), table 178.

18. R. W. Kelsey, "Recent Changes in the Teaching of History in the Colleges and Universities of the Middle States and Maryland," *History Teacher's Magazine* (November 1914): 207–10 and Arthur M. Schlesinger, "The History Situation in Colleges and Universities, 1919–20," *Historical Outlook* 11 (March 1920): 103–6; Milledge L. Bonham Jr., "College Course in General United States History from Another Viewpoint," *Historical Outlook* 13 (January 1922): 14–16; and Sidney R. Packard, "Facts and Fallacies of History Teaching," *Historical Outlook* 15 (March 1924): 110.

19. From a simple tabulation of the faculty information in D. A. Robertson, ed., *American Universities and Colleges*, 5th ed. (Washington, DC: American Council on Education, 1928).

20. The challenges for faculty in these departments is evident in a letter from R. F. Arragon at Reed College to Arthur Schlesinger (errantly addressed to "William" Schlesinger) seeking a second man for the department. He reports that "the emphasis placed here on the correlation of work in history with that of other fields, especially in the curriculum of the first two years, makes breadth of training and experience and an interest in more than a special aspect of history essential." Letter dated January 12, 1928, box UAV 454.8 "History Department: Correspondence and Records c. 1927–c. 1929 A–L," file "Abbott–Austin," Harvard History Department Records.

21. Even though the chronological frame for this chapter ends in 1925, this analysis extends to 1930, since that included programs that started admitting students in 1925, and more accurately reflects the trajectory at the time. Note there is some ambiguity about whether the number of available jobs kept pace. Peter Novick notes some anecdotal evidence of history faculty who felt trapped in poor-paying positions, but it is not clear to me whether this was simply endemic to the system of employment in much of higher education outside of the major research universities. Novick, *That Noble Dream: The "Objectivity Question" and the American Historical Profession* (New York: Cambridge University Press, 1988), 169–70.

22. J. Franklin Jameson, *List of Doctoral Dissertations in History Now in Progress at the Chief American Universities* (Washington, DC: Department of Historical Research, Carnegie Institution of Washington, 1927), 26–28.

23. This is based on a comparison, from 1905 to 1925, of the years of undergraduate degrees included in Jameson, *List of Doctoral Dissertations*, to the years the doctoral degrees were conferred according to Kuehl, *Dissertations in History*. On more recent trends, see Robert B. Townsend, "How Long to the PhD?" *Perspectives* (February 2006): 5.

24. Donald Pritchett Bean, *Report on American Scholarly Publishing* (New York: General Education Board, 1929), 22.

25. "News and Comments," *Mississippi Valley Historical Review* 1 (June 1914): 157 (hereafter cited as *MVHR*); as well as Clarence Alvord to Clarence Paine, December 6, 1912, file 10/13, Organization of American Historians Papers, Ruth Lilly Special Collections and Archives at the Indiana University–Purdue University at Indianapolis University Library, Indianapolis, IN (hereafter MVHA Papers); and circular from Paine (c. 1915), file 10/13, MVHA Papers.

26. "How the Public Received *The Journal of Negro History*," *Journal of Negro History* 1 (April 1916): 225–32; and Charles E. Chapman, "The Founding of the *Review*," *Hispanic American Historical Review* 1 (February 1918): 8. Notably, an effort to create an "American Review of European History" failed as a number of specialists felt their efforts could be better focused on expanding the size of the *AHR*, per George B. Adams to W. S. Ferguson, October 16, 1916, box UA V 454.8, file "Abbott to Ault," Harvard History Department Records;

and W. S. Ferguson to George B. Adams, January 15, 1917, box UA V 454.8, file "Abbott to Ault," Harvard History Department Records.

27. J. Franklin Jameson, memo "American Historical Review Circular to the Board of Editors," February 7, 1921, box 3, file B F752 #18, Guy Stanton Ford Papers, University of Minnesota Archives, Minneapolis, Minnesota (hereafter cited as Ford Papers).

28. "Manual of Historical Literature," n.d., attached to "Report of the Committee on a Manual of Historical Literature, for the year 1920" to the AHA Executive Council, n.d. (c. December 1920), box 458, file "Committee Reports circa 1920," American Historical Association Papers, Manuscript Division, Library of Congress, Washington, DC (hereafter cited as AHA Papers).

29. Bean, *Report on American Scholarly Publishing*, 7.

30. Out of 1,988 reviews published by the *AHR* in the period from 1910 and 1925, 1,760 were on new scholarship, 122 were narrow biographies, 10 were on pedagogy (though all but 3 were reviewed before 1914), and 96 were reviews of works on the tools and materials of research.

31. See, for instance, Carl Becker, "The Reviewing of Historical Books," in *AHA Annual Report, 1920*, 129–36; and the review by Raymond G. Gettell of a festschrift for William A. Dunning, *A History of Political Theories, Recent Times: Essays on Contemporary Developments in Political Theory*, which tries to negotiate the differences between Dunning and his students, *AHR* 30 (April 1925): 574–76.

32. J. Franklin Jameson, "The American Historical Association, 1884–1909," *AHR* 15 (October 1909): 17.

33. Lucy M. Salmon, "The Evolution of the Teacher," [1910], box 472, file "Abstracts of Papers c. 1916," AHA Papers. Despite the name of the file, this was actually delivered to the 1910 meeting.

34. E.g., J. Franklin Jameson to Clarence Bowen, January 11, 1911 (copy of a general circular to the heads of historical societies), box 622, file "Treasurer's File Corres., 1911" (1 of 2), AHA Papers; and J. Franklin Jameson, "Historical Scholars in War-Time," *AHR* 22 (July 1917): 831–35.

35. See, for instance, W. C. Abbott, "Review of *The Last Years of the Protectorate, 1656–1658*," *AHR* 15 (July 1910): 851–53; Arthur Lyon Cross, review of *The Seymour Family, The Cavendish Family, The Cecil Family, and The La Tremoille Family*, *AHR* 20 (January 1915): 396–99; and Victor Hugo Paltsits, "Louisbourg from Its Foundation to Its Fall, 1713–1758," *AHR* 26 (October 1920): 104–5.

36. William Roscoe Thayer, "Historical Writing," *Nation*, July 5, 1915, 67.

37. Wilbur C. Abbott, "The Influence of Graduate Instruction on Historical Writing," in Fling, *Writing of History*, 54. This report was written in 1924 but took almost two years to find its way into print.

38. Abbott, "Influence of Graduate Instruction," 46–47.

39. Benjamin F. Schambaugh to Joseph Schafer, May 19, 1920, box 41, file "B-H [Burrows Fund]," Wisconsin Historical Society Papers, Wisconsin Historical Society, Madison, WI (hereafter cited as WHS Papers).

40. Clarence Alvord, the state historian of Illinois, describes employing up to thirty graduate students to assist with his centennial history of the state, in a letter to Joseph Schafer, May 17, 1920, ibid.

41. Albert Bushnell Hart, "Imagination in History," *AHR* 15 (January 1910): 299.

42. Albert Bushnell Hart, "American Historical Liars," *Harper's Magazine* 131 (October 1915): 731.

43. A copy of Boyd's original request is attached to Carlton J. H. Hayes, "Report of the Sub-Committee to Study and Report on the Proposal to Establish a Committee on Research," December 27, 1921, box 34, folder 10, John Spencer Bassett Papers, Manuscript Division, Library of Congress, Washington, DC (hereafter cited as Bassett Papers).

44. Note that a similar-sounding proposal offered by Fred Morrow Fling in 1912 did not get anywhere in the council. Fling to Charles Homer Haskins, January 9, 1912, box 243, file *"History Teacher's Magazine,"* AHA Papers.

45. Hayes, "Report of the Sub-Committee," 1.

46. Boyd, attachment to Hayes, "Report of the Sub-Committee," 3.

47. William K. Boyd, "Report of the Committee on Historical Research in the Colleges," in *AHA Annual Report, 1925*, 82.

48. The ownership of the *Review* had not formally passed to the association when the council adopted the journal in 1898 (ownership nominally remained with the editorial board), and a small number of members characterized the expenses of the editorial board for travel to their meetings as extravagant. The best summary of events in the uprising is Ray Allen Billington, "Tempest in Clio's Teapot: The American Historical Association Rebellion of 1915,"*AHR* 78 (April 1973): 348–69. The particulars of the discussion are detailed in Frederic Bancroft, Rowland Dunbar, and John H. Latane, *Why the American Historical Association Needs Thorough Reorganization* (Washington, DC: National Capital Press, 1915); and in more personal correspondence, Frederic Bancroft to Albert Bushnell Hart, May 26, 1915, B #1, HUG 4448.17 "A. B. Hart, General Correspondence, 1911–1920, A-L," file "1911–1920," Hart Papers.

49. As noted in chapter 2, correspondence during Adams's tenure was quite explicit about trying to balance members from each region (North, South, and West) on all committees. I could not find any corresponding reflection on these issues in this period.

50. Clarence Paine, the secretary of the MVHA, tacitly supported Rowland (who was then president of the organization) in his use of the organization's membership rosters to distribute a circular protesting the AHA's leadership. C. S. Paine to Rowland, October 15, 1915, file 22/1, MVHA Papers; and C. S.

Paine to Rowland, January 8, 1915, file 22/10, MVHA Papers. The general sense of interest in the issue is also reflected in a letter from an unnamed historian in Minnesota (not Ford) to Clarence W. Alvord, who noted that during a trip through Minneapolis Jameson did not appear "particularly cast down by the recent attack." Anon. to Alvord, August 9, 1915, file 10/13, MVHA Papers.

51. Max Farrand to Albert Bushnell Hart, January 3, 1911, box 1, file "General Correspondence (Misc.), 1910–1918," Hart Papers.

52. Hart to Charles S. Hull (then chair of the Nominating Committee), February 26, 1914, box 1, file "General Correspondence (Misc.), 1910–1918," Hart Papers.

53. Jameson to Dr. James Sullivan, December 18, 1920, box 48, file 51 "AHA Membership Affairs, 1906–20," Jameson Papers.

54. Although notionally the position was consolidated into a single position, this was only made possible by the establishment of a full-time assistant secretary position who handled all day-to-day operations. This is described in Waldo Leland to Bassett, January 7, 1920, file 35/1, Bassett Papers.

55. Victor Paltsits to John Spencer Basset, January 9, 1920, folder 35/1, Bassett Papers.

56. See, for instance, Jameson to I. J. Cox, January 3, 1916, box 50, file 59 "AHA Programmes and Meetings II, 1914–19," AHA Papers; and A. C. Krey to Bassett, September 4, 1925, file 34/6, Bassett Papers.

57. J. Franklin Jameson, "The Meeting of the American Historical Association at Ann Arbor," in *AHA Annual Report, 1925*, 35.

58. Joseph Shafer to J. Franklin Jameson, March 24, 1925, box 126, file "Schafer, Jos.," Jameson Papers.

59. Jameson, "Meeting of the American Historical Association," 37. The correspondence in the AHA papers about how to frame this general effort is voluminous and also appears in the Bassett papers in boxes 34, 36, and 37.

60. Lucy M. Salmon, "Our Greatest Historian," *New York Times*, March 7, 1926, X16.

Chapter Five

1. Victor Paltsits to J. Franklin Jameson, February 25, 1912, box 117, file "Paltsits, V.," J. Franklin Jameson Papers, Manuscript Division, Library of Congress, Washington, DC (hereafter cited as Jameson Papers).

2. The particulars of Paltsits's lost position can be found in correspondence and newspaper clippings in Paltsits's file in the Jameson Papers.

3. Clifford Lee Lord, *Clio's Servant: The State Historical Society of Wisconsin, 1846–1954* (Madison: State Historical Society of Wisconsin, 1967), 239–49.

4. Milo M. Quaife to Carlton Fish, April 2, 1917, box 37, file "Advisory Committee 1915–1918," series 934, Wisconsin Historical Society Papers, Wisconsin Historical Society, Madison, WI (hereafter cited as WHS Papers).

5. Margaret C. Norton to Joseph Schafer, January 27, 1922, box 65, file "MS [Management Staff]," series 934, WHS Papers.

6. Clarence W. Alvord to Joseph Schafer, May 17, 1920, box 41, file "B-H [Burrows Fund]," series 934, WHS Papers.

7. The leaders of the historical societies in the West began to network more actively about developing collections and research services (including networks of "competent workmen" to provide genealogical services) in this period. See, for instance, Milo M. Quaife to Floyd C. Shoemaker (Missouri Historical Society), August 15, 1919, box 64, file "M-R—M-S," WHS Papers.

8. Quaife to Dallas T. Herndon (Arkansas Historical Commission), December 20, 1917, box 38, file "American Historical Society [sic]," WHS Papers.

9. On networks of support for historical societies, see the Committee on Handbook of the Conference of Historical Societies, introduction to *Handbook of American Historical Societies* (Madison, WI: Cantwell, 1926); and Walter Muir Whitehill, *Independent Historical Societies, an Enquiry into Their Research and Publication Functions and Their Financial Future* (Boston: Boston Athenaeum, 1962). On support for academic research, see Frederick Ogg, *Research in the Humanistic and Social Sciences: A Report of a Survey Conducted for the American Council of Learned Societies* (New York: Century, 1928).

10. Waldo G. Leland, "Some Fundamental Principles in Relation to Archives," in *Annual Report of the American Historical Association for the Year 1912* (Washington, DC: Government Printing Office, 1914), 264–68 (hereafter cited as *AHA Annual Report*); Victor Paltsits, "Plan and Scope of a 'Manual of Archival Economy' for the Use of American Archivists," in *AHA Annual Report, 1912*, 253–63. One of the other issues they tried to address was a refinement of the distinction between public archives and historical manuscripts. Waldo Leland to Solon Buck, January 22, 1913, box 623, file "Treasurer's File Corres., 1913," American Historical Association Papers, Manuscript Division, Library of Congress, Washington, DC (hereafter cited as AHA Papers).

11. Leland, "Some Fundamental Principles," 264.

12. Leland, "Some Fundamental Principles," 266; and Paltsits, "Plan and Scope," 258.

13. In describing plans for a chapter on the staffing and employees, Victor Hugo Paltsits reports that "we could wish that politics would not enter into the appointments and that only those who have special fitness would be intrusted with the chief places; that the terms would be during good behavior and efficiency; and that the merit system would prevail as far as possible. Some day we may attain to this millennial state; meanwhile, we have to deal with finite cir-

cumstances—and hope on." "Plan and Scope," 258; Paltsits, "An Historical Resume of the Public Archives Commission from 1899 to 1921," in *AHA Annual Report, 1922,* 156.

14. Waldo G. Leland to Charles Homer Haskins, April 13, 1912, box 18 "Secretary File, Corres. H.," AHA Papers.

15. Thwaites to Thomas L. Montgomery (Pennsylvania Library Association), January 6, 1913, box 26, file "Paxson–Pennsylvania," series 934, WHS Papers.

16. See, for instance, reports to Thwaites from Missouri Historical Society (Idress Head to Thwaites, December 1912).

17. J. Franklin Jameson to R. D. W. Connor (North Carolina Historical Commission), June 8, 1914, box 93, file "Connor, R. D. W., 1910–1928," Jameson Papers.

18. J. Franklin Jameson, John Bach McMaster, and Edward Channing, *Present State of Historical Writing* (Worcester, MA: Davis Press, 1910), 7–9.

19. Worthington C. Ford describes the costs and value of the Photostat machine for the Massachusetts Historical Society in a letter to Milo M. Quaife. Ford to Quaife, November 26, 1915, box 60, file "M-H," series 934, WHS Papers. In a letter sent seven months later, Quaife describes the Wisconsin Historical Society's efforts to imitate "in a small way" the example set by Ford in Massachusetts (Quaife to Ford, July 5, 1916, ibid.).

20. Milo Quaife reports that the society got rid of the old Photostat machine after just six years and purchased a new larger one, "both for ourselves and for such other libraries as may see fit to avail themselves of the service." Quaife to A. E. Cole, March 15, 1918, box 66, file "MV," series 934, WHS Papers.

21. "Principles Governing the Distribution of Documents" offers a useful summary of the state of things before technology facilitated sharing of copies, instead of original files. Statement attached to Quaife to Advisory Committee, January 27, 1916, box 37, file "Advisory Committee 1915–1918," WHS Papers.

22. The first such notice is the acquisition of a Photostat machine at the Library of Congress, in "News and Notes," *American Historical Review* 17 (April 1912), 707 (hereafter cited as *AHR*). Starting in 1916, announcements about the availability of materials "in photostatic form" become increasingly common.

23. Minutes of Conference of Directors of Historical Work in Northwest, October 23, 1915, in box 61, file "M-H," series 934, WHS Papers.

24. Quaife to Alvord, December 10, 1915, box 53, file "I-H," series 934, WHS Papers.

25. See "Proceedings of the Thirteenth Annual Conference of Historical Societies," in *AHA Annual Report, 1916,* 233–35; and "Report of the Secretary of the Council," ibid., 77–78.

26. Note that the Pacific Coast Branch of the American Historical Association was engaged in similar efforts on the West Coast, "Proceedings of the Pacific Coast Branch," in *AHA Annual Report, 1910,* 62–65.

27. Clarence S. Paine to James A. James, July 21, 1913, box 5, file 5/16, Organization of American Historians Papers, Ruth Lilly Special Collections and Archives at the Indiana University–Purdue University at Indianapolis University Library, Indianapolis, IN (hereafter MVHA Papers). Almost a third of the committees established before 1920 were addressed to these sorts of questions, such as considering the roles of museums and historical societies to educational institutions at a variety of levels. See, for instance, "Report of the Secretary-Treasurer, April 1916," in *Proceedings of the Mississippi Valley Historical Association* (Cedar Rapids, Iowa: Torch Press, 1916), 40–46 (henceforth *MVHA Proceedings*); and "Report of the Committee on the Management of Historical Museums" ibid., 9.

28. Milo M. Quaife to Lydia Brauer, July 24, 1918, box 65, file "MS," series 934, WHS Papers; and Waldo G. Leland, "Historians and Archivists in the First World War," *American Archivist* 5 (January 1942): 1–17.

29. Solon Buck describes a variety of efforts by the historical societies under the auspices of the National Board for Historical Service. Solon Buck to Milo M. Quaife, August 23, 1918, box 61, file "M-H," series 934, WHS Papers. See the various state level reports in *AHA Annual Report, 1919*, 204–93; and Karl Singewald and Albert E. McKinley, "Progress in the Collection of War Records by War History Organizations," in *AHA Annual Report, 1920*, 135–52. Curiously, the discussions at the MVHA focused more on the impact the war had on the teaching of history, rather than the impact on the societies. *MVHA Proceedings*, 10 and 11.

30. "Up-to-Date Methods of Illinois Centennial Historian," *New York Times*, July 14, 1918, 53

31. Joseph Schafer, "War Service of Historical Scholars," *American Review of Reviews* (August 1919); and Waldo G. Leland, "The National Board for Historical Service," in *AHA Annual Report, 1919*, 161–89.

32. "Proceedings of the Fourteenth Annual Conference of Historical Societies," in *AHA Annual Report, 1917*, 181.

33. "Report of the Committee on Policy," in *AHA Annual Report, 1920*, 67–73.

34. The deficit ran to $4,500 in an operating budget of $13,500. "Report of the Treasurer, November 30, 1920," in *AHA Annual Report, 1920*, 61. Due to the shortfall in public funds, the annual reports fell as much as three years behind in their publication schedule through the remainder of the decade.

35. "Report of the Committee on Publications," in *AHA Annual Report, 1922*, 64–65.

36. Paltsits, "Historical Resume," 152–163 (quote at p. 160).

37. Waldo Gifford Leland, *Some Early Recollections of an Itinerant Historian* (Worcester, MA: American Antiquarian Society, 1952).

38. Julian P. Boyd, "State and Local Historical Societies in the United States," *AHR* 40 (October 1934): 29.

39. Justin H. Smith to AHA Council, October 29, 1923, p. 4, box 52, file 71, Jameson Papers.

40. Hilary Jenkinson, *A Manual of Archive Administration, Including the Problems of War Archives and Archive Making* (New York: Oxford University Press, 1922). See also the review by Victor Paltsits, *AHR* 28 (April 1923): 524–25.

41. Based on a simple tabulation of the employment listed for the authors of reports published in the AHA annual reports, 1900–1928. Before 1910, twenty-two of thirty-seven reports published by the Public Archives Commission were authored by academics. From 1910 to 1926, just five of twenty-one reports were authored by academics.

42. The Conference of Historical Societies published separate reports of its meetings in the AHA annual reports from 1904 to 1922 and resumed them again from 1929 to its separation from the AHA in 1940. It also distributed copies of the reports to member societies from 1917 to 1940. The Conference of Archivists published reports of its meetings from 1909 to 1922.

43. Dixon Ryan Fox to Joseph Schafer, November 28, 1923, box 1, file "Conference of Historical Societies, June 1922, 1923," Schafer Papers, Wisconsin Historical Society, Madison, WI (hereafter cited as Schafer Papers). The survey attached to the letter goes on to list collections that might be of interest to scholars ("books, manuscripts, and other materials") and asks how many "real scholars" have used them.

44. "American Historical Association Endowment Fund," [1926], box 34, file 5, John Spencer Bassett Papers, Manuscript Division, Library of Congress, Washington, DC (hereafter cited as Bassett Papers).

45. "Historical News," *AHR* 30 (April 1925): 660–61.

46. See correspondence in box 34, file 5 "American Historical Association, Committees, Minutes and Reports, 1920–26 'Endowment,'" Bassett Papers.

47. Cf. Waldo G. Leland to Evarts Greene, April 2, 1925, box 15 "Secretary File," file "Leland 1910–26," AHA Papers; and "Survey and Plan of Fundraising for the American Historical Association" prepared by John Price Jones Corporation, June 3, 1925, box 39, file 3 "American Historical Association Committees, Financial Statements and Reports," Bassett Papers.

48. Examples of the researcher-focused presentations can be found in "Historian Appeals for Research Funds," *New York Times*, March 14, 1926, E4; "Fund of $1,000,000 for History Sought," *New York Times*, May 28, 1926, 23; and "Historical Research Program Outlined: Study of American Family and Inventory of Manuscripts to Be Undertaken First," *New York Times*, September 5, 1926, E3.

49. "Proposed Use of the Increased Endowment of the American Historical Association," February 1926, box 15, file "Leland 1910–26," AHA Papers; and "Campaign Plan," August 1926, box 50, file 51 "AHA Endowment Campaign, 1926–29," Jameson Papers.

50. See, for instance, the editorials "Preserving the Past," *New York Times*,

March 15, 1926, 20; and "Securing Historical Truth," *Washington Post*, March 21, 1926, ES1, which focus primarily on the need to fund the endowment to preserve the documentary record.

Chapter Six

1. J. Franklin Jameson to George B. Adams, November 16, 1911, box 243, file *"History Teacher's Magazine,"* American Historical Association Papers, Manuscript Division, Library of Congress, Washington, DC (hereafter cited as AHA Papers); Charles H. Haskins to Jameson, November 28, 1911, ibid.; and Albert E. McKinley to Haskins, December 7, 1911, ibid; and Circular Letter to Guarantors, January 26, 1912, box 622, file "Treasurer's File Corres., 1912–13," AHA Papers. Notably, while the association took over financial and fiduciary responsibilities for the journal, it did not obtain formal ownership. This created a difficult problem—and two competing social studies magazines—after a falling out with McKinley's heirs twenty-five years later.

2. Henry Johnson to Clarence Bowen, November 20, 1912, box 622 "Treasurer's File Correspondence, 1911–13," file "Treasurer's File Corres., 1912–13 (2 of 2)," AHA Papers, which reports $147 in payments to contributors.

3. Minutes of December 30, 1912, AHA Council meeting, in *Annual Report of the American Historical Association for the Year 1912* (Washington, DC: Government Printing Office, 1914), 132 (hereafter cited as *AHA Annual Report*).

4. Albert McKinley to Charles Homer Haskins, December 7, 1911, box 243, file *"History Teacher's Magazine,"* AHA Papers; and J. F. Jameson to Clarence Bowen, January 9, 1912, box 622, AHA Papers. The list of first guarantors for the magazine's revival was comprised primarily of past presidents of the association and members of the AHA Council (box 243, AHA Papers).

5. The US Bureau of Education also played a critical role in developing and disseminating the work of this committee. The chair of the committee was an employee of the bureau, and he was able to publish the committee's final report and disseminate it through the Government Printing Office. Arthur William Dunn, comp., *The Social Studies in Secondary Education*, Bulletin 1916, no. 28 (Washington, DC: Government Printing Office, 1916).

6. Clarence S. Paine to Benjamin Shambaugh, June 3, 1910, box 20, file 14, Organization of American Historians Papers, Ruth Lilly Special Collections and Archives at the Indiana University–Purdue University at Indianapolis University Library, Indianapolis, IN (hereafter MVHA Papers).

7. Waldo Leland to Clarence S. Paine, March 18, 1915, box 22, file 1, MVHA Papers.

8. Waldo G. Leland, "Activities of the American Historical Association 1884–1920," in *AHA Annual Report, 1921*, 78.

9. Minutes of December 27, 1911, Council meeting, Ledger of AHA Council Minutes 1901–15, p. 117, box 609 "Executive Council File," AHA Papers.

10. "A manuscript written in 1935 by Edgar Dawson on the history of the National Council for Social Studies," box 2007–213/329, file "Reference Notes and Typescript History of NCSS by Edgar Dawson—1934–35," National Council for the Social Studies Records, Dolph Briscoe Center for American History (henceforth designated NCSS Records).

11. Daniel C. Knowlton, "A Decade of Committee Activity," *Historical Outlook* 10 (December 1919): 499.

12. "The Training of High School History Teachers: Two Committee Reports," *History Teacher's Magazine* 4 (January 1912): 22–23.

13. "The Evolution of the Teacher" by Lucy M. Salmon (abstract of paper given to the Indianapolis meeting, December 16, 1916), box 472 "American Historical Association Miscellany," file "Abstracts of Papers c. 1916," AHA Papers.

14. Dawson manuscript, NCSS Records.

15. Frederic L. Paxson, "The Certification of High-School Teachers of History," *History Teacher's Magazine* 4, no. 6 (September 1913): 170.

16. Ibid., 172.

17. Edward L. Thorndike, *The Teaching Staff of Secondary Schools in the United States*, US Bureau of Education Bulletin 1909, no. 4 (Washington, DC: Government Printing Office, 1909), 14–15 and 23. A follow-up committee of the MVHA, also called the Committee on the Certification of High School Teachers of History, expanded on the type of course that should be required to teach pedagogy and came close to arguing for an expansion beyond a single course. "Report of the Committee of the Mississippi Valley Historical Association on the Certification of High-School Teachers of History," *History Teacher's Magazine* 6, no. 5 (May 1915): 150–51.

18. "The Training of High School History Teachers," 23–24.

19. Harlan Updegraff, *Teachers' Certificates Issued under General State Laws and Regulations*, US Bureau of Education Bulletin 1911, no. 18 (Washington, DC: Government Printing Office, 1911), 163–205. See also William Carl Ruediger, *Agencies for the Improvement of Teachers in Service*, US Bureau of Education Bulletin 1911, no. 3 (Washington, DC: Government Printing Office, 1911).

20. See Haven G. Edwards, "Preparation of the High School History Teachers," *History Teacher's Magazine* 11, no. 1 (September 1910): 6–9. And at the 1914 meeting of the AHA's Pacific Coast Branch, for instance, Professor Lull of the Department of Education in the University of Washington was tasked with presenting on the reevaluation of the history course in the schools. "Proceedings of the Special Meeting and the Eleventh Annual Meeting of the Pacific Coast Branch," in *AHA Annual Report, 1914*, 85.

21. The Pacific Coast Branch passed a resolution calling for such a committee, communicated by letter from William A. Morris to Evarts B. Greene, De-

cember 16, 1915, box 460, file "Pacific Coast Branch Correspondence, 1905–16", AHA Papers. According to the minutes, the AHA Council simply accepted their report without comment or action. *AHA Annual Report, 1915*, 107 and 77.

22. Waldo G. Leland, "Proceedings of the Twenty-Fifth Annual Meeting of the American Historical Association," in *AHA Annual Report, 1909*, 39.

23. Johnson discusses his various efforts in his autobiography, *The Other Side of Main Street: A History Teacher from Sauk Centre* (New York: Columbia University Press, 1943). See also Paul Robinson, "The Conventional Historians of the Social Studies," *Theory and Research in Social Education* 8, no. 3 (Fall 1980): 65–88.

24. In fairness, despite his virtues on teaching issues, Johnson was also prone to overcommit to a wide variety of projects and often failed to deliver, as noted by Evarts Greene, who observed, "We committed ourselves quite strongly to some of Henry Johnson's excellent ideas without quite separating the ideas from Johnson's ability to present and also to carry them out." Greene to Guy Stanton Ford, December 13, 1919, box 3, file B F752 #14, Guy Stanton Ford Papers, University of Minnesota Archives, Minneapolis, Minnesota (hereafter cited as Ford Papers).

25. Robert Orrill and Linn Shapiro, "From Bold Beginnings to an Uncertain Future: The Discipline of History and History Education," *American Historical Review* 110 (June 2005): 735–37 (hereafter cited as *AHR*).

26. Clarence D. Kingsley, *College Entrance Requirements*, US Bureau of Education Bulletin 1913, no. 7 (Washington, DC: Government Printing Office, 1913), 26–27.

27. David Warren Saxe, *Social Studies in Schools: A History of the Early Years* (Albany: State University of New York Press, 1992), 77–108; and Diane Ravitch, *Left Back: A Century of Battles over School Reform* (New York: Simon & Schuster, 2001), 120–28. In addition to the pressures from those promoting greater "social efficiency," by this time, the American Political Science Association established a committee on instruction the year it was established (1904), which surveyed what "students know about American government before taking college courses in political science." Suitably appalled by the results, it then established a Committee of Five that followed the procedures and form of the Committee of Seven without explicitly acknowledging it. "Report of the Committee of Five of the American Political Science Association on Instruction in American Government in Secondary Schools," *Proceedings of the American Political Science Association* 5 (Baltimore, MD: Waverly Press, 1908), 219–57. In comparison, the economists would not rouse themselves to take up the issue for another decade. See "Report of Committee on Economics in Secondary Schools," *American Economic Review* 8, no. 1, supplement, Papers and Proceedings of the Thirtieth Annual Meeting of the American Economic Association (March 1918): 308–12. Dunn, comp., *Social Studies in Secondary Education*.

28. Murry R. Nelson, ed., *The Social Studies in Secondary Education: A Reprint of the Seminal 1916 Report with Annotation and Commentary* (Bloomington, IN: ERIC Clearinghouse for Social Studies/Social Science Education, 1994), 44 (p. 36 in the original report).

29. Dunn, comp., *Social Studies in Secondary Education*, 41–43.

30. Nathaniel W. Stephenson, "The Place of History in the Curriculum," in *AHA Annual Report, 1913*, 103.

31. Florence Elizabeth Stryker to Waldo Leland, March 5, 1915, box 31, file "Secretary File, Correspondence—1915 S (first of 2)," AHA Papers. The AHA provided space at its Berkeley meeting in 1915 for a discussion by the California History Teachers' Association on "the teaching of history in schools," which resulted in a thirty-four-page pamphlet on the issue. "Historical News," *AHR* 20 (July 1915): 901; and "Historical News," *AHR* 21 (April 1916): 640.

32. Evarts B. Greene, "Report of the Secretary of the Council," in *AHA Annual Report, 1916*, 76.

33. Box 472 "American Historical Association Miscellany," file "Abstracts of Papers c. 1916," AHA Papers.

34. Dawson manuscript, NCSS Records.

35. David Jenness, *Making Sense of Social Studies* (New York: Macmillan, 1990), 84.

36. William Jasper Kerr, "Education and the World War," *National Education Association of the United States Addresses and Proceedings, 1917* (Washington, DC: Secretary's Office, 1917), 112 and 115–19. This point is made more directly in Edgar Dawson, "History and the Social Studies," *Educational Review* 68 (September 1924): 68.

37. Evarts B. Greene, "The Problems of Historical Scholarship and Teaching as Affected by the War," *National Education Association of the United States Addresses and Proceedings, 1918* (Washington, DC: Secretary's Office, 1918), 200.

38. See the announcement in "Historical News," *AHR* 24 (October 1918): 145; but more generally, see Carol S. Gruber, *Mars and Minerva: World War I and the Uses of the Higher Learning in America* (Baton Rouge: Louisiana State University Press, 1975), 124–26 and 130–36.

39. See, for instance, the discussion of "the adjustment of history teaching to the new conditions caused by the war" in "Historical News," *AHR* 23 (October 1917): 228. W. C. Reavis, "After-the-War Reorganization of History in the Elementary School," *Proceedings of the Mississippi Valley Historical Association* 10 (Cedar Rapids, Iowa: Torch Press, 1919), 144–53; J. H. R. Moore, "Effect of the War on High School Instruction," *Proceedings of the Mississippi Valley Historical Association* 10 (1919), 154–60; Herriott C. Palmer, "How the War Should Affect the Teaching of History," *Proceedings of the Mississippi Valley Historical Association* 11 (Cedar Rapids, Iowa: Torch Press, 1920), 304–11.

40. Based on a survey of 1,032 accredited schools in the North Central Association (which stretched from Ohio to Arizona) that was initiated just before American involvement in the war. Calvin O. Davis, *Accredited Secondary Schools of the North Central Association*, US Bureau of Education Bulletin 1919, no. 45 (Washington, DC: Government Printing Office, 1920), 95 (table 93).

41. Peter Novick, *That Noble Dream: The "Objectivity Question" and the American Historical Profession* (New York: Cambridge University Press, 1988), 127–29; and Joseph Schafer et al., "Report of the Committee on History and Education for Citizenship," *Historical Outlook* 12 (March 1921): 87–93.

42. Palmer, "How the War Should Affect the Teaching of History," 307. A word seems to be missing in the quote, but the text is reproduced as published.

43. R. B. Way, "Reconstructed Courses in History in the Colleges," *MVHA Proceedings*, 1919–1920, 171. See also William T. Laprade, "Concerning the Teaching of History," *Educational Review* 59 (March 1920): 219–25.

44. Arthur M. Schlesinger, "The History Situation in Colleges and Universities, 1919–20," *Historical Outlook* 11 (March 1920): 103. His report is based on survey responses from twenty-one colleges and universities.

45. Albert E. McKinley, "A Decade of History Teaching," *Historical Outlook* 10 (December 1919): 497.

46. Walter H. Cushing, "Associations of History Teachers," *Historical Outlook* 10 (December 1919): 500.

47. Based on tabulations of authors in *Historical Outlook* and speakers listed in the annual *Proceedings* of the New England History Teachers' Assocation and Association of History Teachers of the Middle States and Maryland.

48. "Historical News," *AHR* 24 (October 1918): 145.

49. For instance, Henry Johnson, who served on the committee, completely passes it over in his survey of curricular developments in *Teaching of History in Elementary and Secondary Schools with Application to Allied Studies* ([New York: Macmillan, 1940], 59–73), while David Jenness, in his more comprehensive survey of AHA committees on teaching, passes it off in less than a paragraph and only refers to it as the "Schafer committee" (*Making Sense of Social Studies*, 98).

50. Andrew C. McLaughlin, the chair of the Committee of Seven served in an advisory capacity, but readily conceded that he was "ignorant" and "not entitled to an expert opinion" on the issues before the committee and asked to be excused. McLaughlin to Schafer, May 19, 1919, box 51, file "H C [Committee for Hist. and Ed. in the Schools]," series 934, Wisconsin Historical Society Papers, Wisconsin Historical Society, Madison, WI (hereafter cited as WHS Papers).

51. The ample correspondence from this committee fills boxes 766 and 767 of the AHA Papers.

52. Memo from Joseph Schafer to AHA Council, Report of the Committee on History and Education for Citizenship in the Schools, n.d. [ca. November

1920], box 458, file "Committee Reports," AHA Papers. This language recurred in the published report, Schafer et al., "Report of the Committee on History and Education for Citizenship," 92.

53. "Minutes of the Meeting of the Executive Council on December 29, 1920," in *AHA Annual Report, 1920*, 106. Correspondence in Schafer's papers shows a general descent into chaos as the report approached publication, as various members of the committee pressed for additions and changes. See exchange with Guy Stanton Ford, February 1921, box 50, file "H-C [Committee for Hist. and Ed. in the Schools]," series 934, WHS Papers.

54. Harold Rugg, "On Reconstructing the Social Studies," *Historical Outlook* 12 (October 1921): 251.

55. A. M. Schlesinger to Bassett, December 18, 1922. box 36, file 36/4, John Spencer Bassett Papers, Manuscript Division, Library of Congress, Washington, DC (hereafter cited as Bassett Papers).

56. C. H. Haskins to Waldo G. Leland, February 24, 1921, box 35, file 35/1, Bassett Papers.

57. At its founding, the organization was named the National Council for Teachers of the Social Studies; it dropped "Teachers of" from the title after the first year, reflecting its engagement with a wider constituency. Ironically, this developed in part out of a failed effort by the AHA leadership to promote a "federation of history teachers and associations." Waldo G. Leland to Daniel C. Knowlton, May 9 and May 13, 1919, box 767, file "Committee on History and Education for Citizenship in the Schools: Correspondence 1919," AHA Papers; and Knowlton to A. E. McKinley, June 2, 1919, ibid. The proposal seemed to fall apart over the financial relationship between the organizations. Knowlton and McKinley played key roles in the establishment of the National Council.

58. "Minutes of the Meeting of the Executive Council, December 27, 1921," in *AHA Annual Report, 1921*, 86–87.

59. Edgar Dawson, "National Council for the Social Studies," *AHR* 27 (April 1922): 491–92.

60. Dawson manuscript, pp. 8 and 4 in the addendum, NCSS Records. This finding was based on a survey he had conducted for the US Bureau of Education, published in Edgar Dawson, *Preparation of Teachers of the Social Studies for the Secondary Schools* (Washington, DC: Government Printing Office, 1922).

61. Dawson manuscript, NCSS Records.

62. Minutes of the Executive Council, December 28, 1922, in *AHA Annual Report, 1922*, 84–85.

63. These are discussed in considerable detail in Bessie Louise Pierce, *Public Opinion and the Teaching of History in the United States* (New York: Alfred A. Knopf, 1926), 206–98.

64. *AHA Annual Report, 1923*, 39–40.

65. J. Montgomery Gambrill to Bassett, January 25, 1924, box 36, file 36/6,

Bassett Papers. See also related correspondence, J. Montgomery Gambrill to John Spencer Bassett, March 7, 1924, box 61, AHA Papers; and John Spencer Bassett to William Lingelbach, January 5, 1924, box 36, file 36/6, Bassett Papers.

66. See the minutes of the AHA Council meeting, December 28, 1922, and the report from the Joint Commission published in the *AHA Annual Report, 1922*, 85–90.

67. Bessie L. Pierce, "A Survey of Methods Courses in History," *Historical Outlook* 12, no. 9 (December 1923): 315–18. The survey was conducted of twenty-three "larger universities and colleges"—seemingly to departments with more than five history faculty on staff—and received responses from all departments surveyed.

68. Edgar Dawson, "The Historical Inquiry," *Historical Outlook* 15 (June 1924): 239.

69. "Dr. Edgar Dawson, Hunter Professor [obituary]," *New York Times*, May 1, 1946, 25.

70. Edgar Dawson, "Number Questionnaires Received from High School History Departments in the Respective States to December 10 [1923]," box 34, folder 6, Bassett Papers.

71. Dawson manuscript, addendum, p. 5, NCSS Records.

72. "Historical News," *AHR* 29 (July 1924): 823.

73. Though as Dawson himself noted, the social studies still lacked sufficient coherence at this time to constitute a substantial alternative to the dominance of history in the schools. Dawson, "History and the Social Studies," 69–72.

74. Harry Charles McKown, *The Trend of College Entrance Requirements, 1913–22*, US Bureau of Education Bulletin 1924, no. 35 (Washington, DC: Government Printing Office, 1925), 71 (table 33). Despite the dip, 185 of the 195 institutions that detailed acceptable subjects listed American history, 174 accepted ancient history, and 144 accepted medieval-modern history (72). They also reported New England as slightly more likely to require social sciences (137–38).

Chapter Seven

1. Solon J. Buck, "Proposed Use of the Increased Endowment of the American Historical Association," February 1926, box 15, file "Leland 1910–26," American Historical Association Papers, Manuscript Division, Library of Congress, Washington, DC (hereafter cited as AHA Papers). Note that there is a measure of irony in this recommendation from Buck, since he straddled a growing fissure in the historical enterprise with professional roles as both a professor at the University of Minnesota and superintendent of the Minnesota Historical Society, and in the 1930s he led the archival profession out of the AHA.

2. Dana C. Munro, "Proposed Program for Research and Publication," in

Annual Report of the American Historical Association for the Year 1926 (Washington, DC: Government Printing Office, 1930), 97 (hereafter cited as *AHA Annual Report*).

3. *The Writing of History*, ed. John Spencer Bassett (New York: Charles Scribner's Sons, 1926).

4. "The Meeting of the American Historical Association at Rochester, New York," in *AHA Annual Report, 1926*, 33. Along with Jernegan, the members of the full committee included Dana C. Munro (Princeton Univ.), Carlton J. H. Hayes (Columbia Univ.), Arthur M. Schlesinger (Harvard Univ.), and William K. Boyd (Duke Univ.).

5. "Questionnaire for Doctors of Philosophy," box 38, file 5, John Spencer Bassett Papers, Manuscript Division, Library of Congress, Washington, DC (hereafter cited as Bassett Papers). This survey was sent in spring 1926.

6. Marcus Jernegan, "Productivity of Doctors of Philosophy in History," *American Historical Review* 33 (October 1927): 7–8, http://www.historians.org/projects/cge/Related/Jernegan1927.htm (hereafter cited as *AHR*).

7. Ibid., 21–22.

8. Jameson to Jernegan, December 22, 1926, box 99, file "Jernegan, M. W.," J. Franklin Jameson Papers, Manuscript Division, Library of Congress, Washington, DC (hereafter cited as Jameson Papers).

9. J. Franklin Jameson, "The Meeting of the American Historical Association at Rochester," *AHR* 32 (April 1927): 433–34.

10. "Says Ph.D. Men Lag in Study of History," *New York Times*, October 10, 1926, 13; and "Finds Ph.D.'s Avoid History Research: Association Survey Say Scholars Turn to Teaching Because Other Does Not Pay," *New York Times*, December 28, 1926, 12.

11. "Historical News," *AHR* 33 (January 1928): 462.

12. See, for instance, the follow-up study on the productivity of history PhDs published fifteen years later in section VI of William B. Hesseltine and Louis Kaplan, "Doctors of Philosophy of History: A Statistical Study," *AHR* 47 (July 1942): 790–800.

13. See Jernegan, "Productivity of Doctors of Philosophy in History"; Hesseltine and Kaplan, "Doctors of Philosophy in History"; and Theodore S. Hamerow, *Reflections on History and Historians* (Madison: University of Wisconsin Press, 1987), 57–61.

14. Hesseltine and Kaplan, "Doctors of Philosophy of History," 775 and 778–79.

15. *List of Doctoral Dissertations in History Now in Progress at the Chief American Universities* (J. F. Jameson, 1901–1904; and Washington, DC: Dept. of Historical Research, Carnegie Institution of Washington, 1905–1936).

16. From the 1920s these efforts could be quite blunt, as in a note from Her-

bert E. Bolton (UC, Berkeley) to Guy Stanton Ford, which notes that he has "several men going out this year, with Ph.D.'s. . . . I would like to see one of our men in your department. We could send you a man for either European or American History." Bolton to Ford, April 2, 1923, box 13, file B F752 #88, Guy Stanton Ford Papers, University of Minnesota Archives, Minneapolis, Minnesota (hereafter cited as Ford Papers).

17. Exchange between Joseph C. Schafer and Frederick Paxson, January 1933, box 96, file "PD-PI," series 934, Wisconsin Historical Society Papers, Wisconsin Historical Society, Madison, WI (hereafter cited as WHS Papers).

18. D. A. Robertson, ed., *American Universities and Colleges* (Washington, DC: American Council on Education, 1928); and Clarence Stephen Marsh, ed., *American Universities and Colleges*, 4th ed. (1928; Washington, DC: American Council on Education, 1940).

19. A description of the instructor's workload at Harvard, for instance, consisted of tutorial work for up to forty undergraduates and lectures "on the subjects, approved by the Department, in which they are most interested." William S. Ferguson to Robert P. Blake, March 20, 1920, box UA V 454.8 "History Department: Correspondence and Papers (Ferguson) c. 1915–c. 1920 (box 3 of 21)," file "Babcock to Burbank," Harvard History Department Records, Harvard University Archives, Boston, MA (hereafter Harvard History Department Records).

20. The average history department at a member institution in the American Association of Universities in 1928 had 10.7 faculty. The average rose to 15.6 members of the department by 1948.

21. Edward S. Evenden, Guy C. Gamble, and Harold G. Blue, *National Survey of the Education of Teachers*, vol. II, *Teacher Personnel in the United States* (Washington, DC: Bureau of Education, 1933), 194.

22. Based on a tabulation of award recipients from a brochure on the grants conferred in 1926, 1927, and 1928 by the American Council of Learned Societies (up to $300) and a letter from Guy Stanton Ford to Edwin C. Armstrong, which reports on the twenty-one grant recipients, twelve of which were on historical topics, including faculty at the University of Chicago (4), Princeton (1), and Yale (1). Ford to Armstrong, May 10, 1926, box 1, file B F752 #2, Ford Papers.

23. Evenden, Gamble, and Blue, *Teacher Personnel*, 197 (table 39).

24. See Earle W. Dow, *Principles of a Note-System for Historical Studies* (New York: Century, 1924). The growing use of departmental secretaries to type letters of inquiry becomes more evident in the correspondence with the Wisconsin Historical Society in this period. Previously, references to secretarial assistance had largely been in terms of privately hired assistance. Herman J. Deutsch asks permission to bring a "portable photostat machine" with him on his research, even though it is "about four feet high, about eighteen inches square."

In reply, Joseph Schafer agrees to accommodate the request. Deutsch to Schafer, August 7, 1935, box 86, file "DD-DI," WHS Papers; Schafer to Deutsch, August 12, 1935, ibid.

25. Jernegan, "Productivity of Doctors of Philosophy in History," 4.

26. Among the new titles, *Speculum* for medieval historians began publishing in 1926, the *Journal of Modern History* in 1929, *New England Quarterly* in 1928, the *Pacific Historical Review* and *Church History* in 1932, the *Journal of Southern History* in 1935, the *Journal of Military History* in 1937, and the *Journal of the History of Ideas* in 1940. Data drawn from the Ulrich's Periodicals Directory (http://www.ulrichsweb.com) as tabulated on February 18, 2009. Tabulation limited to Refereed Academic/Scholarly journals published in the United States between 1925 and 1940.

27. Quote from J. Franklin Jameson to Joseph Schafer, April 2, 1925 (concerning establishment of the journal *Agricultural History*), box 126, file "Schafer, Jos.," Jameson Papers.

28. Jameson's successor on the *Review*, Robert Livingston Schuyler, recommended a specialized journal to every author whose article was rejected by the *AHR* in correspondence for period from 1936 to 1941. Suggestions for alternate publications included *Social Education*, the *Journal of Negro History*, the *Journal of Southern History*, and the *Journal of Modern History*. Editorial correspondence in boxes 329 to 334, AHA Papers.

29. See, for instance, The Editors, "History and Historians at Chicago," *AHR* 44 (April 1939): 481–507. The reports were discontinued after 1943.

30. "Report of the Committee on Policy," in *AHA Annual Report, 1929*, 91. The authors of the report observe that "the money scheduled to be paid plays little or no part in determining the purpose of writers to contribute or to have an offering accepted."

31. These terms are laid out in a variety of correspondence between the *Review* editor in the late 1930s and a variety of peer reviewers, e.g., Robert L. Schuyler to Crane Brinton, November 24, 1937; Eleanor D. Smith to Milton R. Hunter, April 8, 1937; and Robert L. Schuyler to M. M. Quaife, January 27, 1938, box 334, file "A.H. Review—ED Corres. 'H' 1936–41," AHA Papers. Notably, the practice of double-blind peer review now in practice at the *AHR* had not begun by the end of this period, as articles were still sent to reviewers with a personal description of the authors.

32. Bernadotte Schmitt to Conyers Read, April 26, 1933, box 85, file "*Journal of Modern History*, c. 1932–38," AHA Papers.

33. The balance of the correspondence in the "*Journal of Modern History*, c. 1932–1938" in box 85, AHA Papers, largely involves articles sent to Conyers Read for scholarly review.

34. "Historical News: Final Report of the Committee of Ten on Reorganization and Policy, December 29, 1939," *AHR* 46 (October 1940): 246.

35. The Editors, "Educating Clio," *AHR* 45 (April 1940): 531.

36. Data from Alexander J. Field, "Books published, by subject: 1880–1999," in *Historical Statistics of the United States, Earliest Times to the Present: Millennial Edition*, ed. Susan B. Carter et al. (New York: Cambridge University Press, 2006), 225–52 (table Dg); and John Tebbel, *History of Book Publishing in the United States: The Golden Age between Two Wars, 1920–1940* (New York: R. R. Bowker, 1978), 684–85. For wider context on the relation between academic and popular writing in this period, see Ian Tyrrell, "Searching for the General Reader," in *Historians in Public: The Practice of American History, 1890–1970* (Chicago: University of Chicago Press, 2005), 45–61.

37. This project was underwritten by a $25,000 grant from the Carnegie Corporation. Munro, "Proposed Program for Research and Publication," 99–100; and "Historical News," *AHR* 32 (January 1927): 380.

38. E. P. Cheyney, "Report of the Carnegie Revolving Publication Fund," in *AHA Annual Report, 1930*, 66–67.

39. The *Pennsylvania Magazine of History and Biography* and the *Wisconsin Magazine of History*, for instance, had barely a handful of reviews in each *volume* in 1925 but included twenty pages of reviews or more in each issue by 1940.

40. Robert L. Schuyler to J. H. Hexter, February 27, 1941, box 334, file "*A. H. Review*—ED. CORRES. 'H' 1936–41 (1 of 2)," AHA Papers.

41. Dexter Perkins to Council, May 18, 1928. See also replies from Verner Crane (May 13, 1930), E. P. Cheyney (May 20, 1930), Worthington Ford (June 1, 1928), and Samuel Eliot Morison (June 1, 1928). Box 70 "Secretary File (Ex.) Corres.; Reports; Etc. 1925–32," file [no label], AHA Papers.

42. Samuel Eliot Morison to Dexter Perkins, June 1, 1928, box 70 "Secretary File (Ex.) Corres.; Reports; Etc. 1925–32," file [no label], AHA Papers.

43. Carlton Russell Fish to Perkins, May 21, 1928, box 70 "Secretary File (Ex.) Corres.; Reports; Etc. 1925–32," file [no label], AHA Papers.

44. Stringfellow Barr, *Cause Celebre or Book Reviewers Reviewed* (Berkeley, CA: Samual T. Farquhar, 1937), 12, 14. This monograph was started as a presentation at the 1935 AHA meeting.

45. Francis Hackett, "On Turning Historian," *Bookman* 69 (August 1929): 575–87 (quote from p. 576); and Wilbur C. Abbott, "New Methods of Writing History: A Criticism," *Current History* 31 (October 1929): 93–98.

46. Allen Sinclair Will, "Our Historians Cut Some Capers: Four Volumes of a New 'Humanized' History of American Life," *New York Times*, February 19, 1928, Book Review 1, 31. The value of the New History approach in this series was rather hotly debated at an AHA session in 1936 (after the final volume had appeared). The papers are recorded in William E. Lingelbach, *Approaches to American Social History* (New York: Appleton Century, 1937). The twelve volumes in the series included Thomas Wertenbaker's *The First Americans* (1927), Allan Nevins's *The Emergence of Modern America* (1927), H. I. Priestley's *The*

Coming of the White Man (1929), Schlesinger's *The Rise of the City* (1933), Carl Russell Fish's *The Irrepressible Conflict* (1934), and Ida M. Tarbell's *The Nationalizing of Business* (1935).

47. Arthur M. Schlesinger, "The History Situation in Colleges and Universities, 1919–20," *Historical Outlook* 11 (March 1920): 223–24.

48. Eugene N. Anderson, "A New Graduate Program in History," *Social Education* 3 (May 1939): 326. Despite the name and date, the program actually started accepting graduate students to the doctoral program around 1932 and conferred the first doctorate in 1936.

49. Harry Elmer Barnes, *History of Historical Writing* (New York: Dover, 1963); Michael Kraus, *History of American History* (New York: Farrar and Rinehart, 1937); William Thomas Hutchinson, ed., *Marcus W. Jernegan Essays in American Historiography* (Chicago: University of Chicago Press, 1937); Allen Johnson, *Historian and Historical Evidence* (New York: Charles Scribner's Sons, 1926); Homer Carey Hockett, *Introduction to Research in American History* (New York: Macmillan, 1931); and Allan Nevins, *The Gateway to History* (New York: D. C. Heath, 1938).

50. In his *Outline of Historical Method* (Lincoln, NE: J. H. Miller, 1899) Fred Morrow Fling did not mention note-taking (though he does discuss the process of developing a bibliography), and in his subsequent *Writing of History: An Introduction to Historical Method* (New Haven, CT: Yale University Press, 1920) he addresses note-taking in just a page and a half. In comparison, Hockett details the process and the characteristics of good notes in ten pages (*Introduction to Research*, 46–55).

51. In Fling's *Outline of Historical Method* the references to libraries are all either distant institutions or the personal libraries "of every student and teacher of history" (69). In contrast, Hockett spends dozens of pages describing how to negotiate library catalogues and bibliographies (*Introduction to Research*, 7–46).

52. Harry Elmer Barnes, "New History," *American Mercury* 5 (May 1925): 68–76; Barnes, *The New History and Social Studies* (New York: Century, 1925); Barnes, "Essentials of the New History," *Historical Outlook* 18 (May 1927): 201–10; Nevins, *Gateway*, 7.

53. An impression of Barnes's general relationship to other members of the discipline was explored in "Historians and the Truth," *Nation*, May 21, 1924, 576–77. He appeared in a number of discussions about potential slots on the AHA's Council and committees, but typically as a negative point of reference (e.g., Joseph Schafer offered his name as someone who could represent a general knowledge of social history, but then averred "though perhaps not altogether like him!"). Joseph Schafer to Waldo G. Leland, October 6, 1925, box 15, file "Leland 1910–26 (3 of 3)," AHA Papers.

54. Kraus, *History of American History*, 238, 356, 411; Fling, *History of Historical Writing*, 204.

55. Arthur Meier Schlesinger et al., *Historical Scholarship in America: Needs and Opportunities* (New York: Ray Long and Richard Smith, 1932), v. The common conference agendas are published on pages 133–37. The entire report is also available online at http://www.historians.org/pubs/archives/HistoricalScholar shipAmerica1932/Findings.htm.

56. Schlesinger et al., *Historical Scholarship in America*, 35.

57. By 1935, for instance, the Committee on Americana for College Libraries was comprised entirely of staff at libraries, while the committees on a bibliography of American travel and historical manuscripts only had one academic historian left on each committee. "Committees for 1936," in *AHA Annual Report, 1935*, 191–92.

58. Dexter Perkins to William Lingelbach, November 19, 1932, box 70 "Secretary File (Ex.) Corres.; Reports; Etc. 1925–32," file "1932," AHA Papers.

59. Memo from Conyers Read to Members of the AHA Executive Committee, March 25, 1937, box 86, file "1933–41," AHA Papers. Read states that this policy was prepared by Charles Beard.

60. Read's appointment and difficulties in his management style are summarized in David D. Van Tassel, "History of the American Historical Association," ([unpublished manuscript, AHA, Washington, DC, 1980], 387–89), and amply evident in the AHA correspondence during his tenure.

61. Detailed in Conyers Read, Memo to Members of the Executive Committee, March 25, 1937, box 86, file "1933–41," AHA Papers. See, more generally, Tyrrell, *Historians in Public*, 45–56.

62. See, for instance, the file "Chattanooga Meeting (Programme)," which despite its label is actually comprised largely of correspondence from members, such as Angie Debo (dated October 1, 1936), resigning for financial reasons, and the file "International Committee of Historical Sciences," which includes a letter from John Howes (October 17, 1936, on the letterhead of Taft Junior College) who observes that "I feel that as a secondary school instructor I am hardly justified in maintaining my membership in the national association." Both files are in box 103 of the AHA Papers.

63. Although the association stopped surveying members until recently, it appears that academics did not comprise more than a majority of the membership until sometime after World War II. Robert H. Knapp noted that staff at the organization reported that academics still comprised just over 50 percent as late as the late 1950s. Knapp, *The Origins of American Humanistic Scholars* (Englewood Cliffs, NJ: Prentice Hall, 1964), 156. More recent studies by the AHA show that around two-thirds of their members are now affiliated with a four-year college or university. Robert B. Townsend, "A Quick Checkup on AHA Mem-

bership," *AHA Today*, June 2, 2008, http://blog.historians.org/news/530/a-quick-checkup-on-aha-membership.

Chapter Eight

1. Arthur Meier Schlesinger, "History," in *Research in the Social Sciences: Its Fundamental Methods and Objectives*, ed. Wilson Gee (New York: Macmillan, 1929), 223 and 225.

2. Jameson to Worthington Ford, May 10, 1928, box 48, file 52 "American Historical Association, 1928–," J. Franklin Jameson Papers, Manuscript Division, Library of Congress, Washington, DC (hereafter cited as Jameson Papers); and Jameson to Ford, December 10, 1928, ibid.

3. Schlesinger to Solon J. Buck, May 16, 1930, HUG 4769.305 box 3 "From Sept. 1, 1925 to Oct. 1, 1928," file "Corresp. 2/30–9/30 B," Schlesinger Papers, Harvard University Archives, Cambridge, MA (hereafter cited as Schlesinger Papers).

4. J. Franklin Jameson to Dana Munro, November 9, 1927, HUG 4769.305 box 3 "From September 1, 1925 to October 1, 1928," file "Corresp. 6/27–10/28 H, I, J," Schlesinger Papers.

5. Payson J. Treat to Dexter Perkins, June 12, 1928, box 70, unmarked file, American Historical Association Papers, Manuscript Division, Library of Congress, Washington, DC (hereafter cited as AHA Papers). Perkins to Council [draft letter], May 17, 1928, ibid. He observed that such projects should not be published in the annual report where they will be forced "into the hands of persons who could not use them." He noted particularly the reports of the Historical Manuscripts Commission, "which, in my case, have been of no value whatever in my work."

6. J. Franklin Jameson to Arthur Schlesinger, April 1, 1931, box 51, file 68 "AHA Planning Committee," Jameson Papers.

7. J. Franklin Jameson to Arthur Schlesinger, April 12, 1931, box 51, file 68 "AHA Planning Committee," Jameson Papers.

8. American Historical Association, *Historical Scholarship in America: Needs and Opportunities* (New York: Ray Long and Richard R. Smith, 1932), 20–24.

9. AHA, *Historical Scholarship in America*, 16–24, 49–50, 60–65, 78–80, 97–102, and 115–19 (quote from page 97).

10. Joseph Schafer to Professor A. C. Cole, October 26, 1925, box 2 "MSS 746," file "Conference of Historical Societies, 1925–Feb 1927," Schafer Papers, Wisconsin Historical Society, Madison, WI (hereafter cited as Schafer Papers); and Schafer to Solon Buck, Nov. 5, 1925, ibid.

11. Nunns and Blume correspondence shows the further changes effected by the development of microfilm technology and the ability to exchange that less expensive form of media. Despite the emergence of microfilm technology, Schambaugh and Schafer were still talking about Photostat exchanges as late as 1938.

12. Joint Committee on Materials for Research, Circular Number I (typescript copy), December 1930, box 83, file "AC–AG," series 934, Wisconsin Historical Society Papers, Wisconsin Historical Society, Madison, WI (hereafter cited as WHS Papers).

13. Lester K. Born,. "History of Microform Activity," *Library Trends* 8 (January 1960): 348–58.

14. See letters and materials in box 83, file "AA [Applications for Jobs]," WHS Papers, which covers the period of the early 1930s.

15. "Proceedings of the Twenty-Fourth Annual Session of the Conference of Historical Societies, December 31, 1928," in *Annual Report of the American Historical Association for the Year 1929* (Washington, DC: Government Printing Office, 1930), 122 (hereafter cited as *AHA Annual Report*).

16. Public Archives Commission, *The Preservation of Local Archives: A Guide for Public Officials* (Washington, DC: AHA, 1932).

17. *AHA Annual Report, 1935*, 48.

18. Circular seeking members of the MVHA (June 20, 1930) aimed specifically at "history teachers," box 66, file "MV," WHS Papers.

19. Conyers Read to Joseph Schafer, April 17, 1934, box 83, file "AH–AI," WHS Papers. Read expresses regret that Schafer's research work while at the Wisconsin Historical Society was not included in a listing, but notes that his method for collecting such information was to send a circular to chairs of the "more important colleges and universities, as well as directors of all the research foundations."

20. Margaret Cross Norton, *Norton on Archives: The Writings of Margaret Cross Norton on Archival & Records Management* (Chicago: Society of American Archivists, 1975), 8. This statement was originally disseminated through the *Bulletin of the American Library Association*. For assessments of the significance of this statement, see Ernst Posner, *American State Archives* (Chicago: University of Chicago Press, 1964), 25; and William F. Birdsall, "The Two Sides of the Desk: The Archivist and the Historian, 1909–1935," *American Archivist* 38 (April 1975): 166–67.

21. Posner, *American State Archives*, 25.

22. I draw this from the general correspondence in the WHS papers with the heads of the other societies, as well as Posner, *American State Archives*.

23. Waldo G. Leland to Avery O. Craven, August 26, 1936, box B-4, file "AHA 1936," American Council of Learned Societies Papers, Manuscript Division, Library of Congress, Washington, DC (hereafter cited as ACLS Papers).

In a letter to Craven a week earlier, he had also cited his role as president of the MVHA and identification "with the historical interests of the Middle West," and his work as editor of the AHA's Bibliography of American Travel. Leland to Craven, August 22, 1936, ibid.

24. "Report of the Special Committee to the Executive Council" (October 15, 1935), in *AHA Annual Report, 1935*, 176.

25. Donald R. McCoy, *National Archives: America's Ministry of Documents, 1934–1968* (Chapel Hill: University of North Carolina Press, 1978), 92–96.

26. Margaret C. Norton to Solon Buck, October 25, 1935, box 7, file "Conference of Archivists," Buck Papers, Manuscript Division, Library of Congress, Washington, DC (hereafter cited as Buck Papers).

27. Solon Buck reports on plans to call a conference of archivists in connection with the dedication of the National Archives building, with the "hope to complete the organization of a 'Society of American Archivists.'" Buck to Joseph Schafer, May 1, 1936, box 111, file "M-S-M-Z," WHS Papers.

28. Memo "Report of the Committee of Ten Appointed to Make Plans for an Organization of American Archivists," December 29, 1936, box 20, file "Society of American Archivists (1936–38)," Buck Papers.

29. "Minutes of the Organization Meeting, December 29, 1936," *Society of American Archivists Proceedings 1936/1937* (Urbana, IL: Society of American Archivists, 1937), 12–13. The SAA's formation is summarized in "Historical News," *American Historical Review* 42 (April 1937): 610–30 (hereafter cited as *AHR*).

30. See Lester J. Cappon, "The Archival Profession and the Society of American Archivists," in *Lester J. Cappon and the Relationship of History, Archives, and Scholarship in the Golden Age of Archival Theory*, ed. Richard J. Cox (Chicago: Society of American Archivists, 2004), 106–7.

31. Victor Hugo Paltsits, "Pioneering for a Science of Archives in the United States," *Society of American Archivists Proceedings, 1936/1937*, 42–43.

32. Samuel Flagg Bemis, "The Training of Archivists in the United States," *American Archivist* 2 (July 1939): 158–59.

33. Minutes of the Committee on the Publication of Archival Material, Society of American Archivists, October 12, 1939, box 20, file "Society of American Archivists (1939–40)," Buck Papers.

34. Posner, *American State Archives*; and Walter Muir Whitehill, *Independent Historical Societies: An Enquiry into Their Research and Publication Functions and Their Financial Future* (Boston: Boston Athenaeum, 1962).

35. Julian P. Boyd, "State and Local Historical Societies in the United States," *AHR* 40 (October 1934): 34. In a letter from Julian Boyd to Joseph Schafer, he describes plans (and apparently still thought it possible) to make the conference a "more effective body." Boyd to Schafer, April 24, 1935, box 85, file "CC–CH," WHS Papers.

36. Ian Tyrrell, *Historians in Public: The Practice of American History, 1890–1970* (Chicago: University of Chicago Press, 2005), 220–21.

37. "The Conference of Historical Societies: Report for 1934," in *AHA Annual Report, 1935*, 217.

38. "The Conference of Historical Societies: Report for 1935," in *AHA Annual Report, 1935*, 218.

39. Boyd, "State and Local Historical Societies in the United States," 36. Perhaps not coincidentally, this was the last article on issues related to the historical societies to appear in the *AHR* until the 1980s.

40. C. C. Crittenden to "All Who Are Interested in the Formation of an Active Organization of American Historical Societies and Agencies," December 12, 1939, box 7, file "Conference of Historical Societies," Buck Papers.

41. "Report of the Conference of State and Local Historical Societies, December 28, 1939," in *AHA Annual Report, 1939*, 103–4.

42. Christopher Crittenden to Stanley Pargellis, September 28, 1942, box 7, file "Conference of Historical Societies," Buck Papers; and "Proceedings of the Policy Committee of the Conference of Historical Societies, June 3, 1940," box PC 188.28, Christopher Crittenden Papers, North Carolina Department of Archives and History.

43. "Report of the Policy Committee of the Conference of State and Local Historical Societies, December 1940," box 7, file "Conference of Historical Societies," Buck Papers.

44. For instance, the Albert J. Beveridge Fund supported document collections on various aspects of American history, the Littleton-Griswold Fund supported the publication of original materials related to American legal history, and a Committee on Americana supported the dissemination of materials to libraries (thanks to a generous grant from Tracy William McGregor, a member of the AHA Board of Trustees). Similarly, the MVHA started publishing documentary collections in the Mississippi Valley thanks to a small endowment left by Clarence Alvord, the first editor of the *MVHR* (indeed, through the Depression years the Alvord Memorial Fund was one of the more productive committees in the organization).

45. C. C. Crittenden to members of the Committee on the Publication of Archival Material, Society of American Archivists, July 10, 1939, box 20, file "Society of American Archivists (1939–40)," Buck Papers.

46. Solon Buck to C. C. Crittenden, July 19, 1939, box 20, file "Society of American Archivists (1939–40)," Buck Papers.

47. "Committee of Ten on Reorganization and Policy: Final Report," in *AHA Annual Report, 1939*, 51.

48. Christopher Crittenden, *Historical Societies in the United States and Canada: A Handbook* (Washington, DC: American Association for State and Local History, 1944).

Chapter Nine

1. John Spencer Bassett to Charles M. Andrews, March 22, 1924, box 36, folder 7, John Spencer Bassett Papers, Manuscript Division, Library of Congress, Washington, DC (hereafter cited as Bassett Papers).

2. Waldo G. Leland to John Spencer Bassett, May 15, 1924, box 15 "Secretary File: Corres., Reports, etc., of Waldo G. Leland," file "Leland 1910–26," American Historical Association Papers, Manuscript Division, Library of Congress, Washington, DC (hereafter cited as AHA Papers).

3. Max Farrand to John Spencer Bassett, May 29, 1925, box 34, file 34/5, Bassett Papers. For a wider perspective on Farrand's views, see Judith Sealander, *Private Wealth and Public Life: Foundation Philanthropy and the Reshaping of American Social Policy from the Progressive Era to the New Deal* (Baltimore: Johns Hopkins University Press, 1997), 31. Like a number of the other most active proponents of an accommodation with the social studies within the AHA (such as Becker, Beard, and Robinson), Farrand later became president of the AHA (in 1940).

4. A. M. Schlesinger to Bassett, August 16, 1924, file 36/9, Bassett Papers.

5. Bassett to C. M. Andrews, September 8, 1924, file 36/9, Bassett Papers.

6. Edgar Dawson to Bassett, November 16, 1924, file 37/2, Bassett Papers. This apparently led to an invitation and meeting with the council and some unstated commitments to proceed with a committee. Dawson to Bassett, November 25, 1924, ibid.; and Bassett to Dawson, November 26, 1924, ibid. Bassett concluded that "I trust that the report of the committee on which you are to serve may give us a definite solution of the matter."

7. Cheyney seems a bit unusual in this context, but Dawson was referring here to his 1923 AHA presidential address, "Law in History," (*American Historical Review* 29 [January 1924]: 231–48 [hereafter cited as *AHR*]), where he argued, "The processes of the minds of men, individually and in groups, are fast being explained by psychological and social laws. Man is simply a part of a law-controlled world."

8. Edgar Dawson, *Teaching the Social Studies* (New York: Macmillan, 1927), x.

9. Bassett to C. M. Andrews, August 22, 1924, file 36/9, Bassett Papers.

10. Bassett to Schlesinger, August 22, 1924, file 36/9, Bassett Papers.

11. Bassett to August C. Krey, January 28, 1925, box 769, file "Developments History and Other Social Studies," AHA Papers.

12. Edgar Dawson to Bassett, January 20, 1925, file 37/4, Bassett Papers.

13. Krey's messages to the council tended to be lengthy. For instance, after sending a lengthy preliminary report to the council, he followed it up with another nine-page letter defending his report. Krey to Bassett, April 11, 1925, box 769, file "Developments History and the Other Social Sciences," AHA Papers.

14. A. C. Krey to the Council of the American Historical Association, November 1925, box 34, folder 6, Bassett Papers, reprinted in slightly abbreviated form in *Annual Report of the American Historical Association for the Year 1925* (Washington, DC: Government Printing Office, 1929), 83–92 (hereafter cited as *AHA Annual Report*).

15. Memo to the Council of the American Historical Association from the Committee on History and Other Social Studies, box 459, file "Cmte Reports Annual Meeting 1926," AHA Papers. An edited version of the report is published in the *AHA Annual Report, 1926*, 107–33. Notably, the committee's rather pointed observations about the potential risks from this sort of study were not included in the published report.

16. Details on the funding and planning of the committee can be found in Bethany Jayne Andreasen, "Reconstructing the Social Order: The American Historical Association Commission on the Social Studies" (PhD diss., Cornell University, 1987); and Truman Beckley Brown, "The American Historical Association and the Schools: A Study of Condescension and Protection in the Twentieth Century" (PhD diss., State University of New York, Buffalo, 1985).

17. "Historical Note," *Proceedings of the National Education Association* 78 (1940): 557 and "Fifth Annual Meeting of the National Council for the Social Studies, *Historical Outlook* 16, no. 4 (April 1925): 135.

18. John Spencer Bassett, "Report of the Secretary for the Council," in *AHA Annual Report, 1925*.

19. Abbie N. Fletcher, "The Salesmanship of a Social Science Department," *Occasional Letter* [of the Southern California Social Science Association] 3, no. 1 (1926): 1–2, 12.

20. Daniel C. Knowlton, *History and the Other Social Studies in Junior and Senior High Schools* (New York: Charles Scribner's Sons, 1926).

21. Frank M. Phillips, *Statistical Summary of Education, 1927–1928*, US Bureau of Education Bulletin 1930, no. 3 (Washington, DC: Government Printing Office, 1930), 15. These findings were confirmed in a closer analysis of schools in the South in Joseph Roemer, *Secondary Schools of the Southern Association*, US Bureau of Education Bulletin 1928, no. 16 (Washington, DC: Government Printing Office, 1928), 62–63 (tables 41 and 42). The survey also provides interesting evidence about perceptions that a disproportionate number of history teachers coached sports teams. While a significant number of the coaches teaching in the schools (15.6 percent) were teaching history, this was actually much smaller than the fields of mathematics (19.9 percent) and science (20.9 percent) (table 55).

22. Edward S. Evenden, Guy C. Gamble, and Harold G. Blue, *National Survey of the Education of Teachers* (Washington, DC: Bureau of Education, 1935), 68–69.

23. "Report of the Committee on History Teaching in the Schools," in *AHA Annual Report, 1925*, 83–92.

24. Julie Koch, "The Social Studies Curriculum in the Junior College," *Social Studies Leaflet* 6, no. 1 (November 1929): 2.

25. This was done as an actual blueprint, prepared in September 1928 by committee staff to guide initial planning efforts and subsequent work. The original can be found in box 769 of the AHA Papers.

26. The often-tortured negotiations about balancing the number of scholars are examined in close detail in Brown, "The American Historical Association and the Schools," 296–307, drawing on information in the Carnegie Foundation's papers.

27. "Report of Progress in the Investigation of the Social Studies in the Schools, Spring 1931," box 769, AHA Papers.

28. Despite his work in history, Beard also served as president of the American Political Science Association in 1926.

29. Charles A. Beard, *A Charter for the Social Sciences in the Schools* (New York: Charles Scribner's Sons, 1932); Commission on the Social Studies, *Conclusions and Recommendations of the Commission* (New York: Charles Scribner's Sons, 1934).

30. Bethany Jayne Andreasen, "Reconstructing the Social Order," 99, 137, 158–72.

31. The best summary of the commission's work can be found in Andreasen, "Reconstructing the Social Order."

32. See, for instance, "Social Study Row Stirred by Report," *New York Times*, May 10, 1934, 23, which reported that a quarter of the commission's sixteen members were refusing to sign on to its "radical" conclusions.

33. Frank W. Ballou, "Statement Concerning the Report of the Commission on the Investigation of History and the Other Social Studies of the American Historical Association," *School and Society* 39, no. 1014 (June 2, 1934): 701–2. This is similar to complaints offered in a series of critical essays published in the *Social Studies* 25, no. 6 (October 1934): 279–94; and Kenneth E. Gell, "Implications of the Report of the Commission on the Social Studies of the American Historical Association," *Proceedings of the National Education Association* 72 (1934): 516.

34. August C. Krey, *A Regional Program for the Social Studies* (New York: Macmillan, 1938).

35. Carl A. Jenssen and Lester B. Herlihy, *Offerings and Registrations in High-School Subjects, 1933–34*, US Bureau of Education Bulletin 1938, no. 6 (Washington, DC: Government Printing Office, 1938), 28 (table 1). In real terms, the report's tabulations of students taking the courses show the massive increase in the numbers of students taking these courses. According to the report, there were 14,915 schools teaching American history to 1,139,860 students; 9,767 schools teaching world history to 557,326 students; 5,660 schools teaching ancient history to 309,591 students; 4,154 schools teaching medieval history to

191,736 students; 1,376 schools teacher modern history to 86,500 students. This compares to just 964 schools with social science studies, with 327,158 students. This shows the relative balance in subjects at this time, and that the subjects were still generally considered in discrete terms at the high school level.

36. Ruth West, the president of the NCSS in 1940, observed that "most social-studies teachers have found the reports of the Commission on the Social Studies of the American Historical Association their most helpful guide in this period of change. The Commission went far toward clarifying problems and giving insight into the methods best adapted to their solution," even though they "felt that the time was not ripe for recommending a 'course of study.'" West, foreword to *The Future of the Social Studies: Proposals for an Experimental Social-Studies Curriculum*, ed. James A. Michener (Cambridge, MA: National Council for the Social Studies, 1939), iii.

37. See "Votes Passed by the Executive Committee," in *AHA Annual Report, 1933*, 3, 12–13, and 18–19; and "Report of the Treasurer," in *AHA Annual Report, 1933*, 96–97.

38. Bessie L. Pierce, the secretary-treasurer of the NCSS at the time, pleaded for a more diplomatic tone with the AHA, "in light of our present financial status," noting that "the depression has made quite an inroad on our membership." Pierce to Edgar Dawson, July 10, 1933, box 329, file "Reference Notes and Typescript History of NCSS by Edgar Dawson—1934–35," National Council for the Social Studies Records, Dolph Briscoe Center for American History (henceforth designated NCSS Records).

39. Edgar Dawson to Bessie L. Pierce, July 14, 1933, box 329, file "Reference Notes," NCSS Records.

40. A memo (dated October 17, 1936) by H. E. Wilson, representing the NCSS in the negotiations, records the discussions at just one meeting descending into "sparring," "considerable impasse," and charges of "unethical behavior," box 266, file "AHA Social Education–Agreements between AHA & NCSS," NCSS Records.

41. "Historical News," *AHR* 41 (April 1936): 594.

42. Jeannette P. Nichols, Morris Wolf, and Arthur C. Bining, eds., *History in the High School and Social Studies in the Elementary School*, Annual Proceedings of Middle States Council for the Social Studies 41 (Philadelphia: Middle States Council for the Social Studies, 1944), 3.

43. When the AHA and NCSS attempted to take the *Social Studies* to a new publishing house and hand more editorial control over to the council, they discovered belatedly that the association lacked full ownership of the magazine (echoing the dispute over the *AHR* in 1915). As a result, the heirs of Alfred E. McKinley took the subscriber list and the name and continued publishing *Social Studies* on their own. *Social Studies* and *Social Education* ultimately merged back together in 1957, published under the former title but by the NCSS.

44. On the differing editorial philosophies of the two journals, see Arthur C. Bining, "Announcement of Change in Editorial Management," *Social Studies* 28, no. 1 (January 1937): 1; and Erling M. Hunt, "Editorial Announcement," *Social Education* 1, no. 1 (January 1937): 1-2.

45. See, for instance, Tyler Kepner, "The Dilemma of the Secondary-School Social-Studies Teacher," *Social Education* 1, no. 2 (February 1937): 81-87; and Conyers Read, "The Dissenting Opinion of Mr. Tyler Kepner," *Social Education* 1, no. 2 (February 1937): 88-93. In a personal letter to Read, the editor of *Social Education* expresses some regret at the "sharpness" of the exchanges and observes that some readers had been objecting to the tone. Erling M. Hunt to Conyers Read, May 5, 1937, box 107, file "Social Education, Correspondence," AHA Papers.

46. Erling P. Hunt to Paul Cram, April 26, 1937, box 266, file "Soc. Ed. Corresp.—1936-1938," NCSS Records.

47. National Education Association, *Proceedings of the National Education Association 1940* (Washington, DC: National Education Association of the United States, 1948), 559-60.

Conclusion

1. The activities and interests of the association can be traced in the annual executive director's reports published in the AHA annual reports. See also William Palmer, *From Gentleman's Club to Professional Body: The Evolution of the History Department in the United States, 1940–1980* (BookSurge, 2008).

2. The society grew from 377 members in 1949 to 2,220 by 1979, with small incremental increases reported in almost every year. Information from annual reports of the secretary in the *American Archivist*. Data for 1979 from "Minutes: Council Meeting, 24 September 1979," *American Archivist* 43, no. 2 (summer 1980): 258.

3. On archival growth, see James M. O'Toole and Richard J. Cox, *Understanding Archives & Manuscripts* (Chicago, IL: Society of American Archivists, 2006), 67-81. For the boom in interest in historical societies, see Clifford Lee Lord, *Clio's Servant: The State Historical Society of Wisconsin, 1846–1954* (Madison: State Historical Society of Wisconsin, 1967), 458-75; and Kevin M Guthrie, *The New-York Historical Society: Lessons from One Nonprofit's Long Struggle for Survival*, 2nd ed. (Houston, TX: Long Tail Press/Rice University Press, 2008), 32-37.

4. Drawn from data from the Survey of Earned Doctorates in Betty D. Maxwell, *Science, Engineering, and Humanities Doctorates in the United States: 1979 Profile* (Washington, DC: National Academy of Sciences, 1980), which found that more than a third of the employed PhDs had jobs outside of academia.

5. See e.g., Albert Somit and Joseph Tanenhaus, *American Political Science: Profile of a Discipline* (New York: Atherton Press, 1964), 99–106; Craig Calhoun and Jonathan VanAntwerpen, "Orthodoxy, Heterodoxy, and Hierarchy: 'Mainstream' Sociology and Its Challengers," in *Sociology in America: A History*, ed. Craig Calhoun (Chicago: University of Chicago Press, 2007); and Stephen P. Turner and Jonathan H. Turner, *The Impossible Science: An Institutional Analysis of American Sociology* (Newbury Park, CA: Sage, 1990), 151–55.

6. One truly puzzling exception to this tendency was the in the rather famous "Lowenheim case"—an accusation by Professor Francis L. Lowenheim (Rice University) that staff at the Franklin Roosevelt Library withheld records to the benefit of a member of the staff. The AHA and OAH established a joint committee to investigate the case without including a single archivist, even though the issue was clearly a matter of professional ethics. Nancy Kegan Smith and Gary M. Stern, "A Historical Review of Access to Records in Presidential Libraries," *Public Historian* 28, no. 3 (summer 2006): 86–87.

7. This is detailed in correspondence between Guy Stanton Ford and Erling Hunt (then secretaries of the AHA and NCSS, respectively). See correspondence in the files "American History, Teaching of" and "American History, Committee on the Teaching of," in box 126, American Historical Association Papers, Manuscript Division, Library of Congress, Washington, DC (hereafter cited as AHA Papers). The precipitating item by Nevins appears in Allan Nevins, "American History for Americans," *New York Times*, May 3, 1942, SM6. This ultimately resulted in the report Edgar B. Wesley, *American History in Schools and Colleges* (New York: Macmillan, 1944), prepared by a leader of the NCSS but ultimately signed on to by the AHA and MVHA.

8. The most notable example is in the report of the program committee chair for the 1969 meeting, who invoked the term seventeen times in a report barely two-and-a-half pages long—an average of more than one use in every two sentences.

9. Robert Weibe's *Search for Order* was particularly significant for the social science fields, as reflected in Thomas L. Haskell, *Emergence of Professional Social Science: The American Social Science Association and the Nineteenth-Century Crisis of Authority* (Baltimore: Johns Hopkins University Press, 2000), 3–4. Robert H. Weibe, *The Search for Order, 1877–1920* (New York: Hill and Wang, 1967), 117–23.

10. Hoff, "Is the Historical Profession an Endangered Species?" Many in the profession shared Hoff's concerns. A committee assessing the future of the AHA in 1972 painted a dire picture for the organization and the profession and fretted over "a decline in historical interest and awareness in the schools and colleges and among the public at large." AHA Review Board, "A Preliminary Report," *AHA Newsletter* 10 (November 1972), http://www.historians.org/pubs/archives/ReviewBoard/ReviewBoard3.cfm.

11. While the objectivity/relativism dispute serves as something of a straight-jacket for his narrative, Peter Novick's account of this period covers the essential details on this subject in *That Noble Dream: The "Objectivity Question" and the American Historical Profession* (New York: Cambridge University Press, 1988), 415–521, particularly when read in parallel with part IV of John Higham's *History: Professional Scholarship in America* (Baltimore: Johns Hopkins University Press, 1989), which was added in 1983. For comparative examples from other disciplines, see Calhoun and Antwerpen, "Orthodoxy, Heterodoxy, and Hierarchy," and David M. Ricci, *Tragedy of Political Science: Politics, Scholarship, and Democracy* (New Haven, CT: Yale University Press, 1984), 291–318.

12. Items about nonteaching careers in the *Newsletter* were limited to occasional short notices and letters until Harriet Warm Schupf, "Alternate Careers for Historians," *AHA Newsletter* 13 (October 1975): 3–5. The program for the 1975 annual meeting included "74. Alternative Careers for A.B.'s and Ph.D.'s in History," *Program of the Ninetieth Annual Meeting* (Washington, DC: American Historical Association, 1976).

13. "New Graduate Program in Public Historical Studies," *AHA Newsletter* 13 (October 1975): 2.

14. John Dichtl and Robert B. Townsend, "A Picture of Public History: Preliminary Results from the 2008 Survey of Public History Professionals," *Perspectives on History* (September 2009): 24–26.

15. Robert Kelley, "Public History: Its Origins, Nature, and Prospects," *Public Historian* 1 (Autumn 1978): 16. This still seems to be the fundamental meaning of the term. A recent AHA task force on public history, comprised of public history specialists, used the same measure. Task Force on Public History, "Public History, Public Historians, and the American Historical Association" (Washington, DC: AHA, 2003), 8, http://www.historians.org/governance/tfph/tfphfinalreport.pdf.

16. Cf. Barbara J. Howe and Emory Kemp, eds., *Public History: An Introduction* (Malabar, FL: Krieger, 1986).

17. See e.g., "First National Symposium on Public History: A Report," *Public Historian* 2 (Autumn 1979): 7–83 (quote from page 57); and the letters gathered in "Reaction to 'The Public Historian,'" (from Robert A. Huttenback, Gary K. Hart, David F. Trask, Knox Mellon, Louis Marchiafava, and Michael G. Schene), *The Public Historian* 1, no. 2 (Winter 1979): 6–7.

18. Examples of some of the better thinking on these issues can be found in Thomas Bender, Philip M. Katz, and Colin Palmer, *The Education of Historians for the Twenty-First Century* (Urbana: University of Illinois Press, 2004); Roy Rosenzweig, *Clio Wired: The Future of the Past in the Digital Age* (New York: Columbia University Press, 2011); and Anthony T. Grafton and Jim Grossman, "Plan C," *Perspectives on History* (November 2011), http://www.historians.org/perspectives/issues/2011/1111/1111pre1.cfm.

19. At the seventy-fifth anniversary meeting of the Society of American Archivists held in Chicago, Illinois, shortly before this book went off to press, a number of current and former presidents of the organization observed with regret the fragmentation of their area of work in very familiar terms. They noted that archivists specializing in business and state and local history separated off during their time as members, leaving an organization seemingly dominated by archivists working at colleges and universities. Comments at "7 x 5 at 75: Presidential Perspectives," August 25, 2011; and the plenary address by current president, Helen Tibbo, August 26, 2011.

20. These complaints can range from agitation about the slow uptake of digital tools, as in Sean Takats, "Adoption of 'New' Media by Historians," *The Quintessence of Ham* (blog), October 28, 2010, http://quintessenceofham.org/2010/10/28/adoption-of-new-media-by-historians/ (last viewed June 12, 2011), to the adoption of new approaches to the subject, such as the recent rise of world history approaches. For the latter, see Patrick Manning, *Navigating World History: Historians Create a Global Past* (New York: Palgrave Macmillan, 2003).

21. The continuing divisions in the discipline are evident in the AHA's recent Task Force on Public History, which found that public historians still feel a "sense of estrangement from, frustration with, even hostility to the organized history profession." Task Force on Public History, "Public History, Public Historians, and the American Historical Association," 5. See also Francis X. Blouin, *Processing the Past: Contesting Authority in History and the Archives* (Oxford: Oxford University Press, 2011), which quite explicitly ties changing professional and historiographical interests to the growing divide between archivists and historians.

Index

Society of American Archivists, 8, 159,
164–66, 182, 197; established, 16–62;
membership demographics, 162
Spencer, Herbert, 17
Stanford University, 137
Stephens, H. Morse, 16, 39, 62
students: college enrollments, 83, 176; high
school enrollment, 61, 172
*Study of History in the Elementary
Schools*, 69

teachers (K–12), history, 1, 5, 7–9, 179; criticisms of, 60; numbers, 172; recognized
in AHA, 58, 81; relation to college faculty, 58, 64; and social studies, 129,
173–77. *See also* social studies
teaching, history: certification requirements, 116–17; at college level, 68–69,
122–23; in elementary schools, 69, 70;
in high schools, 1–2, 31–32; as impediment to research, 16; as professional
identity, 97; professionalization of, 5.
See also American Historical Association (AHA); colleges and universities;
history, as profession; social studies
textbooks, history, criticisms of, 57, 60,
70, 127
Thayer, William Roscoe, 90
Thorpe, Francis, 60
Thwaites, Reuben Gold, 47, 50–52, 54, 101,
102, 104, 108; efforts to organize societies, 48
Trent, William P., 44

Turner, Frederick Jackson, 22, 26, 78, 79,
82, 99, 133
Tyrrell, Ian, 163

US Bureau of Education, 65, 119, 121, 122
US Government Printing Office, 25
US history, as field, 28, 40, 137, 138
University of California, Berkeley, 137
University of Chicago, 137
University of Minnesota, 138, 147
University of North Carolina, 21
University of Pennsylvania, 137; doctoral
program, 23
University of Wisconsin, 137
Upham, Warren, 50

Van Tyne, Claude, 51

Walker, Francis, 14
West, Ruth, 179
Williams, Talcott, 44
Wilson, Woodrow, 15, 59
Winsor, Justin, 29–30
Wisconsin, State Historical Society of, 42,
105; collecting efforts, 41, 104–5; as
model, 38, 50; staff, 102, 158
World War I: and historical societies,
106–7; impact on school reform, 121–23
Writing of History, 134
Writings on American History, 27, 85, 89,
108

Yale University, 21, 82, 139